TARIQ'S GUIDE TO

NEW SHSAT MATH

by Tariq Hussain

ISBN 9781652239550

TABLE OF CONTENT

Topic by Topic Exercise

Practice Tests

Answer Keys & Explanations

Topic by Topic Exercise: Answer Key

Practice Tests: Answer Keys

50

Rules for SHSAT Math

With solved Examples

1. Distance formula (Distance or Work done)

D – Distance

r – Rate

t – Time

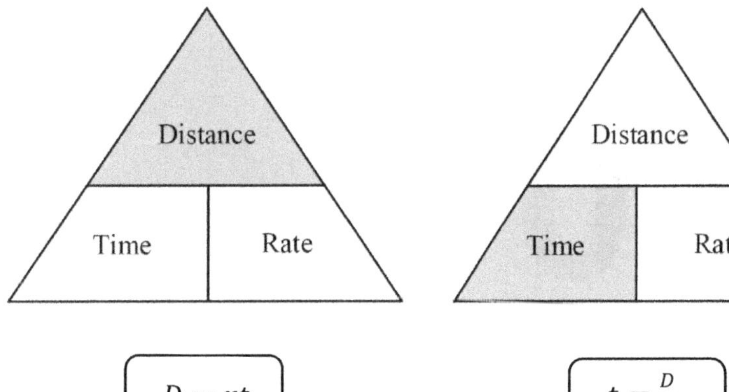

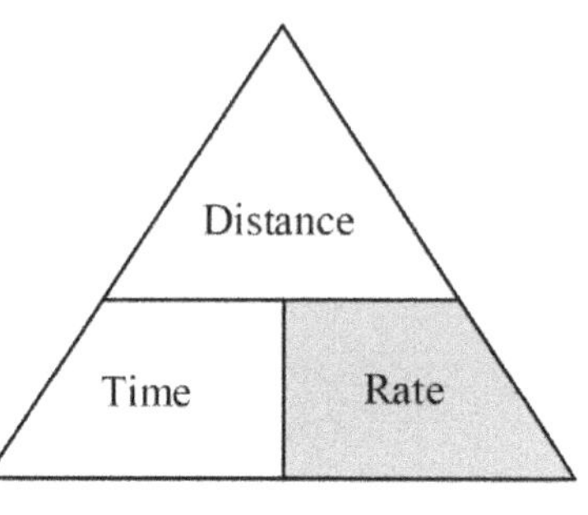

$D = rt$ $\quad t = \frac{D}{r}$ $\quad r = \frac{D}{t}$

If any of the two values among distance, time and rate are given, we can use this formula and find the unknown quantity.

Example: A bike travels at 4 miles per hour for 4 hours. What is the total distance traveled?

Solution:

D = ?
r = 4 mph
t = 4 hrs

$D = rt \Rightarrow D = 4 \cdot 4,\ D = 16$ miles

Answer: The total distance traveled is 16 miles.

Example: The car drove 200 km in 2.5 hours. At what rate did the car go?

Solution:

r = ?
D = 200 km
t = 2.5 hrs

$r = \frac{D}{t} \Rightarrow r = \frac{200}{2.5} = 80$ km/h

Answer: A car drove at 80 kilometers per hour.

Example: Two cyclists start from the same place in opposite directions. First cyclists goes towards north at 12 km/h and the other goes towards south at 15 km/h. What time will they take to be 64.8 km apart?

Solution:

t = ?

D = 64.8 km

r_1 = 12 km/h

r_2 = 15 km/h

$$r = r_1 + r_2 = 12 + 15 = 27 \text{ km/h}$$

$$t = \frac{D}{r} = \frac{64.8}{27} = 2.4 \text{ hours or } 2 \text{ hours } 24 \text{ minutes}$$

Answer: It will take them 2 hours 24 minutes.

2. Average Speed

$$\text{Average Speed} = \frac{\text{Total Distance}}{\text{Total Time}}$$

Example: Mike traveled 4 miles at a rate 2 mph. He then traveled 4 hours at 5 mph. What is Mike's average speed?

Solution:

1st	2nd
$D_1 = 4$ miles	$D_2 = ?$
$r_1 = 2$ mph	$r_2 = 5$ mph
$t_1 = ?$	$t_2 = 4$ hrs

$$t_1 = \frac{D_1}{r_1} = \frac{4}{2} = 2 \text{ hours}$$

$$D_2 = r_2 t_2 = 5 \cdot 4 = 20 \text{ miles}$$

$$\text{Average Speed} = \frac{D_1 + D_2}{t_1 + t_2} = \frac{4+20}{2+4} = \frac{24}{6} = 4 \text{ mph}$$

Answer: Mike's average speed is 4 miles per hour.

3. Difference of Two Squares (D.O.T.S.)

$$a^2 - b^2 = (a-b)(a+b)$$

Example: Evaluate $2{,}019^2 - 2{,}018^2$.

Solution:

$$\begin{matrix} a = 2{,}019 \\ b = 2{,}018 \end{matrix} \Rightarrow 2{,}019^2 - 2{,}018^2 = (2{,}019 - 2{,}018)(2{,}019 + 2{,}018) = 1 \cdot 4{,}037 = 4{,}037.$$

Answer: 4,037.

4. Mean of Consecutive Numbers

When you have a large set of consecutive numbers, or numbers that have a consistent difference, instead of adding all these numbers and dividing them by the amount to find the mean, you could simply add the first number and the last number in the set and divide the sum by 2.

Example: What is the mean of the set of numbers below?

$$3, 6, 9, 12, 15, 18, 21, 24, \dots, 300, 303, 306, 309, 312$$

Solution:

3, 6, 9, 12, 15, 18, 21, …, 300, 303, 306, 309, 312

+3 +3 +3 +3 +3 +3 +3 +3 +3 +3

First number = 3

Last number = 312

$\Rightarrow$ The mean $= \frac{3+312}{2} = \frac{315}{2} = 157.5$

Answer: 157.5.

5. Done and Remaining Method

Done	Remaining

Example: Jessica is working to pay down her debt. She paid $\frac{1}{3}$ of her total debt in May. In June, she paid $\frac{3}{5}$ of the debt she had left. What fraction of her debt does she have left?

Solution:

Done	Remaining
$\frac{1}{3}$	$\frac{2}{3}$
$\frac{2}{5}$	$\frac{4}{15}$

$$1-\frac{1}{3}=\frac{2}{3}$$

$$\frac{3}{5}\cdot\frac{2}{3}=\frac{2}{5}$$

$$\frac{2}{3}-\frac{2}{5}=\frac{10}{15}-\frac{6}{15}=\frac{4}{15}$$

Answer: $\frac{4}{15}$.

6. Arithmetic Sequence

An arithmetic sequence is a sequence of numbers such that the difference of any two successive members of the sequence is a constant.

a_n – n^{th} number in the sequence

a_1 – 1st number in the sequence

d – common difference

n – position of number in the sequence

$$a_n = a_1 + (n-1)d$$

Example: What is the 100th number in the sequence $2, 4, 6, 8, 10, 12, 14, 16, 18, \ldots$?

Solution: 2, 4, 6, 8, 10, 12, 14, 16, 18 ...

+2 +2 +2 +2 +2 +2 +2 +2

$$a_{100} = 2 + (100-1)\cdot 2 \Rightarrow a_{100} = 2 + 99\cdot 2 = 2 + 198 = 200.$$

Answer: 200.

Example: Find a_{30} given that $a_4 = 20, a_8 = -4$.

Solution:

$$\left.\begin{aligned} a_4 &= a_1 + (4-1)d = a_1 + 3d \\ a_8 &= a_1 + (8-1)d = a_1 + 7d \end{aligned}\right\} \quad a_8 - a_4 = a_1 + 7d - (a_1 + 3d) = a_1 + 7d - a_1 - 3d = 4d$$

$$-4 - 20 = 4d \Rightarrow 4d = -24, d = -6$$

$$20 = a_1 + 3 \cdot (-6) \Rightarrow a_1 = 20 + 18 = 38$$

$$a_{30} = a_1 + (30-1) \cdot d = 38 + (30-1) \cdot (-6) = 38 - 29 \cdot 6 = 38 - 174 = -136.$$

Answer: $a_{30} = -136$.

Sum Formula

$$S_n = \frac{a_1 + a_n}{2} \cdot n$$

Example: Find the sum of the first 40 odd integers.

Solution: First 40 odd integers: $1, 3, 5, 7, \ldots$

$$a_1 = 1, d = 2 \Rightarrow a_{40} = 1 + (40-1) \cdot 2 = 1 + 39 \cdot 2 = 1 + 78 = 79$$

$$S_{40} = \frac{1 + 79}{2} \cdot 40 = 1{,}600.$$

Answer: 1,600.

Example: Your father wants you to help him build a shed in the backyard. He says he will pay you \$5 for the first week and add an additional \$2.50 each week thereafter. The project will take 8 weeks. How much money will you earn, in total, if you work for the 8 weeks?

Solution:

$$\left.\begin{aligned} a_1 &= 5 \\ d &= 2.50 \\ n &= 8 \\ S_8 &- ? \end{aligned}\right\} \quad \begin{aligned} a_8 &= 5 + (8-1) \cdot 2.50 = 5 + 7 \cdot 2.50 = 5 + 17.5 = 22.5 \\ S_8 &= \frac{5 + 22.5}{2} \cdot 8 = 110. \end{aligned}$$

Answer: You will earn \$110.

7. Work Formula

If H_1 is 1st hour rate, H_2 is 2nd hour rate and T is together hour rate, then

$$\frac{1}{H_1}+\frac{1}{H_2}=\frac{1}{T}$$

Example: Bob can paint a wall in 5 hours. Tom can paint the same wall in 10 hours. How long it will take them to paint the wall together?

Solution:

$H_1 = 5$ hrs

$H_2 = 10$ hrs

$T =?$

$\frac{1}{T}=\frac{1}{5}+\frac{1}{10}=\frac{2}{10}+\frac{1}{10}=\frac{3}{10}\Rightarrow T=\frac{10}{3}=3\frac{1}{3}$ hours or 3 hours 20 minutes

Answer: It will take them 3 hours 20 minutes.

Example: Three workers A, B, and C can do a piece of work in 8 days. B and C together can do it in 24 days. B alone can do it in 40 days. In what time will it be done by A working alone?

Solution:

$T_{A+B+C} = 8$ days

$T_{B+C} = 24$ days

$H_B = 40$ days

$H_A-?$

$$\frac{1}{T_{B+C}}=\frac{1}{H_B}+\frac{1}{H_C}\Rightarrow\frac{1}{24}=\frac{1}{40}+\frac{1}{H_C},$$

$$\frac{1}{H_C}=\frac{1}{24}-\frac{1}{40}=\frac{5}{120}-\frac{3}{120}=\frac{2}{120}=\frac{1}{60}\Rightarrow H_C=60$$

$$\frac{1}{T_{A+B+C}}=\frac{1}{H_A}+\frac{1}{H_B}+\frac{1}{H_C}\Rightarrow\frac{1}{8}=\frac{1}{H_A}+\frac{1}{40}+\frac{1}{60}$$

$$\frac{1}{H_A}=\frac{1}{8}-\frac{1}{40}-\frac{1}{60}=\frac{15}{120}-\frac{3}{120}-\frac{2}{120}=\frac{10}{120}=\frac{1}{12}\Rightarrow H_A=12$$

Answer: Working alone A can do the work in 12 days.

8. Arrangements

The number of ways of arranging n unlike objects in a line is $n!$

$$n! = 1 \cdot 2 \cdot 3 \cdot 4 \cdot \ldots \cdot (n-2) \cdot (n-1) \cdot n$$

$$0! = 1$$

Example: How many different ways can the letters M, A, T, H be arranged?

Solution: $4! = 1 \cdot 2 \cdot 3 \cdot 4 = 24$.

This is because there are four spaces to be filled: _, _, _, _.

The first space can be filled by any one of the four letters. The second space can be filled by any of the remaining three letters. The third space can be filled by any of the two remaining letters and the final space must be filled by the one remaining letter.

The total number of possible arrangements is therefore $4 \cdot 3 \cdot 2 \cdot 1 = 4! = 24$.

Answer: In 24 different ways.

Example: How many different 5-digit numbers can you create using all digits $0, 1, 2, 3, 4$?

Solution: You can arrange digits $0, 1, 2, 3, 4$ in $5! = 1 \cdot 2 \cdot 3 \cdot 4 \cdot 5 = 120$ different ways. But 5-digit number cannot start with 0, so you have subtracted the number of 5-digit numbers starting with 0. There are $4! = 24$ such numbers, so you can create $120 - 24 = 96$ different 5-digit numbers.

Answer: 96.

9. Combinations (order doesn't matter)

The number of ways of selecting r objects from n unlike objects is

$$C_r^n = \frac{n!}{r! \cdot (n-r)!}$$

Example: How many different ways can you select two letters from the set of letters: A, B, and C? (Hint: In this problem, order is NOT important; i.e., AB is considered the same selection as BA).

Solution: One way to solve this problem is to list all of the possible selections of two letters from the set of A, B, and C. They are: AB, BC, and AC. Thus, there are 3 possible combinations.

Another approach is to use combinations. We have 3 distinct objects so $n = 3$. And we want to arrange them in groups of 2, so $r = 2$. Thus, the number of combinations is:

$$C_2^3 = \frac{3!}{2! \cdot (3-2)!} = \frac{3!}{2! \cdot 1!} = \frac{1 \cdot 2 \cdot 3}{1 \cdot 2 \cdot 1} = 3.$$

Answer: 3 different ways.

Example: There are 10 teams in the WNBA. They play each other twice. How many matches have taken place?

Solution: We have 10 teams, so $n = 10$. And we want 2 teams to play match, so $r = 2$.

$$C_2^{10} = \frac{10!}{2! \cdot (10-2)!} = \frac{10!}{2! \cdot 8!} = \frac{10 \cdot 9 \cdot 8!}{2! \cdot 8!} = \frac{10 \cdot 9}{2} = 45$$

Answer: 45 matches.

10. Probability

Many events can't be predicted with total certainty. The best we can say is how likely they are to happen, using the idea of probability.

$$\text{Probability of an event happening} = \frac{\text{Number of favorable outcomes}}{\text{Number of all possible outcomes}}$$

Tips

- The probability of an event can only be between 0 and 1 and can also be written as a percentage.
- The probability of event A is often written as $P(A)$.
- If $P(A) > P(B)$, then event A has a higher chance of occurring than event B.
- If $P(A) = P(B)$, then events A and B are equally likely to occur.

Example: There are 4 blue marbles and 8 black marbles. What is the probability of picking a blue marble?

Solution:

Number of favorable outcomes $= 4$

Number of all possible outcomes $= 4 + 8 = 12$

$$P = \frac{4}{12} = \frac{1}{3}$$

Answer: $\frac{1}{3}$.

Addition Rule

Two events are called **mutually exclusive** if they cannot occur at the same time. When two events, A and B, are mutually exclusive, the probability that A or B will occur is

$$P(A \text{ or } B) = P(A) + P(B)$$

Example: A single 6-sided die is rolled. What is the probability of rolling 1 or 6?

Solution:

$$\left.\begin{array}{l} P(1) = \frac{1}{6} \\ P(6) = \frac{1}{6} \end{array}\right\} \quad P(1 \text{ or } 6) = \frac{1}{6} + \frac{1}{6} = \frac{2}{6} = \frac{1}{3}$$

Answer: $\frac{1}{3}$.

Multiplication Rule

If the occurrence of the event A has no effect on the probability of the event B, two events A and B are called **independent** events. If A and B are two independent events, then the probability that both events occur simultaneously is

$$P(A \text{ and } B) = P(A) \cdot P(B)$$

Example: Suppose you take out two cards from a standard pack of cards one after another, without replacing the first card. What is probability that the first card is the ace of hearts, and the second card is a spade?

Solution:

The two events are dependent events because the first card is not replaced. There is only one ace of spades in a deck of 52 cards. So,

$$P(1^{st} \text{ card is ace of hearts}) = \frac{1}{52}.$$

If the ace of spaces is drawn first, then there are 51 cards left in the deck, of which 13 are spades. So,

$$P(2^{nd} \text{ card is a spade}) = \frac{13}{51}.$$

Use multiplication rule of probability:

$$P = \frac{1}{52} \cdot \frac{13}{51} = \frac{1 \cdot 13}{52 \cdot 51} = \frac{1}{4 \cdot 51} = \frac{1}{204}.$$

Another way to solve this question is using permutations. We have to choose two cards (order matters), $r = 2$, from the deck of 52 cards, $n = 52$. There are

$$P_2^{52} = \frac{52!}{(52-2)!} = \frac{52!}{50!} = \frac{52 \cdot 51 \cdot 50!}{50!} = 52 \cdot 51 = 2{,}652$$

different ways to choose two cards. There is one way to choose the ace of heart and 13 ways to choose a spade. So,

Number of favorable outcomes $= 1 \cdot 13 = 13$

Number of all possible outcomes $= 2{,}652$

$$P = \frac{13}{2{,}652} = \frac{1}{204}$$

Answer: $\frac{1}{204}$.

11. Midpoint Formula

The midpoint M of the line segment from point $A(x_A, y_A)$ to point $B(x_B, y_B)$ has coordinates

$$M\left(\frac{x_A + x_B}{2}, \frac{y_A + y_B}{2}\right)$$

Example: What is the midpoint of $(4,2)$ and $(-2,6)$?

Solution:

$$\left(\frac{4+(-2)}{2}, \frac{2+6}{2}\right) = \left(\frac{2}{2}, \frac{8}{2}\right) = (1,4)$$

Answer: $(1,4)$.

Example: $M(-2, 5)$ is the midpoint of the line segment AB. A has the coordinates $(1, -2)$, Find the coordinates of B.

Solution: Let the coordinates of B be (x_B, y_B). So,

$$\begin{matrix} \dfrac{1 + x_B}{2} = -2 \\ \dfrac{-2 + y_B}{2} = 5 \end{matrix} \Rightarrow \begin{matrix} 1 + x_B = -4 \\ -2 + y_B = 10 \end{matrix} \Rightarrow \begin{matrix} x_B = -5 \\ y_B = 12 \end{matrix}$$

Answer: $B(-5,12)$.

12. Distance Formula

The distance between points $A(x_A, y_A)$ and $B(x_B, y_B)$ is

$$d = \sqrt{(x_A - x_B)^2 + (y_A - y_B)^2}$$

Example: Find the distance between points $(5, -2)$ and $(-4,9)$.

Solution: $d = \sqrt{\left(5-(-4)\right)^2 + (-2-9)^2} = \sqrt{9^2 + 11^2} = \sqrt{81 + 121} = \sqrt{202}$

Answer: $\sqrt{202}$.

Example: Find all points $(2, y)$ that are 10 units from the point $(-4, -1)$.

Solution: Find the distance between points $(2, y)$ and $(-4, -1)$:

$$d = \sqrt{\left(2-(-4)\right)^2 + \left(y-(-1)\right)^2} = \sqrt{6^2 + (y+1)^2} = \sqrt{36 + y^2 + 2y + 1} = \sqrt{y^2 + 2y + 37}$$

Hence,

$$\sqrt{y^2 + 2y + 37} = 10$$

Square this equation:

$$y^2 + 2y + 37 = 100 \Rightarrow y^2 + 2y - 63 = 0$$

Use quadratic formula:

$$y_{1,2} = \frac{-2 \pm \sqrt{2^2 - 4 \cdot 1 \cdot (-63)}}{2 \cdot 1} = \frac{-2 \pm \sqrt{256}}{2} = \frac{-2 \pm 16}{2} = -9, 7$$

Answer: $(2, -9), (2,7)$.

COORDINATE PLANE

13. Slope Intercept Formula

$$y = mx + b$$

m – slope

b – y-intercept

Example: What is the slope and y-intercept of the line $y = 7x + 3$?

Solution:

Slope $m = 7$

y-intercept $b = 3$ or point $(0,3)$.

Answer: $m = 7, b = 3$.

Example: What is the slope of the line given by the equation $11x + 5y = 32$?

Solution: Rewrite the equation in the slope intercept form:

$$5y = 32 - 11x$$

$$y = \frac{32}{5} - \frac{11}{5}x \Rightarrow y = 6.4 - 2.2x$$

Hence, the slope is $m = -2.2$.

Answer: The slope is -2.2.

14. Slope

If the line passes through the points (x_1, y_1) and (x_2, y_2), then the slope is

$$m = \frac{y_2 - y_1}{x_2 - x_1}$$

Example: Find the slope of the line passing through the points $(0,3)$ and $(5,2)$.

Solution:

$$m = \frac{2-3}{5-0} = -\frac{1}{5} = -0.2$$

Answer: $m = -0.2$.

15. Parallel Lines

Parallel lines have the same slope.

Example: Write the equation of the line parallel to the line $y = -3x + 5$ passing through the point $(3, -10)$.

Solution: The slope of the parallel line is the same as the slope of the given line, so $m = -3$.

Use slope intercept form of the equation:

$$y = -3x + b$$

This line passes through the point $(3, -10)$, so its coordinates satisfy the equation:

$$-10 = -3 \cdot 3 + b$$

$$b = -10 + 9 = -1$$

The equation of the parallel line is $y = -3x - 1$.

Answer: $y = -3x - 1$.

16. Perpendicular Lines

If two lines with equations $y = m_1 x + b_1$ and $y = m_2 x + b_2$ are perpendicular, then

$$m_1 \cdot m_2 = -1$$

Example: Find an equation of the line perpendicular to the line $3x - 9y = 5$ and passing through the point $(1, -3)$.

Solution: Find the slope of the line $3x - 9y = 5$:

$$9y = 3x - 5 \Rightarrow y = \frac{1}{3}x - \frac{5}{9}$$

The slope of the given line is $m_1 = \frac{1}{3}$. If the slope of the perpendicular line is m_2, then

$$\frac{1}{3} \cdot m_2 = -1 \Rightarrow m_2 = -3$$

The slope intercept form of the equation of perpendicular line is $y = -3x + b_2$

This line passes through the point $(1, -3)$, thus

$$-3 = -3 \cdot 1 + b_2 \Rightarrow b_2 = 0 \text{ and } y = -3x$$

Answer: $y = -3x$.

Answer: $(1,5), (4,-1), (3,-2)$.

GEOMETRY

17. Vertical Angles

Vertical Angles are the angles opposite each other when two lines cross.

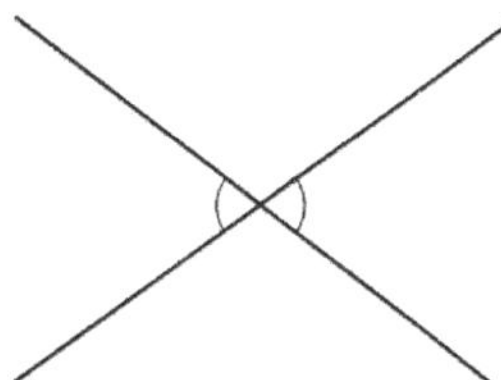

A primary property of vertical angles is that they are **congruent**. In other words, they have the same angle measure.

Example: Two lines a and b intersect. If two opposite angles measure $(2x+40)°$ and $(3x-20)°$, what is the value of x?

Solution: Angles $(2x+40)°$ and $(3x-20)°$ are vertical angles, so

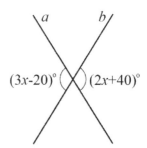

$$2x + 40 = 3x - 20$$

$$40 + 20 = 3x - 2x$$

$$x = 60$$

Answer: $x = 60$.

a b

$(3x\text{-}20)°$ $(2x\text{+}40)°$

18. Complementary angles

Complementary angles are two angles that add to 90 degrees.

Example: The measure of two complementary angles are $(5x-10)°$ and $(x+4)°$. Find the measure of each angle.

Solution:

Complementary angles $\Rightarrow (5x-10)° + (x+4)° = 90°$.

$$6x = 90 + 10 - 4$$

$$6x = 96 \ \Rightarrow \ x = 16$$

Hence, $(5x-10)° = (5 \cdot 16 - 10)° = 70°$

$(x+4)^\circ = (16+4)^\circ = 20^\circ$

Answer: 70° and 20°.

19. Supplementary Angles

Supplementary angles are two angles that add to 180 degrees.

Example: Three lines a, b and c intersect as shown in the diagram. Find the measure of angles $\angle 1, \angle 2$ and $\angle 3$.

Solution:

Angles 2 and $(2x+1)^\circ$ are vertical angles, so

$$\angle 2 = (2x+1)^\circ$$

Angles $(4x+13)^\circ$, $(3x+4)^\circ$ and $\angle 2$ are supplementary angles, so

$$4x + 13 + 3x + 4 + 2x + 1 = 180 \Rightarrow 9x + 18 = 180$$

$$9x = 180 - 18$$

$$9x = 162$$

$$x = 18$$

Now,

- angles 1 and $(3x+4)^\circ$ are vertical $\Rightarrow \angle 1 = (3 \cdot 18 + 4)^\circ = 58^\circ$
- angles 2 and $(2x+1)^\circ$ are vertical $\Rightarrow \angle 2 = (2 \cdot 18 + 1)^\circ = 37^\circ$
- angles 3 and $(4x+13)^\circ$ are vertical $\Rightarrow \angle 3 = (4 \cdot 18 + 13)^\circ = 85^\circ$

Answer: $58^\circ, 37^\circ, 85^\circ$.

20. Parallel lines cut by a transversal

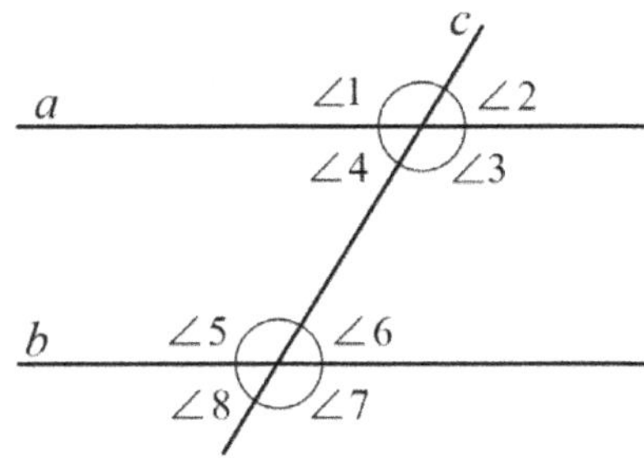

Lines a and b are parallel and they are cut by a line c called **transversal**.

21. Alternate Interior Angles

Alternate interior angles are a pair of angles on the inner side of each of two parallel lines but on opposite sides of the transversal. Alternate interior angles are congruent.

$$\angle 3 \cong \angle 5$$
$$\angle 4 \cong \angle 6$$

22. Alternate Exterior Angles

Alternate exterior angles are a pair of angles on the outer side of each of those two lines but on opposite sides of the transversal. Alternate exterior angles are congruent.

$$\angle 1 \cong \angle 7$$
$$\angle 2 \cong \angle 8$$

23. Corresponding Angles

There are four pairs of corresponding angles. Corresponding angles are congruent.

$$\angle 1 \cong \angle 5$$
$$\angle 2 \cong \angle 6$$
$$\angle 3 \cong \angle 7$$
$$\angle 4 \cong \angle 8$$

24. Same Side Interior Angles

Same side interior angles are a pair of interior angles on the same side of the transversal. Same side interior angles add up to 180°.

$$\angle 3 + \angle 6 = 180°$$
$$\angle 4 + \angle 5 = 180°$$

Example: Two parallel lines a and b are cut by transversal c as shown in the diagram. What are the values of x and y?

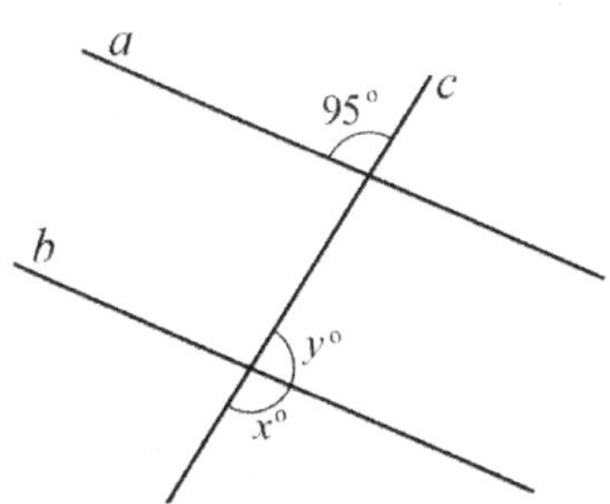

Solution: Supplementary angle to angle $y°$ is corresponding angle with 95° angle, so

$$y° = 180° - 95° = 85°$$

Angles $x°$ and $y°$ are supplementary, thus

$$x° = 180° - 85° = 95°$$

Answer: $x° = 95°, y° = 85°$.

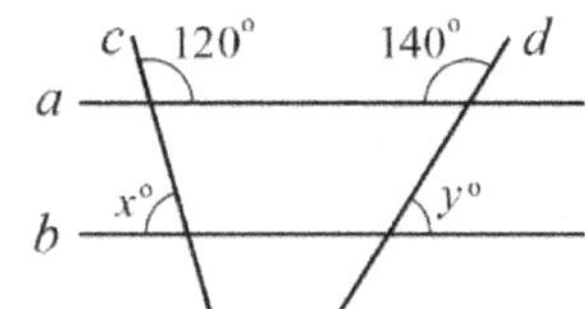

Example: Two parallel lines a and b are cut by two transversals c and d. What are the values of x and y?

Solution:

Supplementary angle to $120°$ angle is alternate interior angle with $x°$ angle, so $x° = 180° - 120° = 60°$.

Supplementary angle to $140°$ angle is alternate interior angle with $y°$ angle, so

$$y° = 180° - 140° = 40°.$$

Answer: $x° = 60°, y° = 40°$.

25. Triangle

A **triangle** is a 3-sided figure formed by joining three line segments together at their endpoints.

A triangle has

- three sides;
- three vertices;
- three angles.

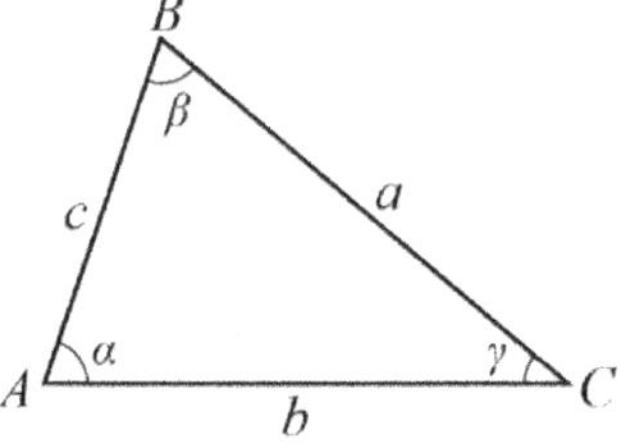

26. Triangle Inequality Theorem

The sum of the lengths of any two sides of a triangle is greater than the length of the third side.

$$a + b > c$$
$$a + c > b$$
$$b + c > a$$

Example: Check whether it is possible to have a triangle with sides lengths of 7 cm, 9 cm and 11 cm.

Solution:

$a = 7$ cm
$b = 9$ cm
$c = 11$ cm

$$7 + 9 = 16 > 11$$
$$7 + 11 = 18 > 9$$
$$9 + 11 = 20 > 7$$

Hence, it is possible to have a triangle with such side lengths.

Answer: Yes.

27. Triangle Interior Angles Theorem

The sum of the measures of triangle's interior angles is always 180°.

$$\alpha + \beta + \gamma = 180°$$

Example: Two interior angles in triangle have measures 135° and 24°. What is the measure of the third triangle's interior angle?

Solution:

$$\left.\begin{array}{l}\alpha = 135° \\ \beta = 24° \\ \gamma = ?\end{array}\right\} \quad 135° + 24° + \gamma = 180° \Rightarrow \gamma = 180° - 135° - 24° = 21°$$

Answer: 21°.

28. Triangle Exterior Angles Sum

The sum of the measures of triangle's exterior angles is always 360°.

29. Exterior Angle Theorem (I. I. E.)

The sum of the two interior angles of the triangle is equal to the exterior angle of the triangle of the third angle.

$$\gamma = \alpha + \beta$$

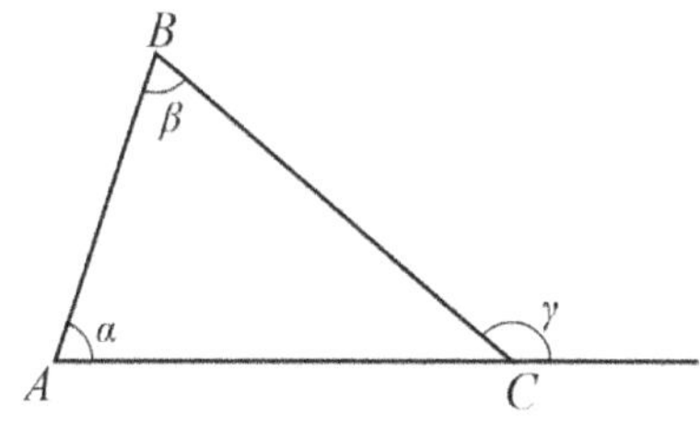

Example: In triangle ABC, two exterior angles have measures 105° and 150°. Find the value of x and y.

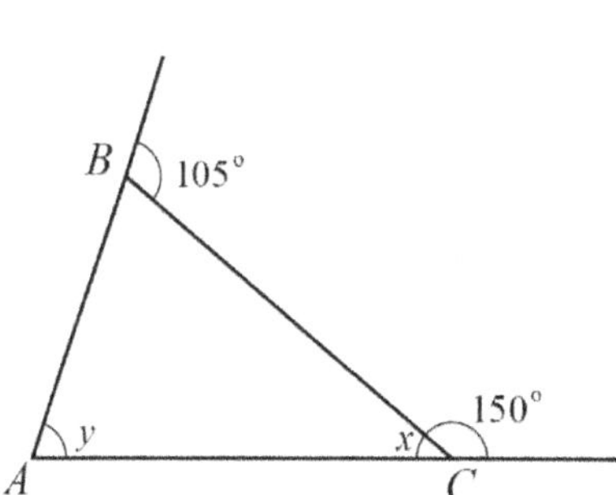

Solution:

Angles with measures x and 150° are supplementary angles, so

$$x + 150° = 180°$$

$$x = 180° - 150° = 30°$$

By the exterior angle theorem,

$$x + y = 105° \Rightarrow y = 105° - 30° = 75°$$

Answer: $x = 30°, y = 75°$.

30. Types of Triangles

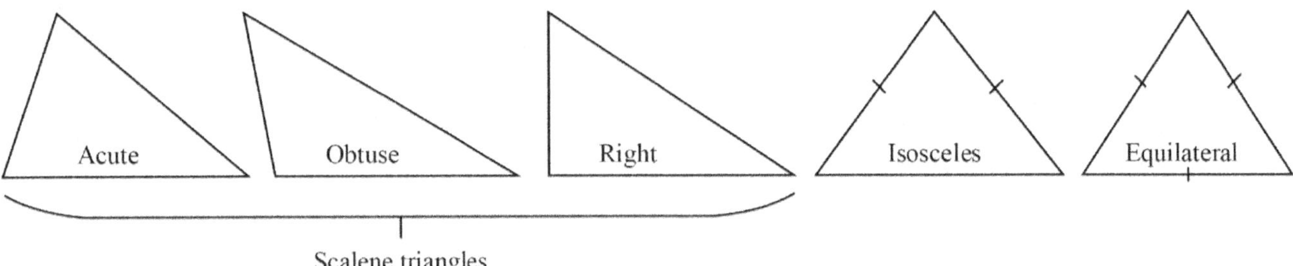

31. Area of the Triangle

$$A = \frac{1}{2} \cdot a \cdot h$$

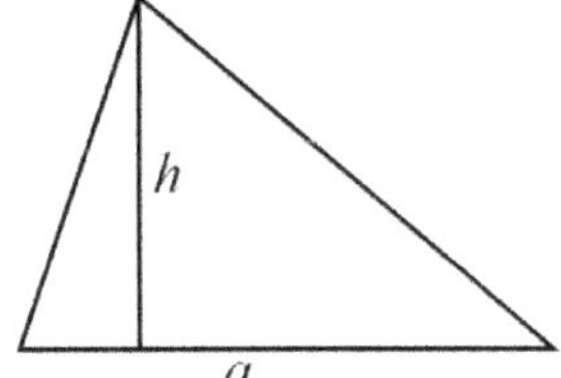

Example: Find the area of an acute triangle with a base of 25 inches and a height of 8 inches.

Solution: Use area formula:

$$A = \frac{1}{2} \cdot 25 \cdot 8 = 100 \text{ in}^2$$

Answer: 100 in^2.

Example: The area of a triangle shaped mat is 36 square feet and the base is 9 feet. Find the height of the mat.

Solution: Use area formula:

$$A = \frac{1}{2} \cdot a \cdot h \Rightarrow 36 = \frac{1}{2} \cdot 9 \cdot h$$

$$h = \frac{36 \cdot 2}{9} = 4 \cdot 2 = 8 \text{ ft}$$

Answer: 8 ft.

32. Isosceles Triangle

A triangle with two congruent sides is called **isosceles triangle**.

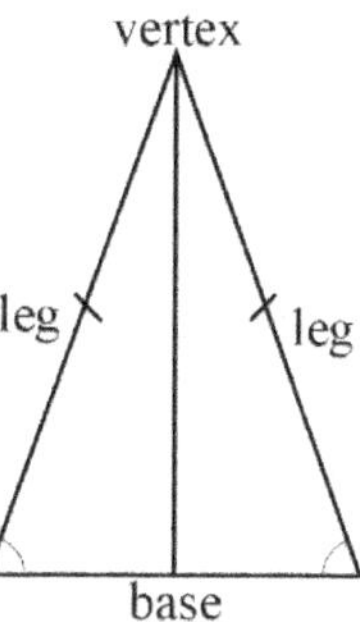

Tips

- has two congruent sides (called legs)
- has two congruent angles adjacent to the base
- has the height which bisects
    - the base at a right angle
    - bisects the vertex angle
    - splits the original isosceles triangle into two congruent triangles

Example: In isosceles triangle $ABC, AB = BC$, BD is the height. If angle ACB has the measure of $54°$, what is the measure of angle DBC?

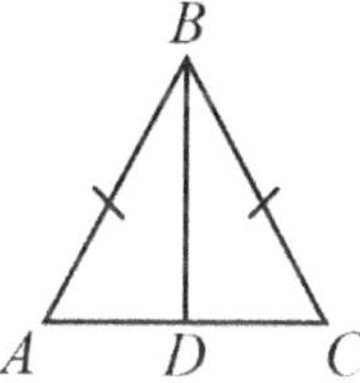

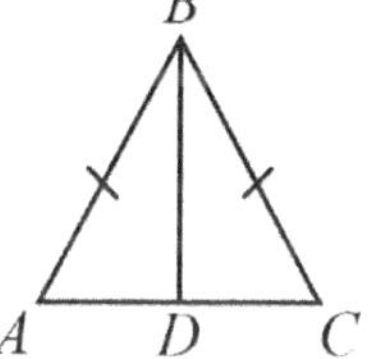

Solution:
Angles BAC and BCA are congruent as adjacent angle to the base AC, so

$$\angle BAC = \angle BCA = 54°.$$

The sum of all interior angles in triangle is always $180°$, thus

$$\angle ABC = 180° - 54° - 54° = 72°$$

The height BD bisects the vertex angle ABC, therefore

$$\angle DBC = \frac{1}{2}\angle ABC = \frac{1}{2} \cdot 72° = 36°$$

Answer: $36°$.

Example: Two isosceles triangles ABC and BED have common point B as shown in the diagram. Find the measure of angle BDE.

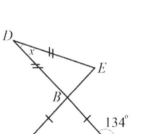

Solution: Supplementary angle BCA to $134°$ angle has measure

$$\angle BCA = 180° - 134° = 46°$$

Two angles adjacent to the base are congruent, so

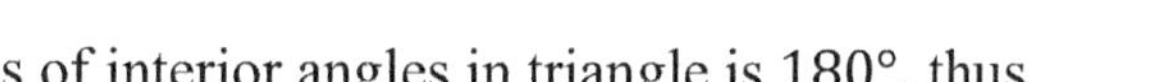

$$\angle BAC = \angle BCA = 46°$$

The sum of the measures of interior angles in triangle is $180°$, thus

$$\angle ABC + 46° + 46° = 180° \Rightarrow \angle ABC = 180° - 46° - 46° = 88°$$

Angles ABC and DBE are vertical, so $\angle ABC = \angle DBE = 88°$.

Angles DBE and DEB are adjacent angle to the base BE of isosceles triangle BED, thus

$$\angle DBE = \angle DEB = 88°$$

The sum of the measures of interior angles in triangle is 180°, thus

$$\angle BDE + 88° + 88° = 180° \Rightarrow \angle BDE = 180° - 88° - 88° = 4°$$

Answer: 4°.

33. Equilateral Triangle

A triangle with three congruent sides is called **equilateral triangle**.

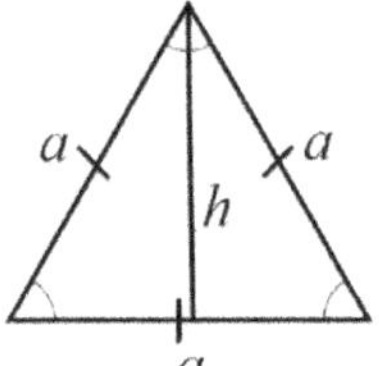

Tips

- has three congruent sides
- has three congruent angles with measure of 60°
- the angle bisectors, the medians, the heights and the perpendicular bisectors of the three sides coincide

- the area of equilateral triangle is $A = \frac{a^2\sqrt{3}}{4}$
- the height of the equilateral triangle is $h = \frac{a\sqrt{3}}{2}$
- the radius of circumscribed circle is $R = \frac{a\sqrt{3}}{3}$
- the radius of inscribed circle is $r = \frac{a\sqrt{3}}{6}$

Example: Find the area of an equilateral triangle whose side is 8 cm.

Solution:

$a = 8$ cm
$A = ?$

$$A = \frac{8^2\sqrt{3}}{4} = 16\sqrt{3}\ \text{cm}^2$$

Answer: $16\sqrt{3}$ cm^2.

Example: If the height of an equilateral triangle is $4\sqrt{3}$ in, what is the perimeter of the triangle?

Solution:

$h = 4\sqrt{3}$ in
$P = ?$

$$4\sqrt{3} = \frac{a\sqrt{3}}{2} \Rightarrow a = 8$$

$$P = 3a = 24 \text{ in}$$

Answer: 24 in.

34. Right Triangle

A **right** triangle is a triangle with a right angle.

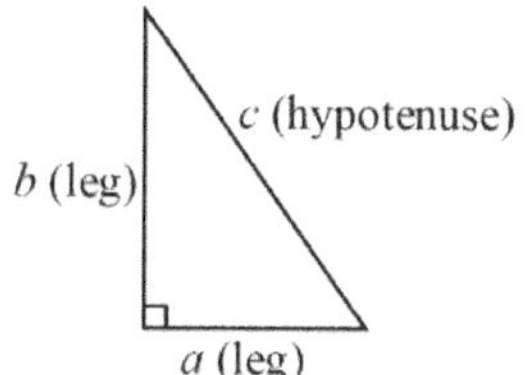

Tips

- one angle is a right angle and two other angles are acute angles
- the longest side is the hypotenuse and is opposite the right angle
- the radius of the circumscribing circle is half the hypotenuse
- the center of the circumscribing circle is the midpoint of the hypotenuse
- the area of the right triangle is $A = \frac{ab}{2}$

Example: In a right triangle, the difference between two acute angles measures is 14°. Find the measures of all angles.

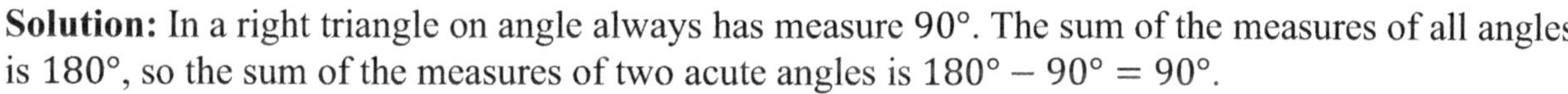

Solution: In a right triangle on angle always has measure 90°. The sum of the measures of all angles is 180°, so the sum of the measures of two acute angles is $180° - 90° = 90°$.

Let $x°$ be the measure of the smaller acute angle, then $(x + 14)°$ is the measure of the larger acute angle. Hence,

$$x° + (x + 14)° = 90°$$

$$(2x)° = 76° \Rightarrow x° = 38°, \qquad (x + 14)° = 38° + 14° = 52°$$

Answer: 38° and 52°.

Example: In a right triangle, one leg is twice greater than the other leg. If the area of the triangle is 36 cm^2, what is the length of the smaller leg?

Solution:

$$\left.\begin{array}{l}\text{Smaller leg} = x \text{ cm} \\ \text{Larger leg} = 2x \text{ cm} \\ A = 36 \text{ cm}^2\end{array}\right\} \quad A = \frac{x \cdot 2x}{2} \Rightarrow x^2 = 36, x = 6 \text{ cm}$$

Answer: 6 cm.

35. Pythagorean Theorem

In any right triangle, the sum of the squared lengths of the two legs is equal to the squared length of the hypotenuse.

$$a^2 + b^2 = c^2$$

Example: Find the length of one side of a right triangle if the length of the hypotenuse is 10 cm and the length of the other side is 8 cm.

Solution:

$$\left.\begin{array}{l} a = 8\text{ cm} \\ c = 10\text{ cm} \\ b = ? \end{array}\right\} \quad a^2 + b^2 = c^2 \Rightarrow b^2 = c^2 - a^2 = 10^2 - 8^2 = 100 - 64 = 36, b = 6\text{ cm}$$

Answer: 6 cm

Example: In a right triangle with hypotenuse 13 in, one leg is 7 in longer than another leg. What is the area of this triangle?

Solution: Let the smaller leg be x in, then the larger leg is $(x + 7)$ in. Use Pythagorean theorem:

$$x^2 + (x + 7)^2 = 13^2$$

$$x^2 + x^2 + 14x + 49 = 169$$

$$2x^2 + 14x - 120 = 0$$

$$x^2 + 7x - 60 = 0$$

By the quadratic formula,

$$x_{1,2} = \frac{-7 \pm \sqrt{7^2 - 4 \cdot 1 \cdot (-60)}}{2 \cdot 1} = \frac{-7 \pm \sqrt{289}}{2} = \frac{-7 \pm 17}{2} = -12, 5$$

The length of the leg cannot be negative, so $x = 5$ in and $(x + 7) = 12$ in.

The area of the triangle is

$$A = \frac{5 \cdot 12}{2} = 30\text{ in}^2$$

Answer: 30 in^2.

Tips

For a triangle with sides a, b and c and c is the longest side:

- If $c^2 < a^2 + b^2$ then it is an acute-angled triangle (the angle facing side c is an acute angle)
- If $c^2 = a^2 + b^2$ then it is a right-angled triangle (the angle facing side c is a right angle)
- If $c^2 > a^2 + b^2$ then it is an obtuse-angled triangle (the angle facing side c is an obtuse angle)

Example: Identify the type of triangle with sides lengths of 5 cm, 8 cm and 11 cm

Solution: Remember c is the greatest side!

$a = 5$ cm

$b = 8$ cm $\quad 5^2 + 8^2 = 25 + 64 = 89 < 121 = 11^2$

$c = 11$ cm

Answer: Acute triangle.

36. Pythagorean Triples

a	b	c
3	4	5
5	12	13
7	24	25
8	15	17
9	40	41

Most used

$3^2 + 4^2 = 9 + 16 = 25 = 5^2$

$5^2 + 12^2 = 25 + 144 = 169 = 13^2$

$7^2 + 24^2 = 49 + 576 = 625 = 25^2$

$8^2 + 15^2 = 64 + 225 = 289 = 17^2$

$9^2 + 40^2 = 81 + 1{,}600 = 1{,}681 = 41^2$

Note that any three numbers proportional to Pythagorean triples is also a Pythagorean triple. For example, $6, 8, 10$ or $10, 24, 26$.

37. Special Right Triangles

$30° - 60° - 90°$ Right Triangle

When a right triangle has interior angles with measures of 30°, 60° and 90°, the side length opposite to the 30° angle is half of the hypotenuse.

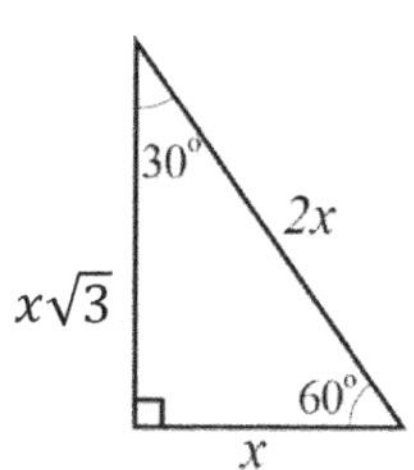

Example: Find the lengths of the other two sides of a right triangle if the length of the hypotenuse is 10 inches and one of the angles is 30°.

Solution: This is special $30° - 60° - 90°$ right triangle.

$$\left.\begin{array}{l} 2x = 10 \text{ in} \\ x = ? \\ x\sqrt{3} = ? \end{array}\right\} \quad 2x = 10 \Rightarrow x = 5 \text{ in}, x\sqrt{3} = 5\sqrt{3} \text{ in}$$

Answer: 5 inches and $5\sqrt{3}$ inches.

$45° - 45° - 90°$ Right Triangle

When a right triangle has interior angles with measures of $45°, 45°$ and $90°$, the sides lengths opposite to the $45°$ angles are equal. This triangle is always isosceles right triangle.

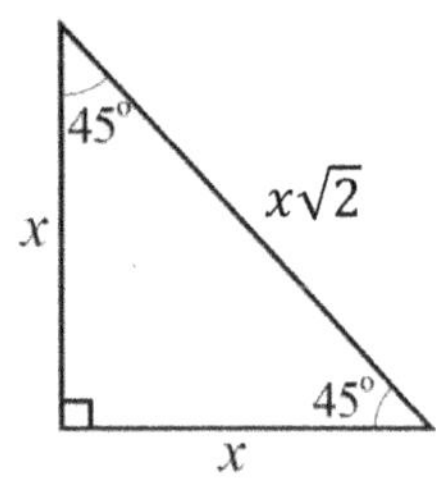

Example: Find the lengths of the other two sides of a right triangle if the length of the hypotenuse is $7\sqrt{2}$ inches and one of the angles is $45°$.

Solution: This is special $45° - 45° - 90°$ right triangle.

$$\left.\begin{array}{l} x\sqrt{2} = 7\sqrt{2} \text{ in} \\ x = ? \end{array}\right\} \quad 7\sqrt{2} = x\sqrt{2} \Rightarrow x = 7$$

Answer: 7 inches and 7 inches.

Example: The height drawn to the hypotenuse in $45° - 45° - 90°$ right triangle is 5 cm. What are the legs lengths?

Solution: This triangle is isosceles triangle, so the height drawn to the hypotenuse is triangle's median and is exactly half of the hypotenuse,

$$\text{hypotenuse} = x\sqrt{2} = 10 \Rightarrow x = 5\sqrt{2} \text{ cm}$$

Answer: $5\sqrt{2}$ cm.

Quadrilaterals

38. Parallelogram

A **parallelogram** is a quadrilateral with opposite sides parallel.

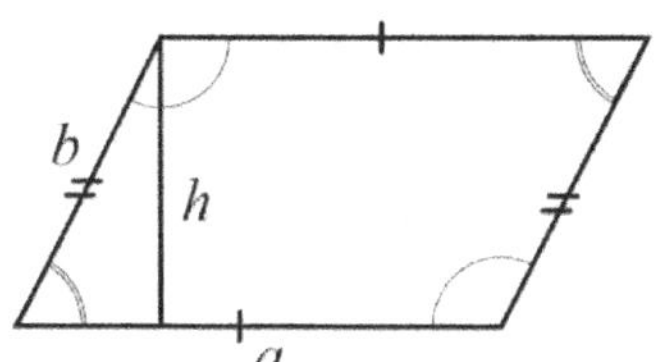

Tips

- opposite sides are parallel
- opposite sides are congruent
- opposite angles are congruent
- two consecutive angles are supplementary
- diagonals bisect each other
- the perimeter of the parallelogram is $P = 2(a + b)$
- area of the parallelogram is $A = a \cdot h$

Example: In parallelogram $ABCD$, angle between height BF and side AB is 22°. Find the measures of all parallelogram's angles.

Solution: Consider right triangle ABF.

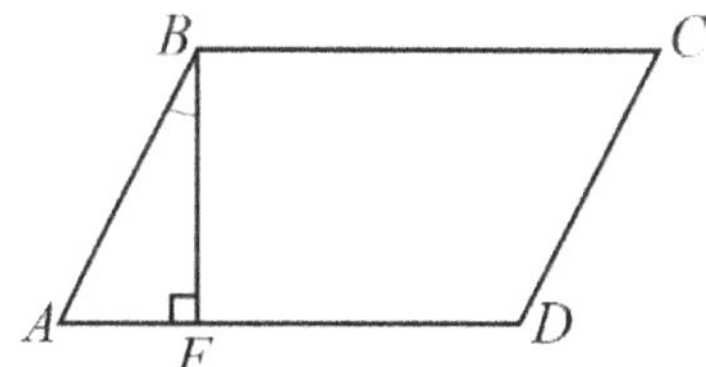

$\angle ABF = 22°$

$\angle AFB = 90°$ $\quad \angle A = 180° - 22° - 90° = 68°$

$\angle A = ?$

Opposite angles in parallelogram are equal, so $\angle A = \angle C = 68°$.

Two consecutive angles in parallelogram are supplementary, thus

$$\angle A + \angle B = 180° \Rightarrow \angle B = 180° - 68° = 112°$$

Angles B and D are equal as opposite angles, $\angle B = \angle D = 112°$.

Answer: $68°, 112°, 68°$ and $112°$.

Example: In parallelogram $ABCD$, height BF bisects the side AD and form isosceles right triangle ABF. If the length of AD is 12 cm, what is the area of the parallelogram $ABCD$?

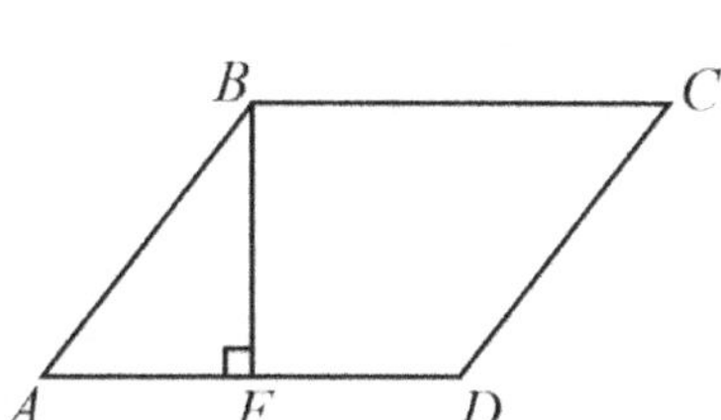

Solution: If BF bisects the side AD, then $AF = 5$ cm.

Triangle ABF is isosceles right triangle, then $AF = BF = 5$ cm.

The area of the parallelogram $ABCD$ is $A = AD \cdot BF = 10 \cdot 5 = 50 \text{ cm}^2$.

Answer: 50 cm^2.

39. Rectangle

A **rectangle** is a parallelogram with four right angles.

Tips

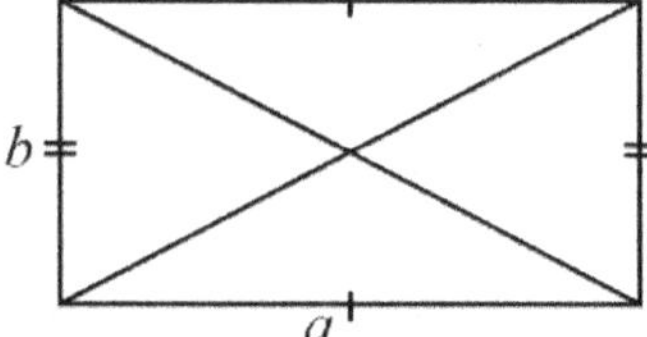

- opposite side congruent
- all angles are right angles
- diagonals are congruent
- diagonals bisect each other
- the perimeter of the rectangle is $P = 2(a + b)$
- the area of the rectangle is $A = a \cdot b$

Example: The area of the rectangle with one side of 8 in is 48 in^2. What is the length of the diagonal of the rectangle?

Solution: Use the area formula to find the length of the second rectangle's side:

$$48 = 8b \Rightarrow b = \frac{48}{8} = 6 \text{ in}$$

Use Pythagorean theorem for the right triangle formed by two consecutive rectangle's sides and diagonal:

$$d^2 = 6^2 + 8^2 = 36 + 64 = 100 \Rightarrow d = 10 \text{ in}$$

Answer: 10 in

40. Square

A **square** is a rectangle with all congruent sides.

Tips

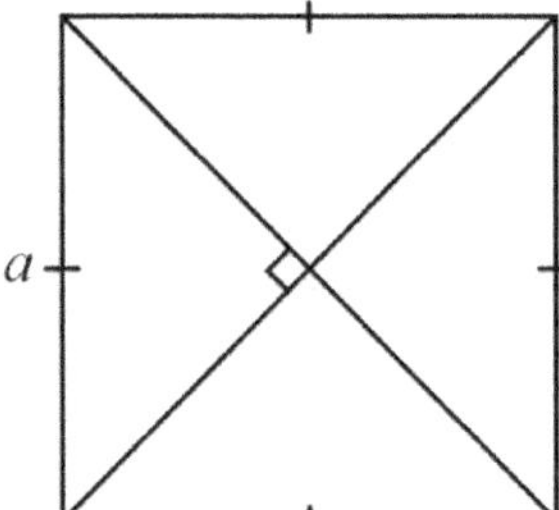

- all sides are congruent
- all angles are right angles
- diagonals are congruent
- diagonals bisect each other
- diagonals are perpendicular and splits the square into four congruent right triangles
- the perimeter of the square is $P = 4a$
- the area of the square is $A = a^2$
- the diagonal of the square has length $d = a\sqrt{2}$

Example: What is the area of the square with diagonal of $12\sqrt{2}$ cm.

Solution:

$d = 12\sqrt{2}$ cm, $a = ?$, $A = ?$

$d = a\sqrt{2} \Rightarrow 12\sqrt{2} = a\sqrt{2}$

$a = 12$ cm

$A = a^2 = 12^2 = 144\text{ cm}^2$

Answer: 144 cm^2.

41. Rhombus

A **rhombus** is a parallelogram with all congruent sides.

Tips

- all sides congruent
- opposite angles congruent
- two consecutive angles are supplementary
- diagonals are perpendicular
- diagonals are angles bisectors
- diagonals bisect each other
- the perimeter of the rhombus is $P = 4a$
- the area of the rhombus is $A = a \cdot h$

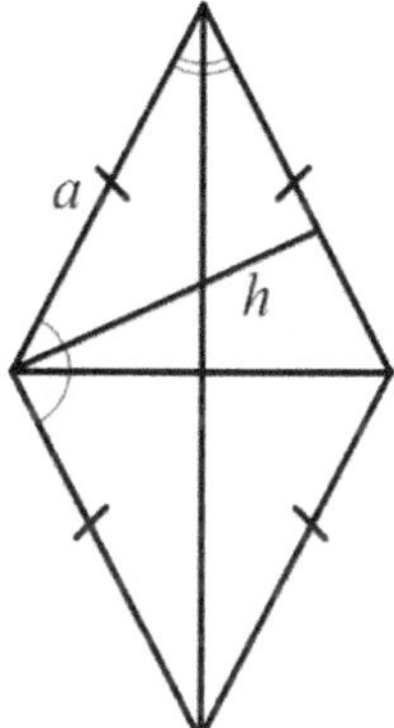

Example: In a rhombus, an acute angle measures 60°. If the height of the rhombus is $5\sqrt{3}$ cm, what is the area of the rhombus?

Solution: Acute and obtuse angles in the rhombus are supplementary angles, so the measure of obtuse angle is $180° - 60° = 120°$. Half of this angle measures 60°. Consider triangle formed by two sides of the rhombus and smaller diagonal (opposite to the acute angle). This triangle is equilateral triangle with the height of $5\sqrt{3}$ cm.

$h = 5\sqrt{3}$ cm, $a = ?$

$$h = \frac{a\sqrt{3}}{2} \Rightarrow 5\sqrt{3} = \frac{a\sqrt{3}}{2}$$

$$a = 10\text{ cm}$$

$a = 10$ cm, $h = 5\sqrt{3}$ cm, $A = ?$

$$A = a \cdot h = 10 \cdot 5\sqrt{3} = 50\sqrt{3}\text{ cm}^2$$

Answer: $50\sqrt{3}\text{ cm}^2$.

42. Trapezoid

A **trapezoid** is a quadrilateral with two parallel opposite sides.

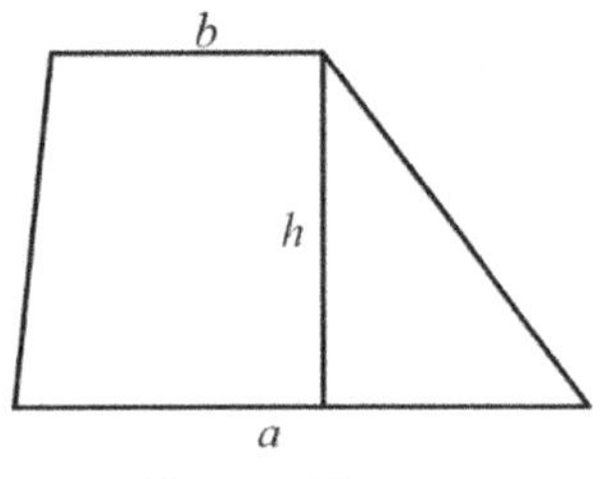

Trapezoid

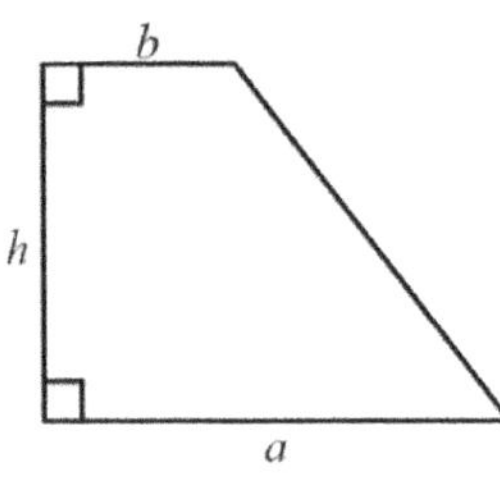

Right trapezoid

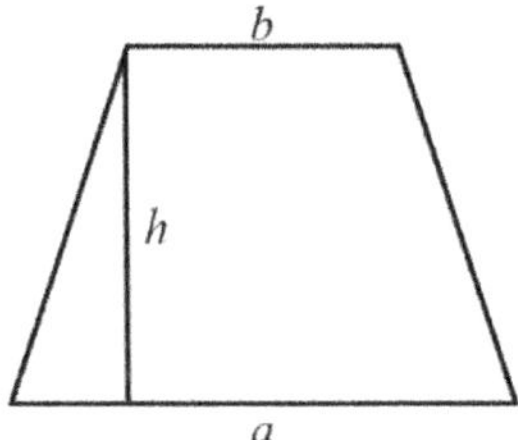

Isosceles trapezoid

Tips

- the bases are parallel
- each lower base angle is supplementary to the upper base angle on the same side
- in isosceles trapezoid the legs are congruent
- in isosceles trapezoid the lower base angles are congruent
- in isosceles trapezoid the upper base angles are congruent
- in isosceles trapezoid the diagonals are congruent
- the area of the trapezoid is $A = \frac{a+b}{2} \cdot h$

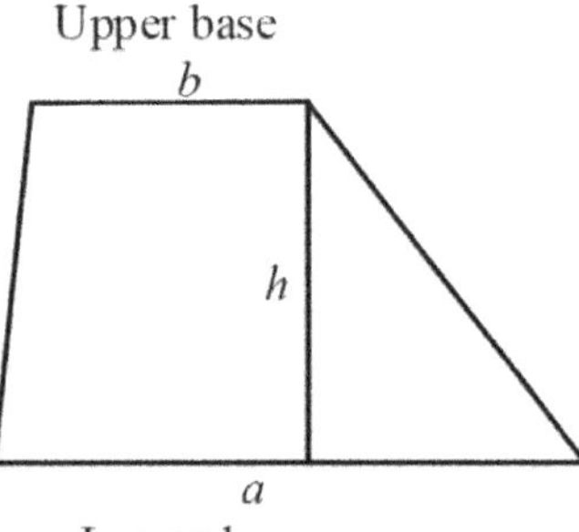

Example: Two angles in trapezoid have measures 46° and 72°. What are the measures of remaining two trapezoid's angles?

Solution: These two angles are not the same side interior angles (their measures do not add up to 180°), so they are adjacent to different trapezoid's legs. Find two supplementary angles to angles of 46° and 72°:

$$180° - 46° = 134°$$

$$180° - 72° = 108°$$

Answer: 134° and 108°.

Example: What is the area of trapezoid with bases of 14 cm and 22 cm and height of 4 cm?

Solution: Use area formula:

$$A = \frac{14 + 22}{2} \cdot 4 = 18 \cdot 4 = 72 \text{ cm}^2$$

Answer: 72 cm^2.

43. Circle

A **circle** is the locus of all points equidistant from a central point.

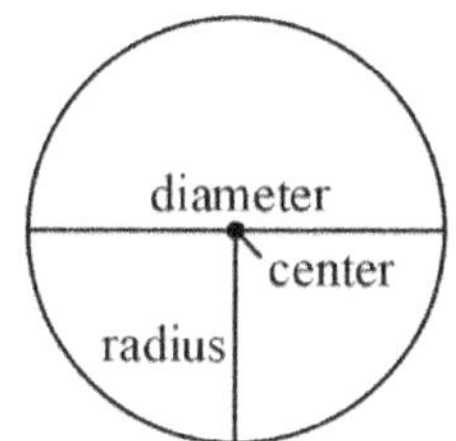

Tips

- the diameter d is twice the radius r
- the circumference of the circle is $c = 2\pi r = \pi d$
- the area of the circle is $A = \pi r^2$

Example: What is the circumference of the circle with diameter 48 cm?

Solution: Use circumference formula:

$$c = \pi d \Rightarrow c = 48\pi \text{ cm}$$

Answer: 48π cm.

Example: What is the area of the circle with circumference of 12π ft?

Solution:

$$\left.\begin{array}{l} c = 12\pi \text{ ft} \\ A = ? \end{array}\right\} \quad \begin{array}{l} c = 2\pi r \Rightarrow 2\pi r = 12\pi, r = 6 \text{ ft} \\ A = \pi r^2 \Rightarrow A = \pi \cdot 6^2 = 36\pi \text{ ft}^2 \end{array}$$

Answer: 36π ft^2.

44. Polygons

The sum of the measures of all interior angles of n-sided polygon is

$$\boxed{(n-2) \cdot 180°}$$

Example: What is the measure of one interior angle of regular hexagon?

Solution:

$n = 6 \Rightarrow$ the sum of the measures of all interior angles is $(6-2) \cdot 180° = 720°$.

All interior angles in regular hexagon are congruent, so the measure of each of these angles is

$$\frac{720°}{6} = 120°$$

Answer: $120°$.

3D Shapes

Surface Area (SA) is the sum of the area of all sides of the shape.

Volume (V) is the measure of the space inside of a solid figure.

45. Cube

Cube is a 3D solid with six square faces.

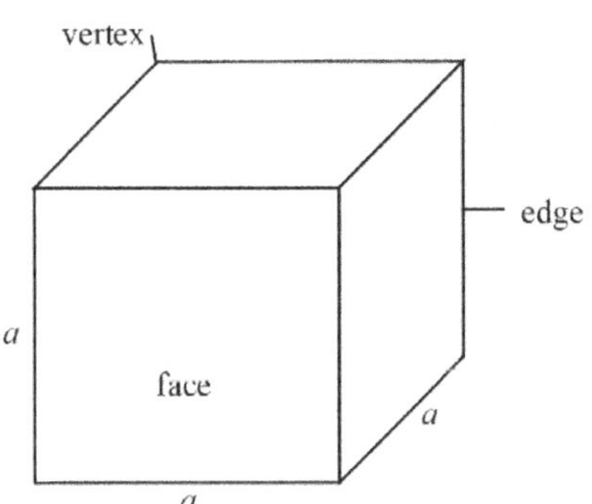

Tips

- has 6 faces
- has 12 edges
- has 8 vertices
- all faces are congruent squares
- the SA of the cube is $SA = 6a^2$
- the volume of the cube is $V = a^3$
- the diagonal of the cube is $d = a\sqrt{3}$

Example: If the SA of the cube is 216 square centimeters, what is the volume of the cube?

Solution:

$SA = 216\text{ cm}^2$, $V = ?$

$SA = 6a^2 \Rightarrow 6a^2 = 216, a^2 = 36, a = 6\text{ cm}$

$V = a^3 = 6^3 = 216\text{ cm}^3$

Answer: 216 cm^3.

46. Rectangular Prism

A **rectangular prism** is a 3D solid, which has six faces that are rectangles.

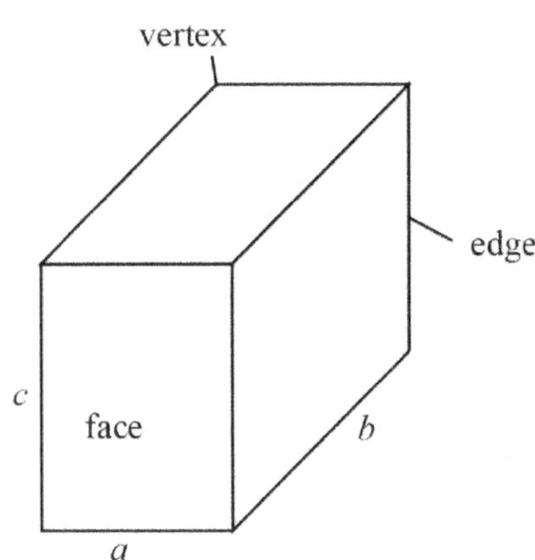

Tips

- has 6 faces
- has 12 edges
- has 8 vertices
- all faces are rectangles
- the SA of the cube is $SA = 2(a \cdot b + a \cdot c + b \cdot c)$
- the volume of the cube is $V = a \cdot b \cdot c$
- the diagonal of the cube is $d = \sqrt{a^2 + b^2 + c^2}$

Example: If three different faces of rectangular prism have area of $24 \text{ cm}^2, 32 \text{ cm}^2$ and 48 cm^2, what is the volume of the prism?

Solution:

$a \cdot b = 24 \text{ cm}^2$

$a \cdot c = 32 \text{ cm}^2$

$b \cdot c = 48 \text{ cm}^2$

$V = ?$

$$(a \cdot b) \cdot (a \cdot c) \cdot (b \cdot c) = 24 \cdot 32 \cdot 48 = 2^3 \cdot 3 \cdot 2^5 \cdot 2^4 \cdot 3$$

$$a^2 \cdot b^2 \cdot c^2 = 2^{12} \cdot 3^2$$

$$V = a \cdot b \cdot c = \sqrt{2^{12} \cdot 3^2} = 2^6 \cdot 3 = 192 \text{ cm}^3$$

Answer: 192 cm^3.

Example: Find the diagonal of the rectangular prism with edges of 3 cm, 4 cm and 12 cm.

Solution:

$a = 3 \text{ cm}$

$b = 4 \text{ cm}$

$c = 12 \text{ cm}$

$d = ?$

$$d = \sqrt{a^2 + b^2 + c^2}$$

$$d = \sqrt{3^2 + 4^2 + 12^2} = \sqrt{9 + 16 + 144} = \sqrt{169} = 13 \text{ cm}$$

Answer: 13 cm.

47. Pyramid

A **pyramid** is a 3D solid with a polygonal base and triangular faces that meet at a common point.

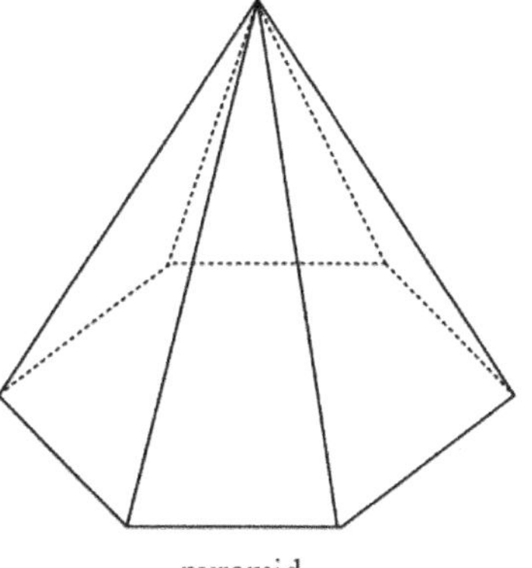

pyramid

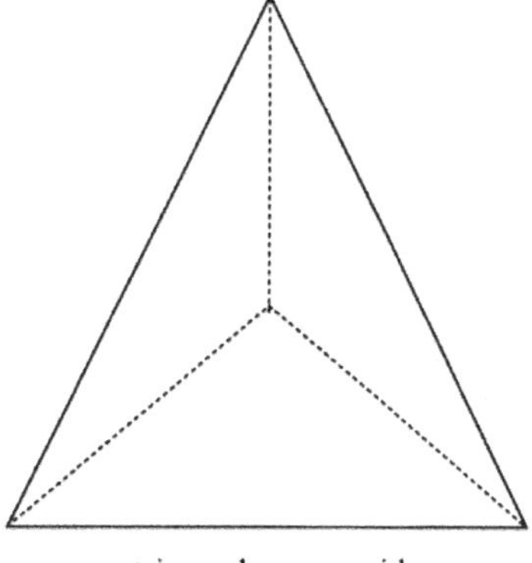

triangular pyramid

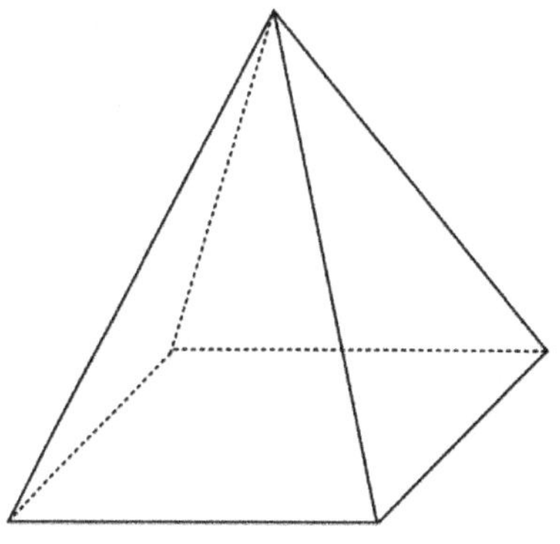

rectangular pyramid

Tips

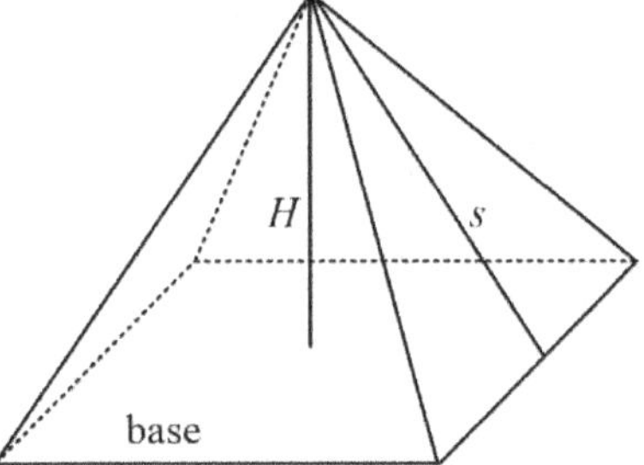

- the volume of the pyramid is $V = \frac{1}{3} \cdot A_{base} \cdot H$
- the surface area of the regular pyramid is
  $SA = A_{base} + \frac{1}{2} \cdot P_{base} \cdot s$, where s is a slant height
- the lateral area of the pyramid is the total area of all lateral faces
- the surface area of an oblique pyramid is
  $SA = A_{base} + A_{lateral\ faces}$

Example: What is the volume of triangular pyramid with base area of 72 square centimeters and height of 8 cm?

Solution:

$A_{base} = 72\text{ cm}^2$

$H = 8\text{ cm}$

$V = ?$

$$V = \frac{1}{3} \cdot A_{base} \cdot H = \frac{1}{3} \cdot 72 \cdot 8 = 192\text{ cm}^3$$

Answer: 192 cubic centimeters.

Example: A regular square pyramid has the base edge of 9 cm and the slant height of 10 cm. What is the surface area of the pyramid?

Solution:

$a = 9\text{ cm}$

$A_{base} = ?$

$$A_{base} = a^2 = 9^2 = 81\text{ cm}^2$$

$a = 9\text{ cm}$

$s = 10\text{ cm}$

$A_{lateral} = ?$

$$A_{lateral} = \frac{1}{2} \cdot P_{base} \cdot s = \frac{1}{2} \cdot (4 \cdot 9) \cdot 10 = 180\text{ cm}^2$$

Hence, $SA = 81 + 180 = 261\text{ cm}^2$.

Answer: 261 cm^2.

48. Cone

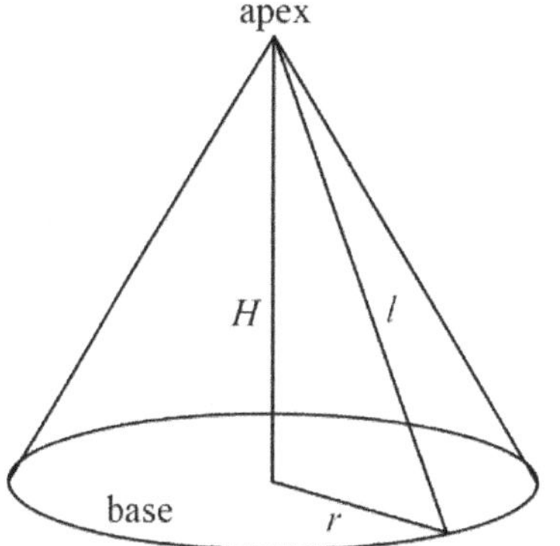

A **cone** is a 3D solid formed when line segments are drawn from vertex (called **apex**) to points on the circle.

Tips

- the lateral area of the cone is $LA = \pi r l$
- the surface area of the cone is $SA = \pi r^2 + \pi r l$
- the volume of the cone is $V = \frac{1}{3}\pi r^2 H$

Example: The height of the cone is 4 in, the radius of the base of the cone is 3 in. What is the volume of the cone? What is the surface area of the cone?

Solution:

$H = 4$ in

$r = 3$ in

$V = ?$

$$V = \frac{1}{3}\pi r^2 H = \frac{1}{3} \cdot \pi \cdot 3^2 \cdot 4 = 12\pi \text{ in}^3$$

Consider right triangle formed by r, H and l. By the Pythagorean theorem,

$$l^2 = r^2 + H^2$$

$$l^2 = 3^3 + 4^2 = 9 + 16 = 25$$

$$l = 5 \text{ in}$$

$H = 4$ in

$r = 3$ in

$l = 5$ in

$SA = ?$

$$A_{base} = \pi r^2 = \pi \cdot 3^2 = 9\pi \text{ in}^2$$

$$LA = \pi r l = \pi \cdot 3 \cdot 5 = 15\pi \text{ in}^2$$

$$SA = A_{base} + LA = 9\pi + 15\pi = 24\pi \text{ in}^2$$

Answer: volume is 12π cubic inches, the surface area is 24π cubic inches.

49. Cylinder

A **cylinder** is a 3D solid formed by connecting two parallel congruent circles with perpendicular lines.

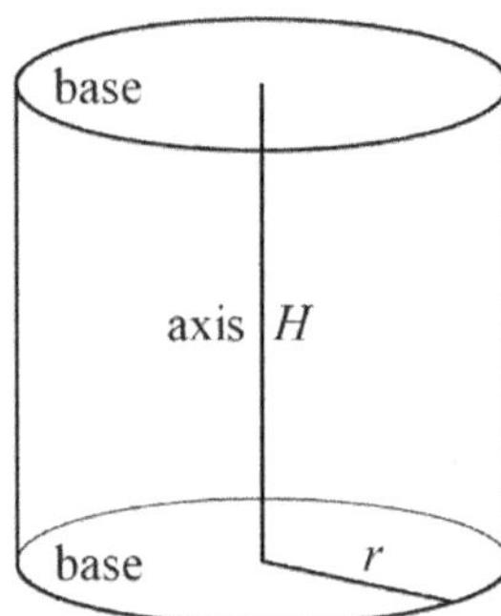

Tips

- the lateral area of the cylinder is $LA = 2\pi rH$
- the surface area of the cylinder is $SA = 2\pi r(r + H)$
- the volume of the cylinder is $V = \pi r^2 H$

Example: The height of the cylinder is 10 cm, the radius of the base of the cylinder is 6 cm. What is the volume of the cylinder? What is the surface area of the cylinder?

Solution:

$H = 10$ cm
$r = 6$ cm
$V = ?$

$$V = \pi r^2 H = \pi \cdot 6^2 \cdot 10 = 360\pi \text{ cm}^3$$

$H = 10$ cm
$r = 6$ cm
$SA = ?$

$$SA = 2\pi r(r + H) = 2\pi \cdot 6 \cdot (6 + 10) = 192\pi \text{ cm}^2$$

Answer: volume is 360π cubic centimeters, the surface area is 192π cubic centimeters.

Example: If the height H of the cylinder is 5 times greater than the radius r of the cylinder's base, what is the volume of the cylinder in terms of r?

Solution:

$H = 5r$
$V = ?$

$$V = \pi r^2 H = \pi r^2 \cdot (5r) = 5\pi r^3 \text{ un}^3.$$

Answer: $5\pi r^3$ un^3.

50. Sphere

A **sphere** is the locus of points at a fixed distance from a given point. This point is known as the **center** of the sphere.

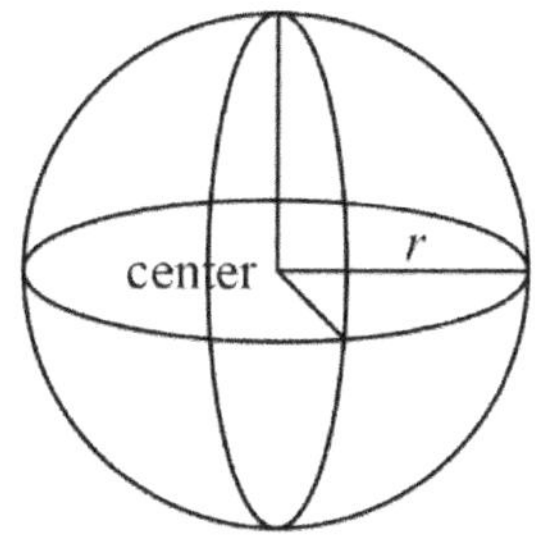

Tips

- the surface area of the sphere is $SA = 4\pi r^2$
- the volume of a sphere is $V = \frac{4}{3}\pi r^3$

Example: A sphere has the radius of 12 cm. What is the volume and surface area of the sphere?

Solution:

$r = 12$ cm

$V = ?$ $\qquad V = \frac{4}{3}\pi r^3 = \frac{4}{3}\pi \cdot 12^3 = 2{,}304\pi \text{ cm}^3$

$SA = ?$ $\qquad SA = 4\pi r^2 = 4\pi \cdot 12^2 = 576\pi\ cm^2$

Answer: the volume is $2{,}304\pi$ cubic centimeters, the surface area is 576π square centimeters.

TOPIC BY TOPIC PRACTICE EXERCISE

EXERCISE 1: RATIO & PROPORTION

---

1. A set of playing cards contains 4 cards with the letters A, K, Q and J written on them. There are 9 more cards numbered 2 through 10. What is the ratio of odd-numbered cards to the other cards?

A) 4 : 9 B) 4 : 13 C) 5 : 9 D) 5 : 13

---

2. Base your answer on the following chart showing the number of students obtaining 1, 2, 3 or 4 A's on their monthly assessment tests.

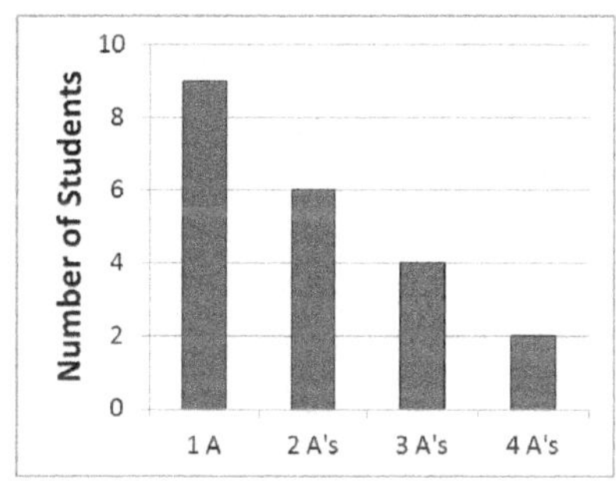

What is the ratio of students obtaining 3 or more A's to the number of students obtaining fewer than 3 A's?

A) 2 : 7 B) 2 : 5 C) 2 : 9 D) 4 : 15

---

3. In a class of 24 students, 3 out of 8 are left-handed. How many right-handed students are there in the class?

A) 5 B) 9 C) 12 D) 15

---

4. What fraction of the largest triangle is shaded?

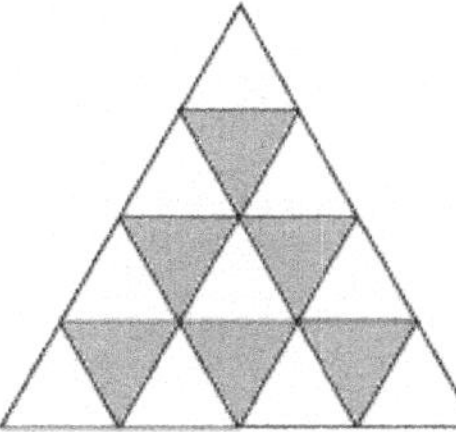

A) $\frac{1}{2}$ B) $\frac{3}{8}$ C) $\frac{5}{8}$ D) $\frac{7}{16}$

---

5. Base your answer to this question on the image below:

What is the ratio of the stars to the rest of the shapes?

A) 1 : 2 B) 4 : 5 C) 4 : 9 D) 5 : 9

6. The table below shows the colors of horses participating in a race.

Color	Number of Horses
Brown	7
Black	9
White	4

What is the ratio between the numbers of black and white horses?

A) 4 : 9 B) 9 : 20 C) 1 : 5 D) 9 : 4

7. A racecar driver adds a special additive to his fuel in the ratio 1 : 10 for high-performance. Which of the following is the correct combination of additive and fuel he can use?

A) 2 liters of additive to 10 liters of fuel
B) 10 liters of additive to 1 liter of fuel
C) 2.5 liters of additive to 25 liters of fuel
D) 1 liter of additive to 10.5 liters of fuel

8. Each student, in a class of 50, must choose a foreign language for study. 27 students chose Spanish, 5 chose German and the rest chose French. What is the ratio of the students who chose Spanish to the students who picked French?

A) $\frac{2}{3}$ B) $\frac{1}{10}$ C) $\frac{3}{2}$ D) $\frac{9}{25}$

9. At a party, 28 people are wearing a jacket and 21 are wearing a hat. If there are 7 people who are wearing both a jacket and a hat, what is the ratio of people wearing only a hat to people wearing only a jacket?

A) $\frac{2}{3}$ B) $\frac{3}{4}$ C) $\frac{3}{2}$ D) $\frac{4}{3}$

10. In a parking lot, the ratio of cars to trucks is 7 : 2. Which of the following is an equivalent fractional form of this ratio?

A) $\frac{2}{7}$ B) $\frac{2}{9}$ C) $\frac{7}{9}$ D) $\frac{21}{6}$

11. A small square pond is surrounded by square tiles as shown in the figure below. What is the ratio of the area of the pond to the area of the tiles?

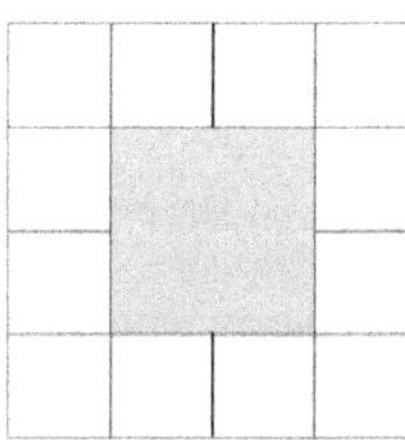

A) $\frac{1}{4}$ B) $\frac{1}{3}$ C) $\frac{1}{2}$ D) $\frac{2}{5}$

12. A sum of $70 is to be divided among three children in the ratio 2 : 5 : 7. What is the largest share that a child receives?

A) $5 B) $10 C)$25 D) $35

13. A cake recipe uses flour and butter in the ratio of 3 : 1. The ratio of butter to milk is 2 : 5. What is the ratio of flour to milk?

A) 2 : 3 B) 5 : 6 C) 3 : 5 D) 6 : 5

14. The length and width of a cube are 6 cm and 5 cm respectively. If the ratio of the length to the height of the cube is 3 : 1, what is the ratio of the width to the height of the cube?

A) 5 : 2 B) 2 : 5 C) 1 : 2 D) 5 : 1

15. The salaries of Allan and Bob are in the ratio 3 : 5. The salaries of Bob and Charles are in the ratio 3 : 7. What is the ratio of the salaries of Allan, Bob and Charles?

A) 9 : 15 : 35 B) 3 : 5 : 7 C) 3 : 7 : 3 D) 9 : 35 : 15

16. A mountaineer is climbing at an average rate of 5 ft per minute. How long will it take him to reach the top of a hill that is 400 ft high?

A) 20 minutes B) 40 minutes C) 1 hour 20 minutes D) 1 hour 40 minutes

17. For every 5 meters that Allison covers on her bicycle, Bryan walks 2 meters. At this rate, how much distance would Bryan have covered when Allison has travelled 340 meters?

A) 68 m B) 136 m C) 272 m D) 850 m

18. The ratio of flowering plants to non-flowering plants in a park is 4 : 9. If the number of non-flowering plants is 2,754, what is the number of flowering plants?

A) 306 B) 847 C) 1,224 D) 6,196

19. A boat builder can build 3 boats in 4 months. How many boats can he produce in two years?

A) 12 B) 6 C) 18 D) 32

20. A beverage-filling machine can fill 250 cans in 3 minutes. What is the number of cans that it can fill in one hour?

A) 83 B) 2,500 C) 750 D) 5,000

21. Murielle bakes clay pots, in an oven, in batches of 11 pots. If a batch takes 20 minutes to bake, how many pots can she bake in her 8-hour shift during which she takes a 40-minute lunch break?

A) 88 B) 242 C) 264 D) 800

22. A moneychanger exchanges 4 Canadian dollars (CAD) for 3 US dollars (USD)? How many USD will a man get for CAD 630?

A) USD 2,520.00 B) USD 1,890.00 C) USD 840.00 D) USD 472.50

23. The ratio of white sheep to black in a herd is 13 : 3. If there are 39 black sheep what is the size of the herd?

A) 130 B) 169 C) 208 D) 247

24. Carlton starts depositing money in his empty bank account. He deposits $45 every 2 months. What is the minimum number of full months after which he will have sufficient money in his account to pay for a $300 gaming console?

A) 6 B) 7 C) 13 D) 14

25. The table below shows the number of students and the number of teachers in 3 different schools.

School	Students	Teachers
X	440	40
Y	480	60
Z	210	30

Which of the following lists the three schools in ascending order of teacher to student ratio?

A) X, Y, Z B) Z, Y, X C) Z, X, Y D) Y, X, Z

---

26. A box of chocolates contains 16 pieces. If 7 chocolates have been eaten, what percentage of the chocolates is left?

A) 6.25% B) 31.25% C) 43.75% D) 56.25%

---

27. A dress with a price tag of $140 is being offered at a discount of 45%. What is the new price of the dress?

A) $63 B) $77 C) $95 D) $134

---

28. In a school, every student is required to choose one sport: 12.5% students play football, 25% play basketball and the rest participate in swimming. What is the ratio of students who play basketball to the students who participate in swimming?

A) 1 : 5 B) 2 : 5 C) 3 : 8 D) 1 : 4

---

29. A boy is downloading a large video file from the internet at a rate of 5% every 3 minutes. Given that 35% of the file has already been downloaded, how much additional time is required to complete the download?

A) 39 minutes B) 60 minutes C) 65 minutes D) 108 minutes

---

30. Jane scored 26 points out of 40 on her math test. On the following test she scored 37 points out of 50. What is her combined percentage for the two tests?

A) 63% B) 69% C) 70% D) 74%

EXERCISE 2: NUMBER SYSTEM

1. Simplify $-2(3-2)+3(1-2)$

   A) -5
   B) -1
   C) 1
   D) 5

---

2. Given that $a=-2, b=3$ and $c=-5$, calculate $ab-bc$

   A) -21
   B) -9
   C) 9
   D) 21

---

3. A submarine test fired an anti-aircraft missile from a depth of 35 meters, which hit the target at an altitude of 127 meters above sea level. How far did the missile travel vertically?

   A) 70 m
   B) 92 m
   C) 162 m
   D) 184 m

---

4. The temperature in Rochester on Sunday, at 12:00 AM, was $-2°C$. Over the next four days, the temperature changed by $+2°C$, $-7°C$, $+3°C$ and $-4°C$ respectively, from the previous day. What was the 12:00 AM temperature in Rochester on Thursday?

   A) $-11°C$
   B) $-8°C$
   C) $0°C$
   D) $4°C$

---

5. At a temperature of $-195.79°C$, nitrogen gas turns into a liquid. The liquefaction temperature of oxygen is $-182.96°C$. What is the absolute value of the difference between the liquefaction temperatures of nitrogen and oxygen?

A) -378.75
B) -12.83
C) 8.75
D) 12.83

6. Which of the following numeric sequences does not fit the sequence represented by the algebraic expression below?

$$x - 1, x + 1, x + 5, x + 13$$

A) $-10, -8, -4, 4$
B) $-6, -4, 0, 8$
C) $-1, 1, 5, 13$
D) $4, 6, 10, 17$

7. The sum of two numbers a and b is twice their difference. Which of the following expressions relate a and b?

A) $a = 3b$
B) $2a = 3b$
C) $a = -3b$
D) $a = 2b$

8. Given that $ab \geq 0$, which of the following cannot be true regarding a and b?

A) $a > 0$ and $b > 0$
B) $a < 0$ and $b < 0$
C) $a < 0$ and $b = 0$
D) $a > 0$ and $b < 0$

9. Simplify: $t - 3(t - 8) + 6(3t + 4)$

A) $15t$
B) $16t$
C) $16t + 48$
D) $15t + 48$

---

10. Evaluate $5^2 \times (55 \div 550) \times (12 \div 60) \div 1^5$

A) $\frac{1}{10}$
B) $\frac{1}{5}$
C) $\frac{5}{11}$
D) $\frac{1}{2}$

---

11. Given that $x > 0$, how does $\frac{1}{x}$ compare with x?

A) $x > \frac{1}{x}$
B) $x < \frac{1}{x}$
C) $x > \frac{1}{x}$ when $x > 1$, $x < \frac{1}{x}$ when $x < 1$
D) $x < \frac{1}{x}$ when $x > 1$, $x > \frac{1}{x}$ when $x < 1$

---

12. The number y is at a distance of 4 units from point x. Which of the following gives the possible value(s) of y?

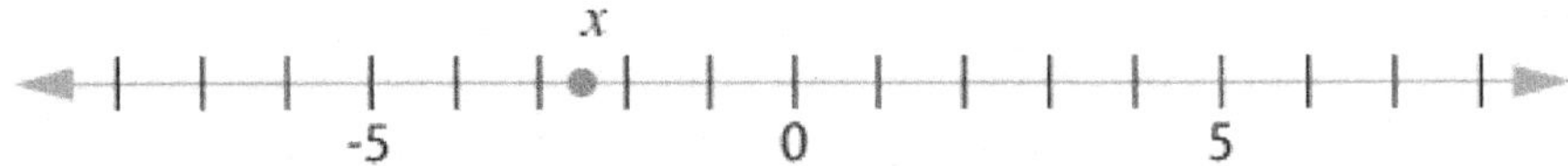

A) 1.5 only
B) -6.5 and 1.5
C) -1.5 and 6.5
D) -4 and 4

---

13. Which expression has the same value as $15.5 + 27.8$?

A) $-(-15.5 - 27.8)$
B) $-(-15.5 + 27.8)$
C) $-15.5 - 27.8$
D) $-15.5(-27.8)$

---

14. Which of the following is equivalent to the number $\frac{77}{15}$?

A) 5.133
B) $5.1\overline{3}$
C) $5.\overline{133}$
D) $5.\overline{13}$

---

15. For what values of x the expression $3 - x$ is always negative?

A) $x > 3$
B) $x < 3$
C) $x < -3$
D) $x > -3$

---

16. Which statement correctly describes the decimal equivalent of $\frac{1}{32}$?

A) The decimal form terminates after 4 decimal places
B) The decimal form terminates after 5 decimal places
C) The decimal form has repeating digits of 0312
D) The decimal form has repeating digits of 03125

---

17. Jimmy had \$19.40 in his savings box at the start of the month. Which of the following sets of transactions, during the month, will leave him with exactly \$25 at the end of the month?

A) Receiving an allowance of \$6.90 and spending \$12.50
B) Receiving an allowance of \$12.90 and spending \$6.50
C) Receiving an allowance of \$12.50 and spending \$6.90
D) Receiving an allowance of \$6.50 and spending \$12.90

---

18. Tom is 3 years old. Jerry is thrice as old as Tom. Elmer's age is two years less than twice Jerry's age. What is the sum of their ages?

A) 16
B) 25
C) 28
D) 30

---

19. What is the value of the following expression?

$$\left(-\frac{12}{7}\right) \times \left(3\frac{2}{3}\right) \div \left(-\frac{6}{7}\right)$$

A) $7\frac{1}{3}$
B) $6\frac{2}{3}$
C) $5\frac{19}{49}$
D) $-7\frac{2}{3}$

---

20. A group of 3 students wants to donate \$500 to a charity project. The status of their fund raising campaign is given below:

- The money raised so far is \$283.50
- They have incurred fund raising expenses of \$19.70 which they must also recover from the funds raised.
- Each student will contribute \$25.00 from his own pocket.

How much more money do they need to collect?

A) \$121.80
B) \$161.20
C) \$171.80
D) \$211.20

---

21. Following the instructions on a treasure map, Jim walked 20 paces north, 9 paces east, 11 paces south and 5 paces west. Which of the following gives Jim's current location?

A) 9 paces North and 4 paces West of the starting point
B) 11 paces South and 4 paces East of the starting point
C) 4 paces North and 9 paces East of the starting point
D) 9 paces North and 4 paces East of the starting point

---

22. What is the fractional equivalent of the decimal number 5.125?

A) $\frac{5}{8}$
B) $4\frac{1}{8}$
C) $5\frac{1}{4}$
D) $\frac{41}{8}$

---

23. The table below shows the banking transactions performed by Carol over five days.

Monday	Deposited $158 into the account
Tuesday	Deposited $95 into the account
Wednesday	Withdrew $203 from the account
Thursday	Withdrew $275 from the account
Friday	Deposited $50 into the account

What is her average daily transaction during the period?

A) A deposit of $35 per day
B) A withdrawal or $35 per day
C) A deposit of $101 per day
D) A withdrawal of $239 per day

---

24. Which of the following does NOT result in a change in value of zero?

A) An aircraft climbing 235 feet, then dropping by 305 feet and climbing again by 70 feet.
B) A temperature drop of 5°C followed by another drop of 7°C and a rise of 12°C
C) A 10% increase in profit followed by a 10% decrease in profit next year.
D) Sales increasing from $1,000 to $2,000 but getting halved the following year

---

---

25. Buttercup, Bubbles and Blossom earned the following points on their math test:

- Buttercup scored 69 points
- Bubbles scored $\left(\frac{2}{3}\right)^{\text{rd}}$ of the points scored by Buttercup
- Blossom score 11 points more than Bubbles

What is the total number of points scored by the three girls?

A) 103
B) 126
C) 172
D) 195

---

26. Which expression can be placed in the blank to make the equation hold true?

$$3(-2.9) - 3.1 - \_\_\_\_\_ = 0$$

A) -11.9
B) $2(-2.3 - 3.6)$
C) $2(1.9 + 4.0)$
D) $3(4) - 0.2$

---

27. x and y are two positive integers. The midnight temperature on January, 1 was $-x$, the noon temperature on the same day was y. What was the increase in temperature?

A) $y + x$
B) $y - x$
C) $-x - y$
D) $x - y$

---

28. Bobby has 279 matchsticks. He uses each stick to make one side of an independent shapes as follows:

- He makes 36 triangles
- He makes 24 squares
- He uses the remaining sticks to make pentagons

Which of the following expressions can be used to calculate the number of pentagons he makes?

A) $[279 - 4(36) - 3(24)] \div 5$
B) $[279 - 3(36) + 4(24)] \div 5$
C) $[279 - 3(36) - 4(24)] \div 4$
D) $[279 - 3(36) - 4(24)] \div 5$

---

29. A scientist measured the lengths of five fish. If the length of 4 of these fish were $3\frac{1}{4}, 4\frac{1}{8}, 5$ and $4\frac{1}{2}$ and the average length was $4\frac{1}{4}$, what was the length of the fifth fish?

A) $3\frac{3}{8}$
B) $4\frac{1}{8}$
C) $4\frac{1}{2}$
D) $4\frac{3}{8}$

---

30. Which of the following sequences lists the numerical values in an ascending order?

A) $\frac{15}{32}, 0.5, \frac{31}{64}, \frac{3}{4}$
B) $\frac{15}{32}, \frac{31}{64}, 0.5, \frac{3}{4}$
C) $\frac{3}{4}, 0.5, \frac{31}{64}, \frac{15}{32}$
D) $0.5, \frac{15}{32}, \frac{31}{64}, \frac{3}{4}$

EXERCISE 3: EXPRESSIONS & EQUATIONS

1. Simplify the expression: $7 + 2(3 - 9)$

   A) -5
   B) 15
   C) 18
   D) 19

---

2. Which expression makes the following equation true for all values of x?

   $$9x - 15 = 3 \cdot (\,?\,)$$

   A) $-6x$
   B) $9x - 5$
   C) $3x - 15$
   D) $3x - 5$

---

3. Which of the following options is an equivalent form of the equation below?

   $$\frac{3}{y-3} = -\frac{5}{x+2}$$

   A) $3x + 2 = -5y - 3$
   B) $3(x + 2) + 5(y - 3) = 0$
   C) $3(x + 2) = 5(y - 3)$
   D) $5(x + 2) = -3(y - 3)$

---

4. A baker wants to bake 45 cakes. Each cake requires 3 eggs to prepare. If the baker already has 28 eggs and eggs are sold in packs of 12, what is the minimum number of packs he must buy?

   A) 8
   B) 9
   C) 12
   D) 107

---

5. Which of the following expressions is a simplified form of the following expression?

$$\frac{2}{3}(2x+1)-\frac{1}{6}(2x+9)$$

A) $x-8$
B) $\frac{5}{3}x-\frac{5}{6}$
C) $x-\frac{5}{6}$
D) $x+\frac{5}{6}$

---

6. The price of a jacket was reduced to p dollars, after a discount of 35% during a sale. Which of the following expressions represents the price of the jacket before the discount?

A) $\frac{165p}{100}$
B) $\frac{135p}{100}$
C) $\frac{100p}{65}$
D) $\frac{65p}{100}$

---

7. Which expression is equivalent to the expression below?

$$-5\left(\frac{2}{3}+h\right)+\frac{11}{3}h$$

A) $-\frac{2}{3}(5+2h)$
B) $\frac{2}{3}(5+13h)$
C) $-\frac{2}{3}(10+2h)$
D) $-\frac{2}{3}(5h+2)$

---

8. A rectangular piece of paper had sides of lengths x cm and y cm. A strip of paper with width w cm was cut out along the length y cm. Which of the following is an expression for the perimeter of the remaining rectangle?

A) $x + y - w$
B) $2(x + y) - w$
C) $x + y - 2w$
D) $2(x + y - w)$

---

9. The net wealth of three friends, Allan, Brandon and Charles is $(3.3x - 5y)$, $(2.9y - 2.8z)$ and $(3.7z - 2.1x)$ respectively. What is their average net wealth?

A) $5.4x - 7.9y + 6.5z$
B) $0.3x + 0.4y - 0.7z$
C) $0.4x - 0.7y + 0.3z$
D) $1.2x - 2.1y + 0.9z$

---

10. Jerry bought some apples and oranges for \$3.40. Given that an apple costs \$0.25, an orange costs \$0.20 and that the number of apples he purchased was a, which of the following is the expression for the number of oranges?

A) $\frac{3.40-0.20a}{0.25}$
B) $\frac{3.40-0.25a}{0.20}$
C) $3.40 - 0.45a$
D) $\frac{3.40}{0.20} - a$

---

11. Which of the following equations is NOT equivalent to the equation below?

$$y = \frac{2}{3}x + 1$$

A) $3y - 2x = 3$
B) $6y = 4x + 6$
C) $\frac{3}{2}y = x - \frac{3}{2}$
D) $\frac{3}{2}(y - 1) = x$

12. An item with a regular price of p dollars is being offered at a discount of 35% during a sale. Customers with a shopper's club card receive an additional 10% discount on the discounted price. Which of the flowing gives the price that a customer with a shopper's club card would pay?

A) $(0.90)(0.65)p$
B) $0.45p$
C) $(0.65)(0.10)p$
D) $(0.35)(0.10)p$

13. Which of the following is the numeric value of the following expression?

$$\frac{2.3 - 9.2}{3} + \frac{0.25(11.9 + 4.1)}{-2}$$

A) -5.825
B) -4.3
C) 0.3
D) 10.425

---

14. A marathon runner covered a distance of x miles during the first hour. During the second hour the distance covered decreased by 25%. During the third hour the distance covered was 80% of the distance covered during the second hour? What was the total distance covered in 3 hours?

A) $0.60x$
B) $1.75x$
C) $1.90x$
D) $2.35x$

---

15. Which expression is equivalent to $6\pi - (-72)$?

A) -66π
B) $6(\pi + 12)$
C) 78π
D) $6\pi + 12$

---

16. Tom and Jerry completely filled up an empty bucket, which can hold 32 liters of water. Tom poured 18 full jugs of water into the bucket. Jerry used a jug of capacity 0.5 liters to fill the bucket. If Tom's jug can hold 1.5 liters of water, which of the following expressions gives the number of full jugs that Jerry poured?

A) $(32 \div 1.5) - 18(0.5)$
B) $(32 - 18(0.5)) \div 1.5$
C) $(32 - 18(1.5)) \div 0.5$
D) $(32 - 18) \div 0.5$

---

17. The average rainfall in New York increases by 21% from June to July and decreases by 9.6% from July to August. If the average rainfall in June 2018 was 3.5 inches, which expression represents a strategy for the estimating the rainfall in August 2018?

A) $3.5(20)(10)$
B) $3.5(1.2)(0.9)$
C) $3.5 + 2 - 1$
D) $3.5(1.2)(1.1)$

---

18. Which expression is equivalent to the expression $j + 3 - (0.91j + 1.32) \cdot 2$?

A) $-0.46j$
B) $-0.36 + 0.82j$
C) $0.18j + 3.36$
D) $-0.82j + 0.36$

---

19. Which expression is equivalent to the expression $\frac{3}{5}(3a + 10b) - \frac{4}{7}(7a + 14b)$?

A) $-\left(\frac{11}{5}a + 2b\right)$
B) $\frac{11}{5}a - 2b$
C) $-\left(\frac{11}{5}b + 2a\right)$
D) $-\frac{12}{35}(10a + 24b)$

---

20. Carol is throwing darts at a circular dartboard.

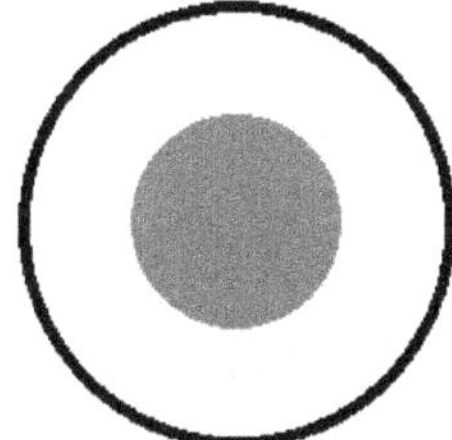

- She earns 25 points for hitting the gray region in the center;
- She earns 10 points for hitting the white outer region;
- She needs to score more than 180 points to win the prize.

Given that she has already scored 45 points, which inequality gives the minimum number of additional throws t, she needs to win the prize?

A) $180 \leq 10x + 45$
B) $180 + 45 \leq 25x$
C) $180 \geq 25x + 45$
D) $180 \leq 25x + 45$

21. A shoe store is offering sneakers at a 40% discount. Donald has a discount coupon, which entitles him to get an additional \$5 off the discounted price. If the original price of the sneakers was s, how much does Donald have to pay?

A) $0.6s$
B) $s - 0.6s - 5$
C) $s - 0.6 - 5$
D) $s - 0.4s - 5$

22. A mini golf course charges \$5.00 for a 30-minute game and \$1.75 every 10 minutes, if the game goes over 30 minutes. George had \$52 to spend on mini golf. Which of the following inequalities can be used to determine x, the maximum number of *additional* games, he can play if the first game lasted for 1 hour?

A) $5x \geq 41.75$
B) $6.75x \leq 52$
C) $10.25 + 5x \leq 52$
D) $5 + 1.75x \leq 52$

23. Chris had 255 beads. She made 12 identical necklaces from these beads and was left with 27 beads. How many beads did she use per necklace?

A) $(255 - 27) \div 12$
B) $255 \div 12 - 27$
C) $255 - 27 \div 12$
D) $(255 - 12) \div 27$

24. Jennifer prepared 5 kg of batter to bake some cakes for a birthday party. She used 1.5 kg to make a large cake, $\frac{2}{7}$ of the remaining to make a medium-sized cake and used the left over batter to make 10 small cakes of equal size. Which of the following expressions gives the weight of batter in each small cake?

A) $(5 - 1.5) \times \frac{2}{7} \div 10$
B) $(5 - 1.5) \times \frac{5}{7} \div 10$
C) $(5 - 1.5) \times \frac{2}{7} \times 10$
D) $5 \times \frac{5}{7} \div 10$

25. The town of Altimus is located 251 m above sea level. The town of Lowplains is located 27 m below sea level. How many meters above Lowplains is Altimus located?

A) $251 + (-27)$
B) $251 - (-27)$
C) $251 - 27$
D) $27 - 251$

26. Two sticks of lengths x and y are tied together as shown in the figure below.

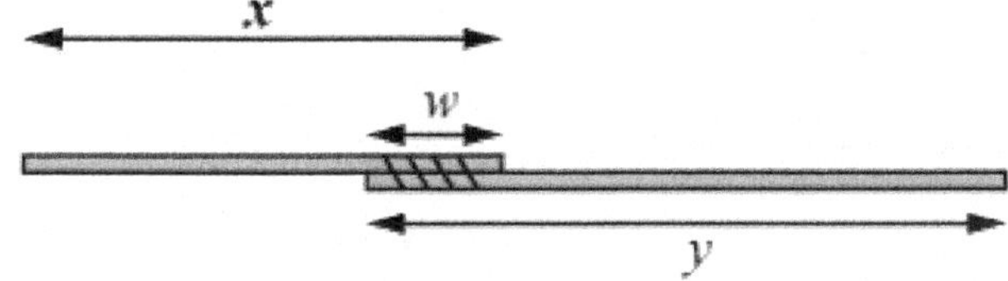

Which of the following expressions gives the total length of the joined sticks?

A) $x + y$
B) $x + y - 2w$
C) $x + y - w$
D) $x + y + w$

---

27. The following minimum temperatures were recorded on the seven days of a week in a city:

$$1°C,\ 3°C,\ 0°C,\ -7°C,\ -9°C,\ -11°C,\ -5°C$$

Which of the following gives the highest temperature rise between two successive days during the week?

A) 2°C
B) 6°C
C) 7°C
D) 9°C

---

28. Which of the following is the correct value of the expression $2 + 5 \cdot 8 - 3$?

A) 15
B) 35
C) 39
D) 53

---

29. Given that $x \div 3 = a$ and $x \div \frac{1}{3} = b$, which of the following gives the relationship between a and b?

A) $a = 3b$
B) $a = 9b$
C) $3a = b$
D) $9a = b$

---

30. Use the equation below to answer the following question?

$$xy = z$$

Given that $z > 0$, which of the following statements CANNOT be true?

A) x and y are both positive
B) x and y are both negative
C) x is negative and y is positive
D) x is equal to y

EXERCISE 4: GEOMETRY

(Use $\pi = 3.14$ unless otherwise specified)

1. The diameter of a round table is 70 cm. Which of the following is the approximate area of the table?

   A) 220 cm^2
   B) 440 cm^2
   C) 3,850 cm^2
   D) 15,400 cm^2

---

2. A bicycle tire has circumference of 107 cm. Which of the following is the best estimate for its diameter?

   A) 17
   B) 34
   C) 54
   D) 336

---

3. A merry-go-round has a diameter of 25 feet. Its outer edge moves at an average speed of 4 feet per second. One ride consists of 20 revolutions of the merry-go-round. Approximately how long does the ride take?

   A) 20 seconds
   B) 195 seconds
   C) 390 seconds
   D) 780 seconds

---

4. A truck wheel has a radius of 40 cm. If the truck moves a distance of 100 m, how many complete revolutions will the wheel make?

   A) 2.5
   B) 20
   C) 30
   D) 40

---

5. The circumference of a circular dinner plate is 80 cm. What is the approximate area of the dinner plate?

A) $510\ \text{cm}^2$
B) $2{,}039\ \text{cm}^2$
C) $5{,}024\ \text{cm}^2$
D) $20{,}096\ \text{cm}^2$

6. The figure below shows the proposed model of a shopping mall with a residential tower in the middle. Which of the following is a view from a point directly above the building?

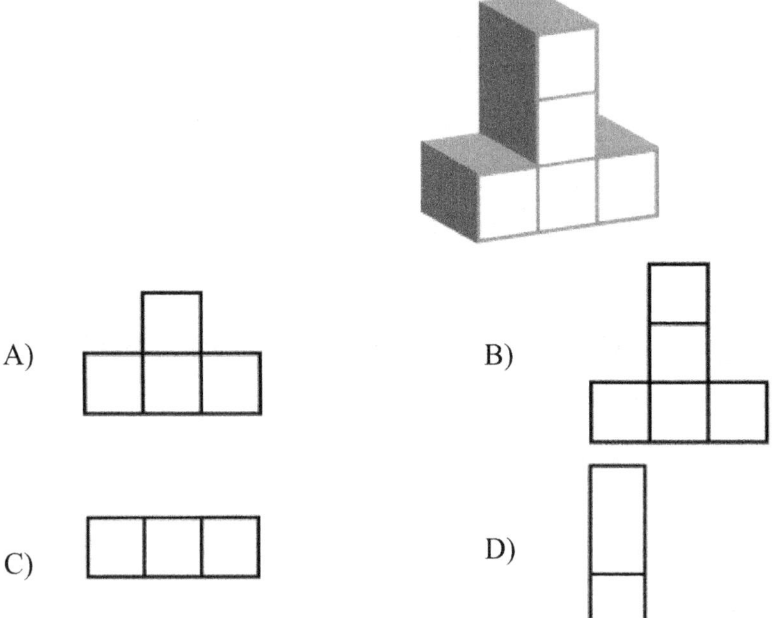

7. Which line segment is not equal to the diameter of the circle in the following figure?

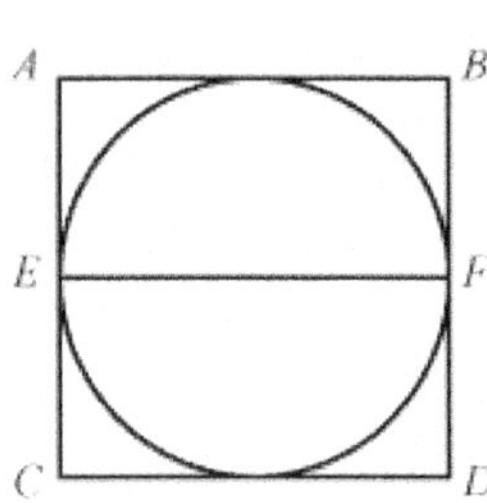

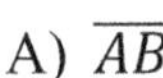

A) $\overline{AB}$
B) $\overline{AD}$
C) $\overline{CD}$
D) $\overline{EF}$

8. Which of the following shows the shape of the intersection of the cone and the plane?

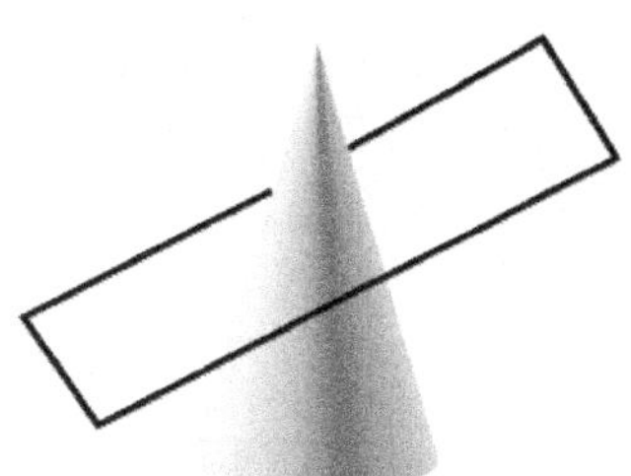

A) 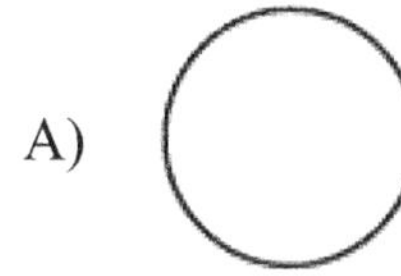

B) 

C) 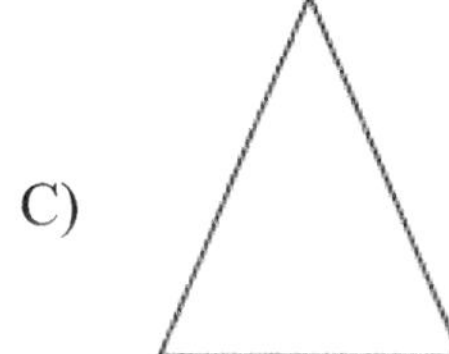

D) 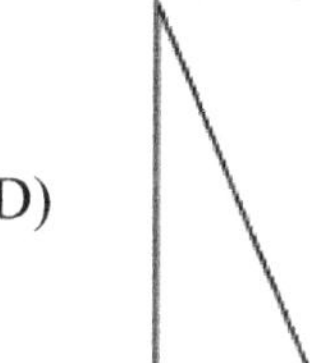

9. A 12-inch in diameter pizza is cut up into 8 equal slices. What is the approximate length of the curved edge of each slice?

A) 1.5 inches
B) 4.7 inches
C) 9.4 inches
D) 37.7 inches

10. A teacher asked a group of students to stand shoulder-to-shoulder, such that every student is exactly 10 feet away from her. The students, in this arrangement, would be standing on the edge of which of the following shapes?

A) A square with a side length of 10 feet
B) A square with a side length of 20 feet
C) A circle with a diameter of 10 feet.
D) A circle with a diameter of 20 feet

11. The figure below shows four cylindrical cans tied together by a piece of string. The diameter of each can is 10 cm. What is the approximate length of the string around the cans?

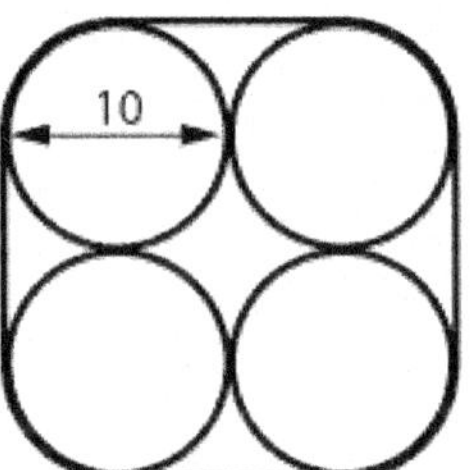

A) 31
B) 51
C) 71
D) 126

12. The figure below shows a rectangle and a parallelogram between two parallel lines. Which of the following statements is true about the areas of the two shapes?

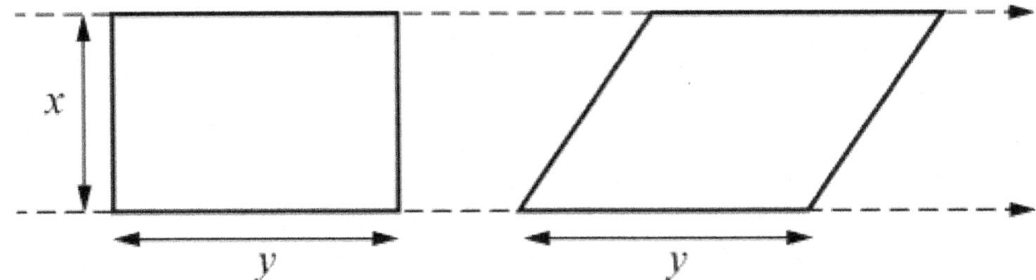

A) The area of the rectangle is greater than the area of the parallelogram.
B) The area of the rectangle is less than the area of the parallelogram.
C) The area of the rectangle is equal to the area of the parallelogram.
D) If $x > y$ then the area of the rectangle is greater than the area of the parallelogram.

13. The figure shows a circle in which $\overline{OD}$ is the radius and $\overline{AC}$ is the diameter. What is the perimeter of the triangle ABC?

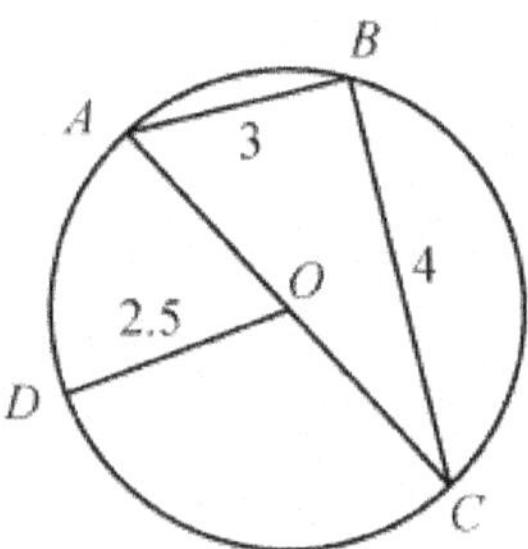

A) 12
B) 9.5
C) 8
D) 7

14. What is the perimeter of a rectangle with an area of 143 cm^2 and a side length of 13 cm?

A) 11 cm
B) 24 cm
C) 37 cm
D) 48 cm

15. Which outline below shows the view of the following 3-dimensional object from the side?

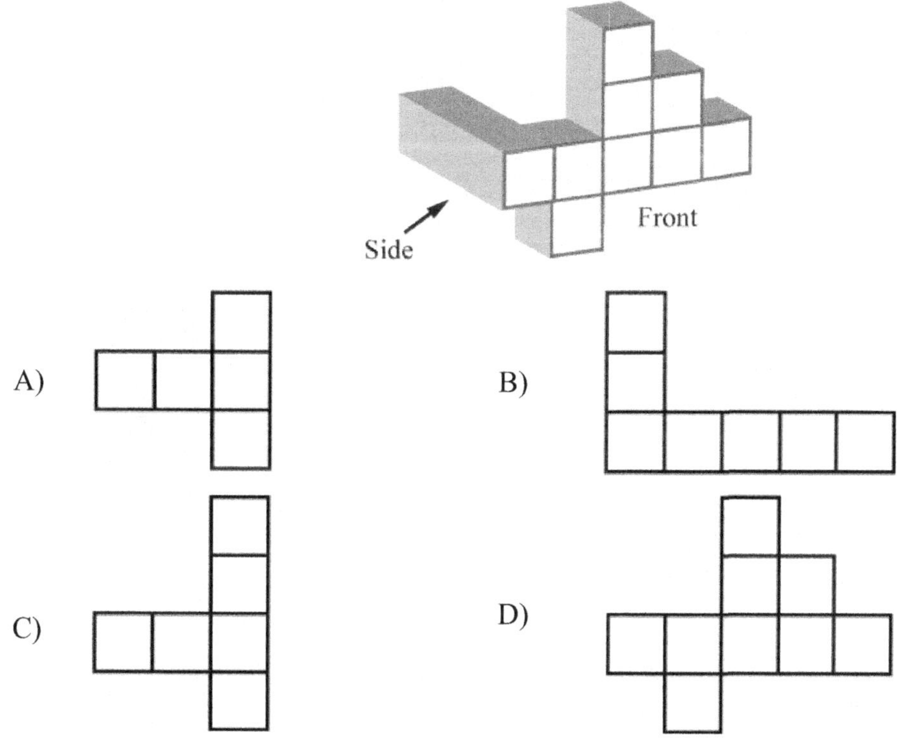

16. The figure below shows the scaled drawing of a house. Given that the height h of the window is 3 feet, what is the width w of the house?

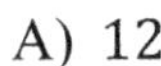
A) 12

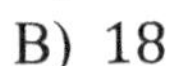
B) 18

C) 24

D) 36

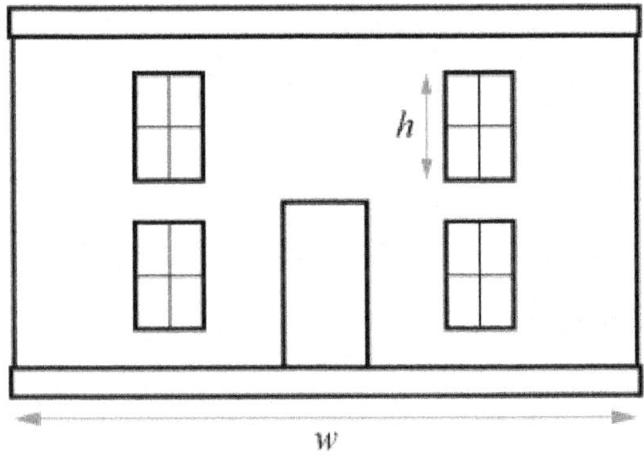

17. The scale drawing shows the outline of an aircraft with a length of 120 feet. Use the figure to estimate the wingspan w of the aircraft.

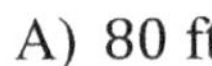
A) 80 ft

B) 96 ft

C) 120 ft

D) 150 ft

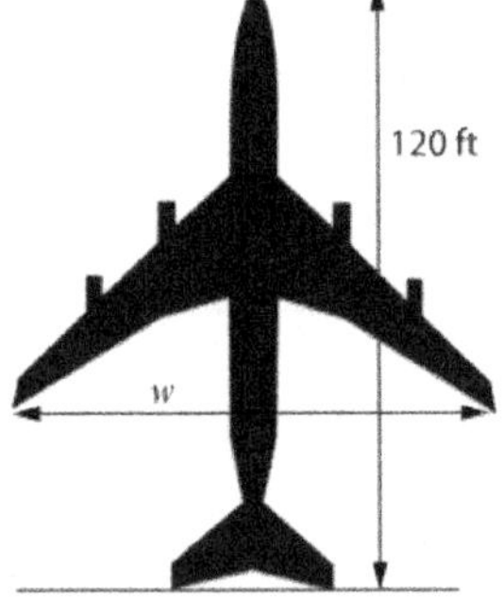

18. The figure shows the dimensions, in cm, of an aquarium that is partially filled with water. If the level of water is 3 cm below the top of the aquarium what is the volume of water in the aquarium? (1 liter = 1,000 cm^3)

A) 40.5 liters

B) 45.0 liters

C) 405 liters

D) 450 liters

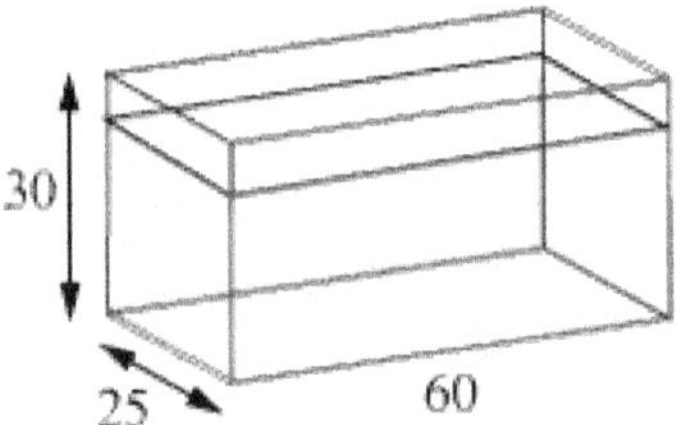

19. A $1 : 120$ scale drawing of a swimming pool shows the length of the pool as 5.0 cm. What would be the length of the pool in a $1 : 25$ scale drawing of the pool?

A) 1.04 cm
B) 12.5 cm
C) 24 cm
D) 25 cm

20. The area of a square garden on a $1 : 40$ scaled drawing is $36\ \text{cm}^2$. What is the area of the actual garden in m^2?

A) 1.44
B) 5.76
C) 1,440
D) 57,600

21. Which of the following sets of side lengths cannot be used to draw a triangle?

A) $3, 4, 5$
B) $7, 9, 14$
C) $9, 5, 12$
D) $12, 18, 31$

22. Consider a triangle ABC. Which of the following sets of measurements do not define a unique triangle?

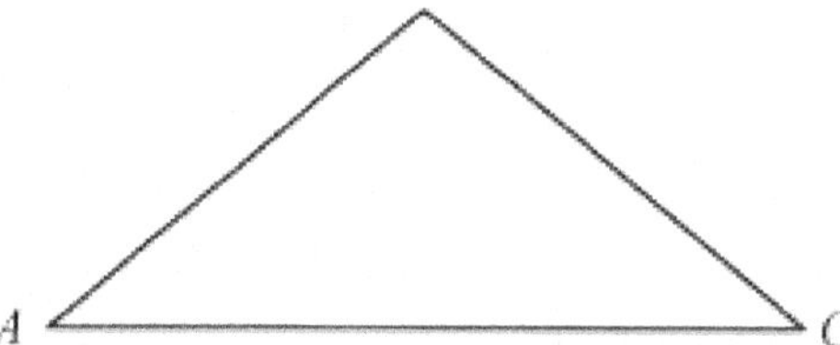

A) $\overline{AB} = 6,\ \overline{BC} = 8,\ \overline{AC} = 10$
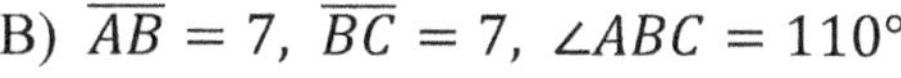
B) $\overline{AB} = 7,\ \overline{BC} = 7,\ \angle ABC = 110°$
C) $\overline{AB} = 8,\ \angle CAB = 45°,\ \angle ABC = 100°$
D) $\angle ABC = 100°,\ \angle BCA = 45°,\ \angle CAB = 35°$

23. The figure shows the view from above of a right rectangular pyramid. A plane cuts the pyramid vertically down along the line l. Which of the following shows the correct planer section of the pyramid?

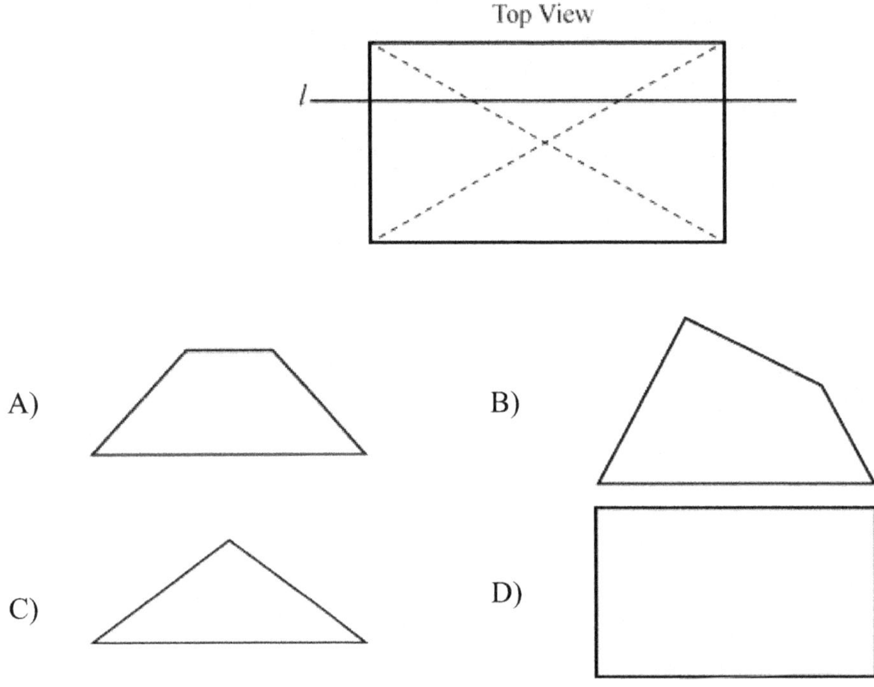

24. The right rectangular prism in the figure below was sliced with a plane perpendicular to the base as shown. Which of the following gives the dimensions of the resulting rectangular slice of the prism (the shaded area)?

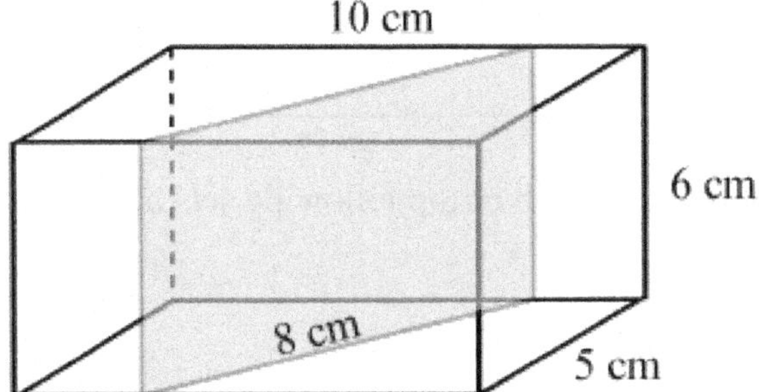

A) 10 cm × 6 cm
B) 8 cm × 6 cm
C) 8 cm × 5 cm
D) 10 cm × 8 cm

25. What is the value of x?

A) 12.5°
B) 25°
C) 35°
D) 50°

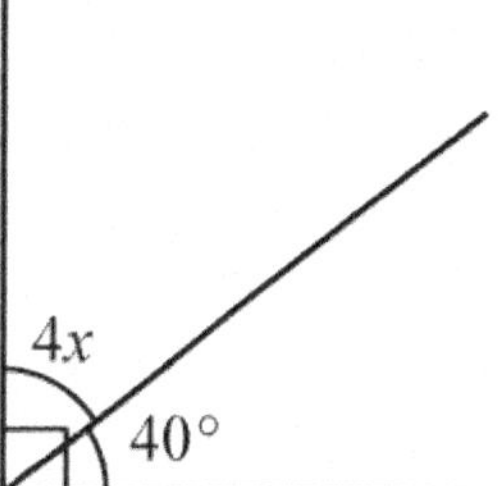

26. What is the value of x?

A) 6°
B) 12°
C) 20°
D) 24°

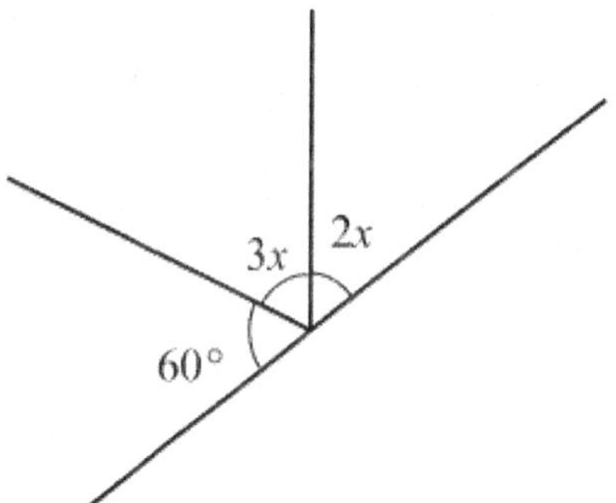

27. Given that $\angle AOC = 68°$ and $\angle AOB = 35°$, what is the measure of $\angle BOC$?

A) 22°
B) 33°
C) 55°
D) 103°

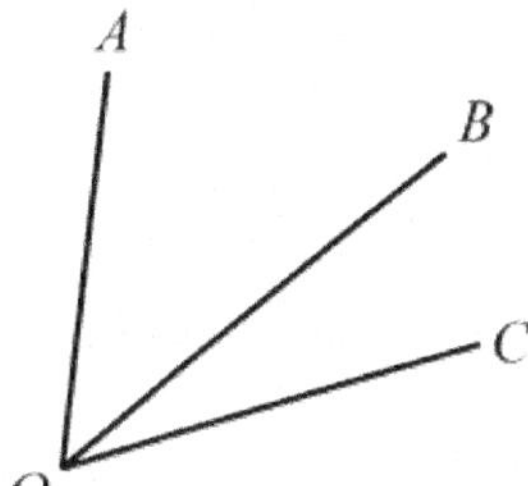

---

28. The figure shows a cuboid from which a corner has been cut away. All angles on the object are right angles. What is the total surface area of all the faces of the resulting object?

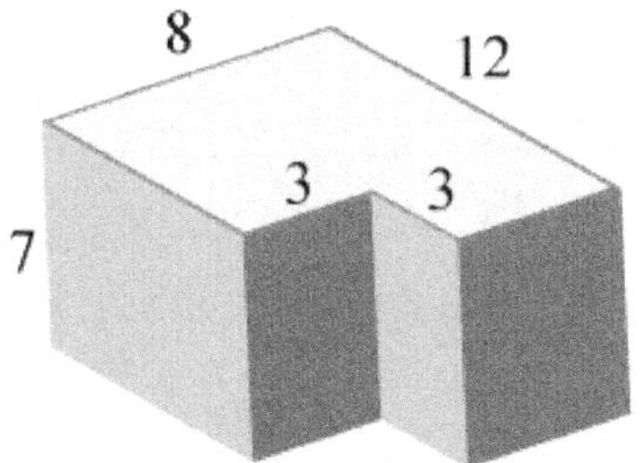

A) 236
B) 367
C) 454
D) 472

---

29. The figure shows a warehouse, which consists of a triangular prism on top of a cuboid. The dimensions of the warehouse, in meters, are indicated on the Figure.
What is the volume of the warehouse?

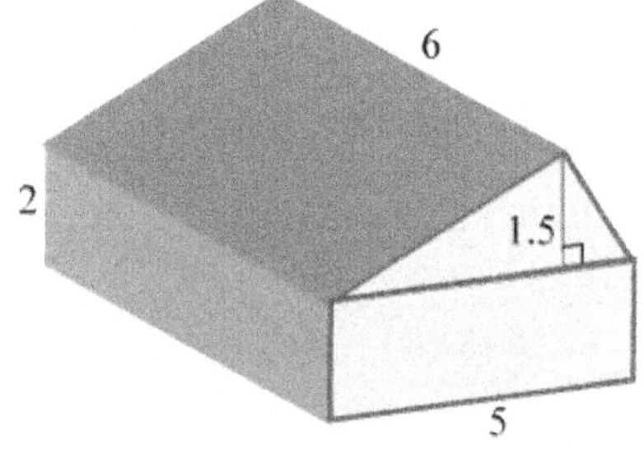

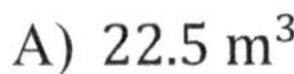
A) 22.5 m^3
B) 60.0 m^3
C) 82.5 m^3
D) 105 m^3

---

30. George wants to build a bird cage by bending a piece of metal wire in the shape shown below. He needs 18 such pieces to build the entire cage. What is the total length of wire he must buy? $\left(\pi \approx \frac{22}{7}\right)$

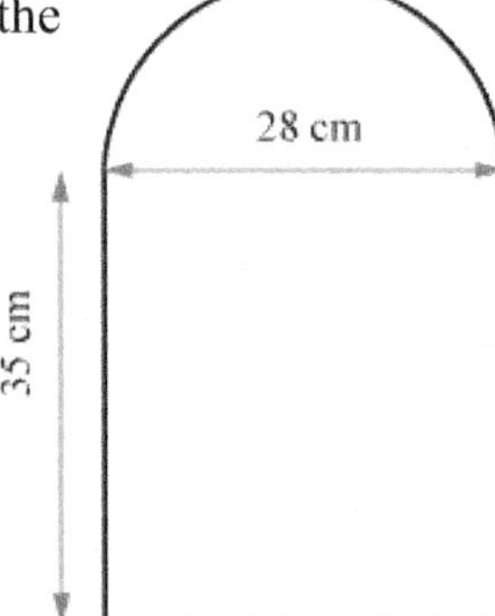

A) 142 cm
B) 256 cm
C) 2,268 cm
D) 2,556 cm

EXERCISE 5: STATISTICS & PROBABILITY

1. A box of chocolates contains 5 chocolates with caramel filling, 7 with coconut filling, 4 with cream filling and 8 with no filling. What is the probability that a randomly selected chocolate contains a filling?

A) $\frac{1}{6}$

B) $\frac{5}{24}$

C) $\frac{1}{3}$

D) $\frac{2}{3}$

---

2. The probabilities of scoring a three-pointer from a shot, for four different players on a basketball team are as follows:
   - Scottie: $\frac{1}{3}$
   - Michael: $\frac{2}{5}$
   - Shaquille: $\frac{7}{20}$
   - Kobe: $\frac{3}{10}$

Which player is most likely to score a three-pointer?

A) Scottie

B) Michael

C) Shaquille

D) Kobe

---

3. A teacher wants to assign one of two topics to each student for a term paper. She placed 40 slips of paper, 20 with each topic, in a jar from which students take turns to draw a slip without replacement. Given that 13 students have already drawn Topic I and 9 students have drawn Topic II what is the probability that the next student will be assigned to Topic II?

A) $\frac{1}{2}$

B) $\frac{11}{20}$

C) $\frac{11}{18}$

D) $\frac{13}{18}$

---

4. A food company wants to conduct a survey in the city of Pasadena to find out where the residents of the city purchase their bread. Which of the following sampling strategies will lead to the best results?

   A) Have a representative interview visitors at major Pasadena supermarkets
   B) Send a survey form by post to 1000 random people living in California
   C) Interview every car owner in the parking lot at a Pasadena sporting event
   D) Use the map of Pasadena to randomly identify houses for survey.

5. A set of 13 cards consists of 9 cards numbered 2-10 and 4 cards with the letters A, K Q and J written on them. What is the probability that a card drawn at random is a numbered card divisible by 3?

   A) $\frac{1}{13}$
   B) $\frac{3}{13}$
   C) $\frac{4}{13}$
   D) $\frac{9}{13}$

6. A soccer team manager collected the following data regarding the corner at which the opposing team's striker has directed his last 30 penalty shots on goal:
   - 12 shots were directed at the top-left corner
   - 8 shots were directed at the top-right corner
   - 6 shots were directed at the bottom-left corner
   - 4 shots were directed at the bottom-right corner

   What is the probability that the strikers next shot will be directed towards the right of the goal?

   A) $\frac{2}{15}$
   B) $\frac{4}{15}$
   C) $\frac{2}{5}$
   D) $\frac{3}{5}$

7. John rolls a regular die (numbered 1-6) every day. He puts the same number of quarters (25¢ coins) as the number shown on the dice into his savings box. Which of the following is a reasonable estimate for the amount of money in the savings box after 30 days?

   A) \$26.25
   B) \$22.50
   C) \$21.00
   D) \$5.25

---

8. A town has a total of 10,000 residents of which 1,500 wear glasses 500 residents attended a town fair. How many at the fair are likely to be wearing glasses?

A) 15
B) 75
C) 120
D) 150

---

9. A bag filled with 4 types of sweets contains a total of 500 sweets. 80 sweets were randomly drawn from the bag and the results were recorded in the table below. All the sweets were replaced in the bag. What is the probability that the next sweet drawn will be lemon flavored?

Flavor	Number of Sweets
Orange	22
Strawberry	12
Lemon	18
Pineapple	28

A) $\frac{9}{40}$
B) $\frac{4}{25}$
C) $\frac{1}{18}$
D) $\frac{9}{250}$

---

10. A hen hatched 10 chicks with hatch weights in grams shown in the list below. What is the median hatch weight?

$$34, 37, 45, 35, 39, 36, 42, 36, 38, 48$$

A) 36.0
B) 37.0
C) 37.5
D) 39.0

---

11. A pediatrician gathered data regarding the age of children who visited him for treatment during a week. The figure below shows the box plot of the data he collected. Which of the following statements is NOT true, based on the figure?

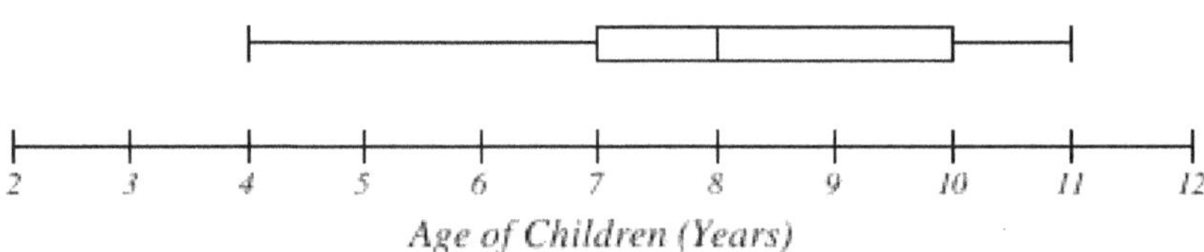

A) The youngest child to visit him was 4 years old.
B) The median age of the children was 8 years.
C) Half of the children visiting him were between the ages of 7 and 10.
D) The oldest child to visit him was 10 years old.

---

12. A game show uses the spinner in the figure below. During the first season, the spinner was spun 250 times and pointed to Red 90 times, Blue 80 times, Green 60 times and Pink 20 times. The spinner is expected to be used 400 times in the second season. How many times is the spinner likely to point to the Blue section?

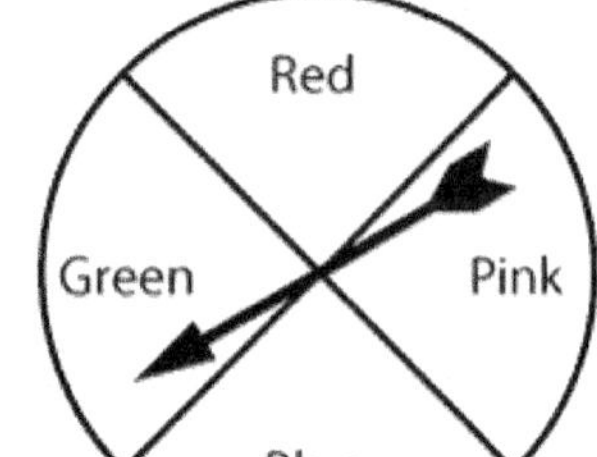

A) 50
B) 96
C) 100
D) 128

---

13. Scientists have detected that a large asteroid is heading in Earth's direction. They however predict that it is very unlikely that the asteroid will collide with Earth. Which of the following could be the probability of the asteroid will pass Earth without colliding?

A) 0.000
B) 0.001
C) 0.999
D) 1.000

---

14. A math teacher compiled the results of her 35 students. The lowest score was 30, the highest score was a 100, the average score was 60, and the median score was 70. Which of the following could be a box plot of this data?

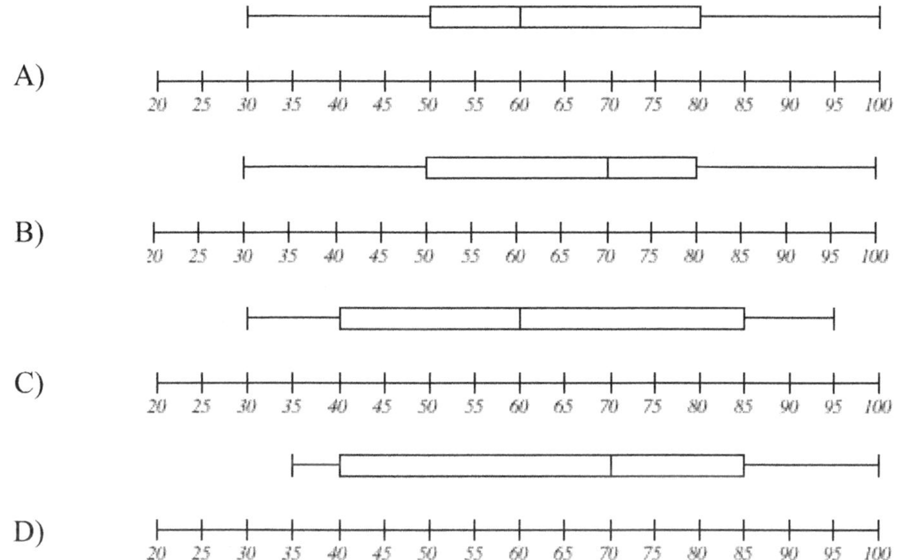

15. Four runners are running laps around a track. The table below shows the times in seconds for each of the four laps, completed by each runner:

Runner 1	Runner 2	Runner 3	Runner 4
64	62	64	70
69	61	66	72
72	64	65	75
74	61	65	80

Based on the data in the table, which runner is running the fastest average lap around the track?

A) Runner 1
B) Runner 2
C) Runner 3
D) Runner 4

16. Base your answer to the following question on the shapes below:

Quinton closes his eyes and randomly puts his finger on a shape in the figure. If he repeats this 80 times, how many times is he likely to choose a pentagon?

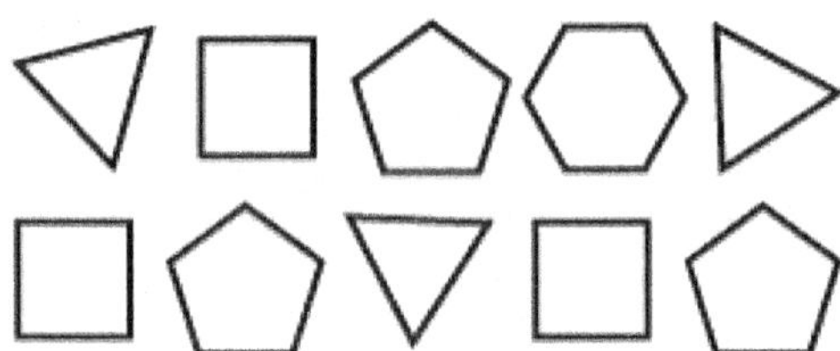

A) 16
B) 24
C) 30
D) 32

17. A representative survey of the population was conducted in Rochester and Buffalo in which the residents were asked if they preferred watching basketball or football; the table below shows the results of the survey. Which of the following conclusions can be drawn from this data?

	Basketball	Football	Total
Buffalo	90	60	150
Rochester	100	150	250

A) Residents of both Rochester and Buffalo prefer basketball to football
B) Residents of both Rochester and Buffalo prefer football to basketball
C) Residents of Rochester prefer basketball whereas residents of Buffalo prefer football
D) Residents of Buffalo prefer basketball whereas residents of Rochester prefer football

18. Consider the set of numbers shown below. How will the median change if one of the numbers, 27, is replaced by the number 22?

$$23, 27, 29, 24, 28, 31, 35, 21, 27, 32$$

A) The median will decrease by 1
B) The median will decrease by 0.5
C) The median will increase by 0.5
D) The median will not change

19. A bag contains 3 blue balls, 5 green balls and 7 black balls. What is the probability that a ball drawn at random is not black?

A) $\frac{8}{15}$
B) $\frac{1}{3}$
C) $\frac{1}{5}$
D) $\frac{1}{15}$

20. A drug maker is testing a health supplement on mice to see if the life expectancy can be increased by use of the supplement. Mice were divided into two groups: both were fed the same diet but only one group received the supplement. The figure below shows the lifespan data in months for the two groups.

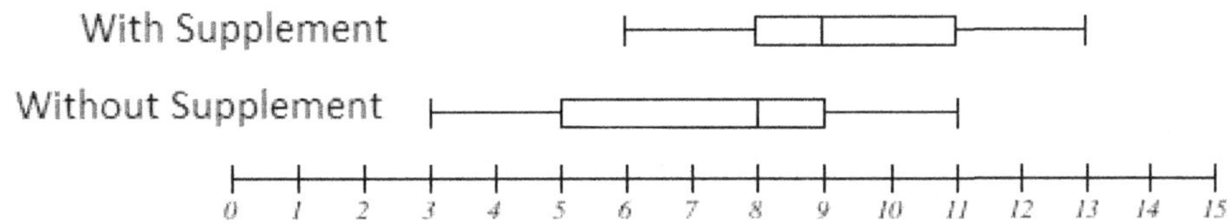

Which of the following is a valid claim, which can be made based on this data?

A) The lifespan of all the mice who were fed the supplement was greater than the mice that were not fed the supplement.
B) The use of the supplement had no effect on the lifespan of mice.
C) The median lifespan of the group which was fed the supplement was 1 month greater than the median of the group which was not given the supplement.
D) The average lifespan of the group which was fed the supplement was 1 month greater than the group which was not given the supplement.

---

21. Consider the spinner shown in the figure with equal sections. Which two numbers is the spinner equally likely to select?

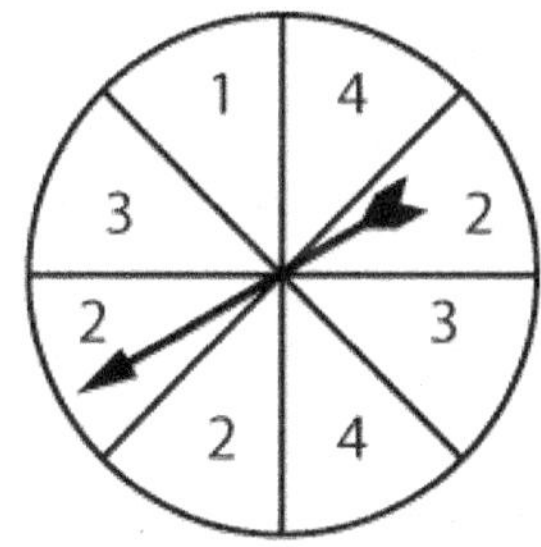

A) 1 and 2
B) 2 and 4
C) 2 and 3
D) 3 and 4

---

22. A fair, six-faced die, with the numbers 1-6, was rolled 9 times and showed the following numbers:

$$3, 1, 4, 2, 5, 6, 6, 6, 6$$

What is the probability that the die will show another 6 on the 10th roll?

A) 0
B) $\frac{1}{6}$
C) $\frac{1}{2}$
D) $\frac{2}{27}$

23. A teacher divided the students in his class into two equal groups; the Lions and the Tigers. He awarded 1-5 stars to each student based on the overall performance during the academic year. The figure below shows the number of students who received 1-5 stars in each group.

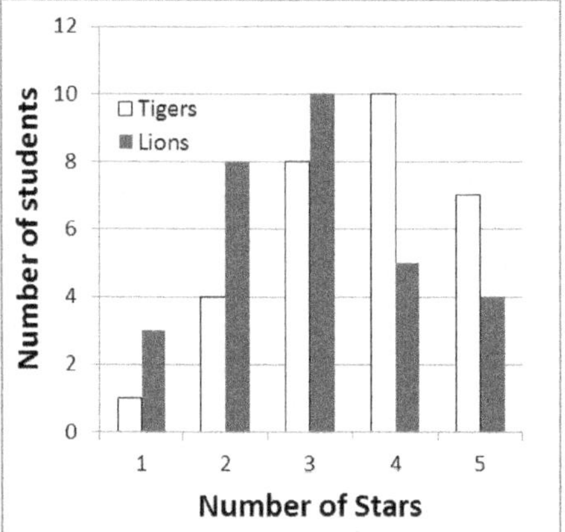

Which of the following is not a valid observation from this figure?

A) More Tigers received 5 starts than the Lions
B) Fewer Tigers received 3 stars than the Lions
C) The average rating for the Tigers was higher than the average rating for the Lions.
D) The mode score for the Lions was 3 stars.

24. Brenda setup a game at the school fair, which costs \$1 to play. A ball is dropped onto a set of 9 holes, as shown in the figure below. If the ball falls into the middle hole the player wins \$5. Given that the player is equally likely to hit each of the nine holes, how much money will Brenda earn or lose if a total of 54 games are played?

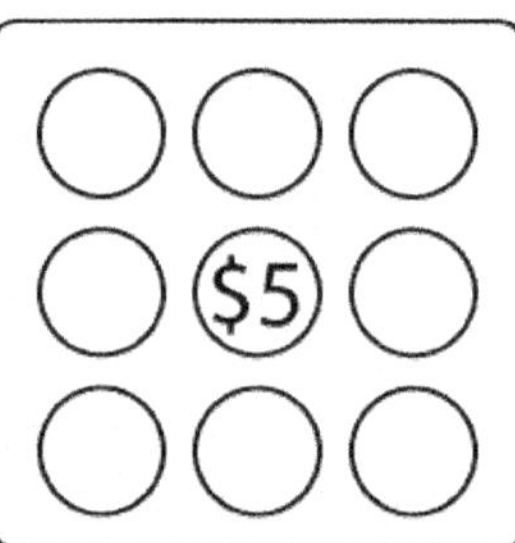

A) Win \$24
B) Lost \$9
C) Lost \$24
D) Win \$54

25. Jack's flock has only pure black or pure white sheep. The probability that a sheep picked at random is black is $\frac{1}{19}$. If there are a total of 12 black sheep, how many white sheep are there in the flock?

A) 209
B) 216
C) 228
D) 240

---

26. Two regular dice are rolled together. What is the probability that the sum of the two numbers is greater than or equal to 9?

A) $\frac{1}{36}$

B) $\frac{1}{12}$

C) $\frac{1}{6}$

D) $\frac{5}{18}$

---

27. A pizza shop allows the customer to choose 1 of 2 types of cheese, 1 of 3 types of crust and 1 of 6 types of toppings for $9.99. How many different pizzas can be ordered?

A) 10

B) 18

C) 36

D) 72

---

28. Carla wants to simulate the probability of a baseball player hitting a home run. If the probability of hitting the home run on a given pitch is 0.15, which of the following will be a valid simulation of this probability?

A) Putting 3 red marbles and 17 black marbles in a bag where randomly selecting a red marble represents a home run.
B) Putting 3 red marbles and 17 black marbles in a bag where randomly selecting a black marble represents a home run.
C) Putting 3 red marbles and 20 black marbles in a bag where randomly selecting a red marble represents a home run.
D) Putting 3 red marbles and 20 black marbles in a bag where randomly selecting a red marble represents a home run.

---

29. A standard deck of cards contains a total of 52 cards, 4 of which are aces. A bag contains 5 red marbles and 50 blue marbles. How many blue and red marbles should be added to the bag to simulate drawing an ace from the deck of cards?

A) 1 Red marble and 15 blue marbles
B) 0 Red marble and 10 blue marbles
C) 0 Red marble and 15 blue marbles
D) 1 Red marble and 10 blue marbles

---

30. A die is rolled twice. What is the probability that the number on the second roll is greater than the number on the first roll?

A) $\frac{1}{6}$

B) $\frac{1}{2}$

C) $\frac{5}{12}$

D) $\frac{7}{12}$

PRACTICE TEST 1

GRID-IN QUESTIONS

Questions 58 – 62

58.

In the above figure, $\overrightarrow{BD}$ is perpendicular to $\overrightarrow{BE}$. If $\angle ABD = 30°$, what is the measure of the angle CBE?

59. The ratio of the girls to the boys in a school is 5 : 6. What is the total number of students in the school if there are 150 girls?

60. If $4x + 18 = 30$, then $x =$?

61. A teacher wants to create a schedule for Monday. There are 5 subjects: Math, Art, Sport, English, and Logic. How many different combinations of the schedule are possible?

62. Emily uses $1\frac{4}{25}$ kg of flour to bake a cake. Express this number in decimal form.

MULTIPLE CHOICE QUESTIONS

Questions 63 – 68

63. In the figure below, a right triangle with legs 6 and 8 is inscribed in a circle. What is the perimeter of the shaded region?

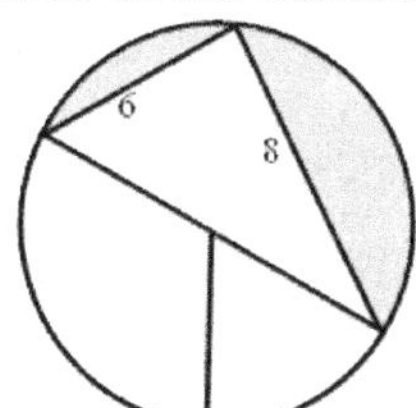

A. $14 - 5\pi$
B. $14 - 10\pi$
C. $14 + 5\pi$
D. $14 + 10\pi$

64. Students' Scores in Math Test

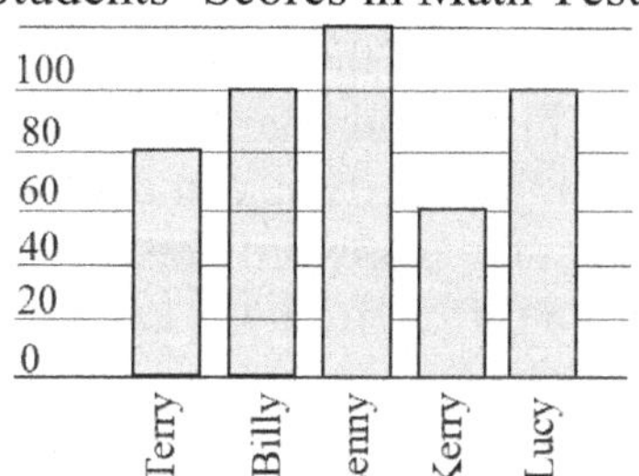

According to the graph above, by what percent does Kerry's score decrease from Terry's score?

E. 75%
F. 80%
G. 25%
H. 20%

65. A farmer sold 60 sheep and geese altogether at the farmer festival. Each sheep costs \$32 and each goose costs \$3.50. If the farmer sold all his animals for \$609, how many sheep did he sell?

A. 14
B. 24
C. 46
D. 36

66. Find the value of the expression: $(5 * 3) * 1$, such that operation $*$ converts the pair of natural numbers n and m to $2^{|n-m|}$?

E. 2
F. 4
G. 8
H. 16

67. In square ABCD, MP ∥ CD and RN ∥ BC. If MN = 5, MO = 4 and RO = 12, what is the area of the square ABCD?

A. 256 sq. units
B. 225 sq. units
C. 289 sq. units
D. 81 sq. units

68. If $a = 5$, $b = -2$ and $c = -3$, what is the value of the expression below?

$$(b \cdot (a - c) + 2)^2$$

E. -196
F. -4
G. 4
H. 196

Questions 69 – 74

69. The daughter's age is $\frac{1}{12}$ of the sum of her parents' ages. After 4 years her age will be $\frac{1}{8}$ of the sum of her parents' ages. How old will the daughter be after 4 years?

A. 6
B. 8
C. 10
D. 11

70. Three friends bought a Christmas tree for \$96 collectively. They made a cash contribution of $3:5:8$. Two friends who invested less, decided to return the third friend money so that their cash contributions become the same. What is the ratio of the money returned by the first person to the money returned by the second person?

E. 7 : 1
F. 5 : 3
G. 8 : 5
H. 3 : 5

71. In a mixture of 120 liters, the ratio of juice to water is 4 : 1. How much water should be added so that the ratio of juice to water is 1 : 4?

A. 300 liters
B. 320 liters
C. 340 liters
D. 360 liters

72. If a and b are positive integers and

$$a^2 - b^2 = 200,$$
$$a^2 + b^2 = 1258,$$

find $\frac{a+b}{a-b}$.

E. 12
F. 12.5
G. 13
H. 13.5

73. John forgot the password of his Facebook profile. He remembers that it consists of the same numbers and letters as his car number GH406. How many combinations he can attempt if he knows that the password doesn't start with 0 and differs from his car number?

A. 95
B. 96
C. 119
D. 120

74. If $2^x \cdot 3^y = 6912$, then $\frac{x+y}{x-y} = ?$

E. 1.5
F. 1.6
G. 2
H. 2.2

Questions 75 – 80

75. There are 12 basketball players in the team. In order to complete the main composition of the team for the game, the coach can choose any 5 players from the team. How many different combinations of the main composition the coach can choose?

A. 396
B. 792
C. 120
D. 256

76. If $2x - 6y = 11$, what is y in terms of x?

E. $y = \frac{x}{3} - \frac{11}{6}$
F. $y = \frac{11}{6} - \frac{x}{3}$
G. $y = \frac{11}{2} - 3x$
H. $y = \frac{2x}{11} - 2$

77. What is the prime factorization of 240?

A. $8 \cdot 3 \cdot 2 \cdot 5$
B. $2^3 \cdot 3 \cdot 5$
C. $2^3 \cdot 6 \cdot 5$
D. $2^4 \cdot 3 \cdot 5$

78. James eats a jar of jam in 6 minutes. His father eats the same jar of jam twice as fast. How long will it take both the son and his father to eat the same jar of jam together?

E. 1 minute 20 seconds
F. 2 minutes
G. 2 minutes 10 seconds
H. 3 minutes

79. The average of three consecutive integers is 396. Find the sum of the largest and the smallest integer among the three.

A. 792
B. 793
C. 794
D. 796

80. Samantha has 3 yellow balls, 4 red balls, 5 blue balls and 6 green balls. She selects 2 balls at random without replacement. What is the probability that the first ball is red and the second ball is green?

E. $\frac{2}{27}$
F. $\frac{1}{24}$
G. $\frac{2}{9}$
H. $\frac{4}{51}$

Questions 81 – 86

81. If each side length of the square PLAN is 10 units, find the area of shaded region?

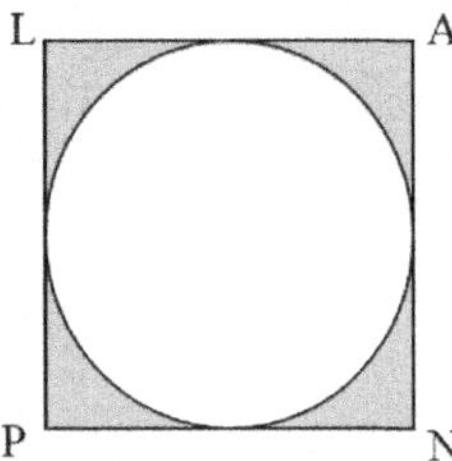

A. $100 - 100\pi\ units^2$
B. $100 - 75\pi\ units^2$
C. $100 - 50\pi\ units^2$
D. $100 - 25\pi\ units^2$

82. On the number line below, the position of c is 2.5, $a \cdot b = -4.08$ and $a \cdot c = -8.5$. What is the position of b?

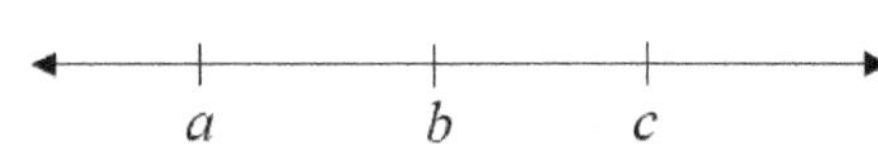

E. -3.4
F. 3.4
G. 1.2
H. -1.2

83. A grocery store announced a promotion: If you buy 3 units of stock product (each for $\$v$), then each next unit will cost you $\$u$ less. What is the cost, in dollars, for buying w units of stock product, where w is greater than 3?

A. $w \cdot v - 3 \cdot u$
B. $w \cdot v - w \cdot u$
C. $w \cdot v - (w - 3) \cdot u$
D. $(w - 3) \cdot v - w \cdot u$

84. If $\frac{a+2b}{c} = \frac{c}{2a}$, what is the value of b in terms of a and c?

E. $\frac{c^2}{4a} - \frac{a}{2}$
F. $\frac{a}{2}$
G. $\frac{a}{2c} - \frac{c}{4}$
H. $\frac{4}{ac} - \frac{a}{2}$

85. Sofia has 5 times as many coins as Steve has and 3 times as many coins as Tom has. What fraction of Tom's number of coins is the Steve's number of coins?

A. $\frac{1}{3}$
B. $\frac{5}{3}$
C. $\frac{3}{5}$
D. $\frac{1}{5}$

86. Anna and Kallie passed an exam. Anna secured 33 points more than Kallie. Her points were 155% more than Kallie's score. How many points did each of them score?

E. 90 and 57
F. 93 and 60
G. 90 and 63
H. 96 and 63

Questions 87 – 92

87. Luis uses a map, where two cities have a distance of $\frac{5}{6}$ cm between them. If $1\text{ cm} = 864\text{ km}$ on the map, what is the distance, in km, between these cities?

A. 1008 km
B. 644 km
C. 748 km
D. 720 km

88. In the isosceles trapezoid ABCD, the bisectors of angles B and C meet at point O that lies on the base AD. If AB = 6 cm, what is the perimeter of the trapezoid ABCD?

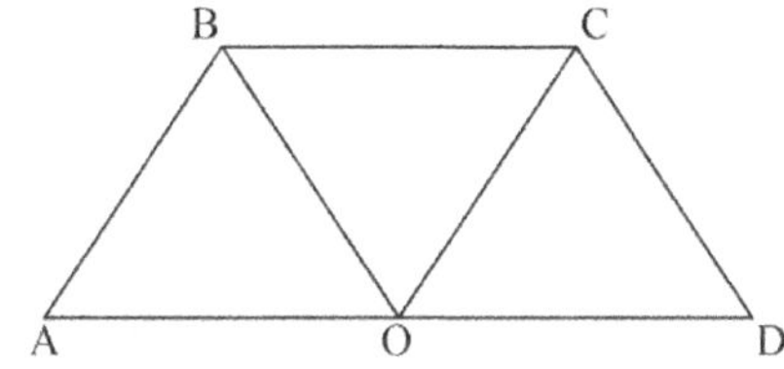

E. 30 cm
F. 36 cm
G. 28 cm
H. 35 cm

89. The diagram below shows the number of pets owned by 600 children. How many children have 2 or more pets?

Pets of 600 Children

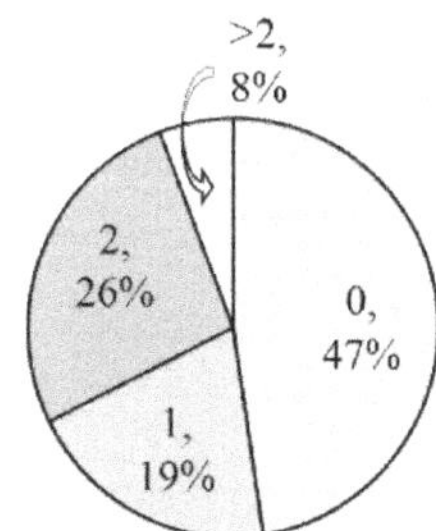

A. 210
B. 156
C. 204
D. 48

90. If x is an even integer and $48 - 7x < 5$. What is the least possible value for x?

E. 6
F. 7
G. 8
H. 9

91. There are 2 boxes. The first box contains 5 red balls and 4 black balls. The second box contains 3 blue balls and 6 pink balls. Dylan picks a ball randomly from the second box and places it in the first one. Then he picks a ball randomly from the first box. What is the probability that the ball he picks from the first box is red?

A. $\frac{1}{2}$
B. $\frac{5}{9}$
C. $\frac{5}{18}$
D. $\frac{2}{5}$

92. The table below shows how the prices (in dollars) of washing gel changed during a week in two supermarkets.

	Monday	Tuesday	Wednesday	Thursday	Friday	Saturday	Sunday
I	35	36	38	37	36	35	35
II	37	36	34	34	33	35	36

What is the difference between the average prices in two supermarkets?

E. \$1.00
F. \$1.25
G. \$0.75
H. \$0.50

Questions 93 – 98

93. What is the area of the figure shown below?

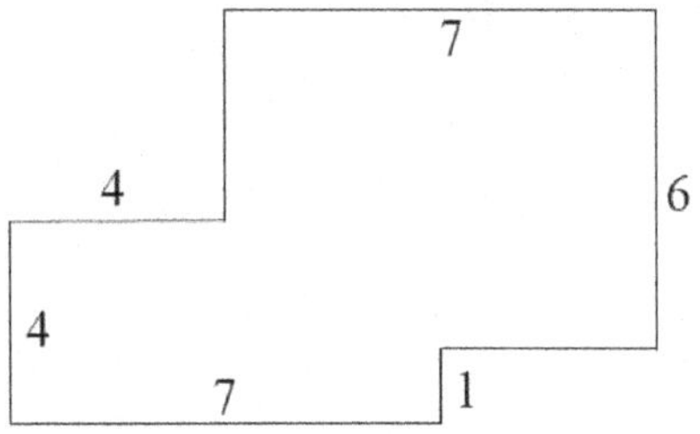

A. 66
B. 77
C. 71
D. 61

94. Which of the following repeating decimals is equivalent to the fraction $2\frac{4}{9}$?

E. $2.\overline{42}$
F. $2.\overline{4}$
G. $2.\overline{24}$
H. $2.\overline{45}$

95. What is $\frac{1}{625}$ of 5^{10}?

A. 5^8
B. 5^7
C. 125^3
D. 25^3

96. There are 36 students in 6th grade. 17 students learn French, 18 students learn German, 6 students learn both languages. Students, who do not learn French and German, learn Japanese. How many students learn Japanese?

E. 5
F. 6
G. 7
H. 8

97. If $a = -2$, $b = 3$, find the smallest number in the set below?

$$ab,\ a^2b,\ ab^2,\ a^3b,\ ab^3$$

A. ab
B. ab^2
C. a^3b
D. ab^3

98. How many multiples of 4 are in between 105 and 357?

E. 62
F. 63
G. 64
H. 65

Questions 99 – 104			
99.	If the number of apples is 20% of the number of pears, then the number of pears is what percent of the number of apples? A. 200% B. 250% C. 400% D. 500%	102.	Find the number of diagonals of a polygon, if the sum of the measures of its interior angles is 1980°? E. 62 F. 65 G. 68 H. 70
100.	For what value of x, the expression $\frac{x^2-4}{(x-2)^3}$ is undefined? E. $x = 2$ F. $x = -2$ G. $x = 2$ or $x = -2$ H. $x = 8$	103.	The distance from Mars to the Sun is $2.297 \times 10^8\ km$ and the distance from Neptune to the Sun is $4.459 \times 10^9 km$. How many times Mars is closer to the Sun than Neptune? A. 0.05 B. 0.52 C. 1.94 D. 19.41
101.	The price of the petrol first increases by 20% and then decreases by 20%. Which statement is true? A. The final price and initial price are the same. B. The final price decreases from the initial price by 4%. C. The final price increases from the initial price by 4%. D. It depends on petrol's price.	104.	On the coordinate plane, the coordinates of points A and B are $(-2, 8)$ and $(-10, -4)$. What are the coordinates of the point C lying on the line segment AB such that, AC : BC = 1 : 3? E. (-4,5) F. (-6,2) G. (-8,-1) H. (-3,-6)

Questions 105 – 110

105. A man standing in a queue is the 17th from the end and the 35th from the beginning of the queue. How many people are in the queue?

A. 50
B. 51
C. 52
D. 53

106. Triangles ABC and KLN, shown below, are similar. What is the perimeter of the triangle KLN?

B
28
21
L
4
5
A
C
K
N

E. 11
F. 12
G. 13
H. 14

107. Two planes 3000 miles apart, are flying towards each other. Their speeds differ from each other by 80 mph. If they pass each other after 6 hours, find the speed of the plane moving at a higher rate.

A. 210 mph
B. 260 mph
C. 290 mph
D. 300 mph

108. In the right trapezoid ABCD, AB = 13, AH = 5 and BCDH is a square. What is the area of the trapezoid ABCD?

E. 144
F. 164
G. 174
H. 194

109. A mathematical quiz contains 50 questions of 2 points each. Each correct answer allows you to move on and answer the next question. After the 1st mistake, you are allowed to continue the test, but all the next questions will be worth 1 point each. After the 2nd mistake, the quiz stops. You made the 1st mistake answering the 24th question and the 2nd mistake answering the 39th question. What is your score on the quiz? (You do not get any points for the wrong questions.)

A. 72
B. 70
C. 77
D. 78

110. A train runs over a bridge at a speed of 1 km 500 meters per minute. How long is the train if it passes by a telegraph pole in 9 seconds?

E. 200 m
F. 225 m
G. 250 m
H. 275 m

Questions 111 – 114

111.	In a school café, 5 different types of buns, 4 different kinds of drinks and 6 different types of cakes are sold. In how many different ways a student can choose 1 bun, 1 cake and 1 drink? A. 100 B. 110 C. 120 D. 150	113.	In the rhombus ABCD given below, $AB = BD = 8$. What is the area of the rhombus ABCD? 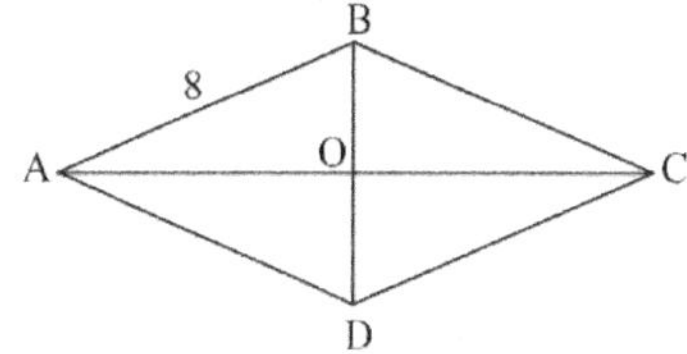 A. $16\sqrt{3}$ B. $48\sqrt{3}$ C. $64\sqrt{3}$ D. $32\sqrt{3}$
112.	If $\frac{A}{120} = B$ and $B < -2$, which of the following statements is true? E. $A < -240$ F. $A > -240$ G. $A < -120$ H. $A > -120$	114.	Sam goes on a road trip to spend his holidays. He drives at an average of 60 miles per hour for the first 6 hours. The next 6 hours he drives a total of 400 miles. If his car covers 19 miles per gallon and each gallon costs $3.25, how much does his entire trip cost him? E. $120 F. $130 G. $140 H. $150

PRACTICE TEST 2

GRID-IN QUESTIONS			
Questions 58 - 62			
58.	A standard deck of cards consists of 52 cards. What is the probability that a card selected at random is a face card or a black ace?	61.	The sum of two consecutive even integers is -46. What is the absolute value of the difference of the squares of these two numbers?
59.	Two boys play a barter trading game and use different items to exchange goods: if 2 Lego cubes = 5 matches 1 apple = 4 Lego cubes 3 pears = 2 apples. According to their rules of exchange, how many matches does one boy need to exchange to get 6 pears?	62.	Pamela goes swimming and training at the gym. In the last 28-day period, Pamela went swimming $\frac{2}{7}$ of all the days and she had a rest from the trainings for $\frac{1}{14}$ of the whole period. Pamela went to the gym on the remaining days. How many days did Pamela go to the gym during the 28-day period?
60.	In the parallelogram SPAM, the segment SV is angle S's bisector. If the sides SP and PA have lengths 5 and 8 cm, what is the length of the midline of the trapezoid SVAM? P V A S M		

MULTIPLE CHOICE QUESTIONS

Questions 63 - 68

63. A theater expected to earn a profit of \$4,450 from a premiere show performance. In fact, the profit earned was 76% of what was expected. How much money did the theater actually earn?

    A. \$3,382
    B. \$3,482
    C. \$1,068
    D. \$1,069

64. Oil flows out of a tank at a rate of 2.6 gallons per minute. At this rate, how long (in minutes) would it take to fill a tub that has a capacity of 221 gallons?

    E. 80 minutes
    F. 85 minutes
    G. 90 minutes
    H. 95 minutes

65. The table below gives the height of 5 basketball players. Which of the following is Steve's height if the mean height of these basketball players is 190 cm?

Player	Height
Chris	192
Steve	x
Tom	188
Larry	190
John	186

    A. 192 cm
    B. 193 cm
    C. 194 cm
    D. 195 cm

66. A survey about how the temperature causes insomnia says that among 4,000 interviewed people 1,800 cannot sleep when the temperature is too high, 2,400 cannot sleep when the temperature is too low and 600 people cannot sleep in both cases. How many people's sleep is not affected by the temperature?

    E. 100
    F. 200
    G. 300
    H. 400

67. How many different 3-letter words can be created using the letters from the word "LAPTOP", if the letters cannot repeat?

    A. 720
    B. 360
    C. 120
    D. 60

68. If $\frac{k+2m}{a-4} = \frac{2k-m}{4}$, what is the correct expression for a in terms of k and m?

    E. $\frac{4(3k+m)}{2k-m}$
    F. $\frac{4k^2+3km-2m^2+16}{4}$
    G. $\frac{4(k+2m)}{2k-m}$
    H. $\frac{2k^2-2m^2+16}{4}$

Questions 69 - 74

69. Which of the following system of inequalities represent the solution set shown on the number line below?

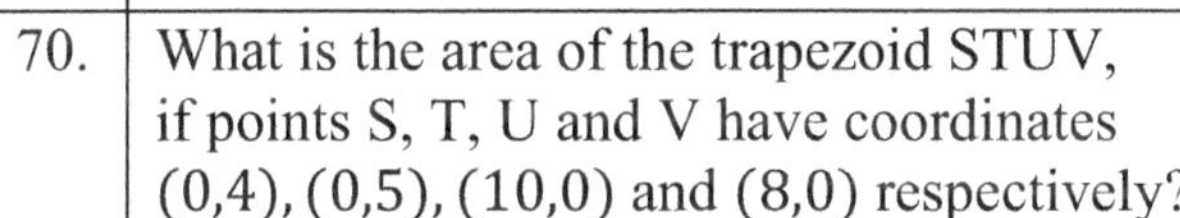

A. $\begin{cases} 2x - 7 < 0 \\ 4x + 12 \leq 0 \end{cases}$

B. $\begin{cases} 2x - 7 \geq 0 \\ 4x + 12 < 0 \end{cases}$

C. $\begin{cases} 2x - 7 < 0 \\ 4x + 12 \geq 0 \end{cases}$

D. $\begin{cases} 2x - 7 \leq 0 \\ 4x + 12 > 0 \end{cases}$

70. What is the area of the trapezoid STUV, if points S, T, U and V have coordinates (0,4), (0,5), (10,0) and (8,0) respectively?

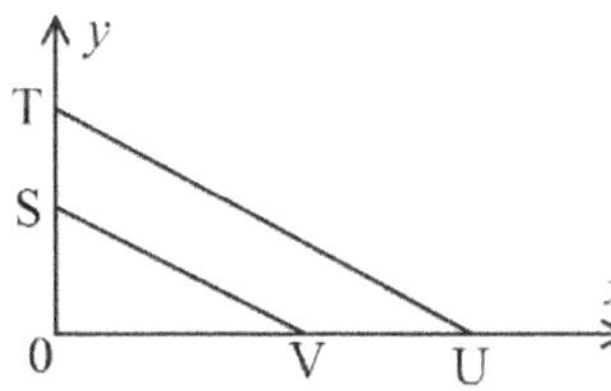

E. 9 $units^2$.
F. 10 $units^2$.
G. 12 $units^2$.
H. 14 $units^2$.

71. Two fair dice are rolled. What is the probability that the sum of the rolled numbers is an even number greater than 7 and both numbers are odd?

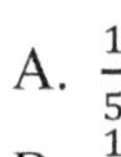

A. $\frac{1}{5}$
B. $\frac{1}{9}$
C. $\frac{1}{12}$
D. $\frac{1}{15}$

72. The fraction $\frac{47}{x}$ can be written in decimal form as 2.9375. What could be the possible value of x?

E. 16
F. 18
G. 20
H. 22

73. In the isosceles right triangle SAD, the length of its hypotenuse SD is 24 cm. What is the area of the shaded region?

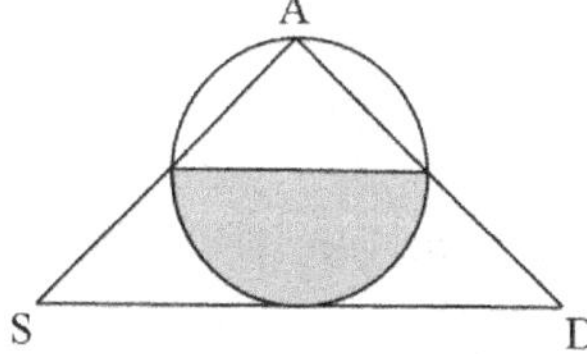

A. $36\pi\ cm^2$
B. $12\pi\ cm^2$
C. $18\pi\ cm^2$
D. $144\pi\ cm^2$

74. Point M divides segment AB in the ratio 3 : 4. If points K and L are midpoints of the segments AM and MB, what is the ratio $AK: KB$?

E. 3:4
F. 3:7
G. 3:11
H. 3:14

Questions 75 - 80

75. How many different 6-digit numbers can be created using the digits 0, 1, 2, 3, 4 and 5 without repeating any of these digits in the number and the number cannot start with 0?

A. 720
B. 600
C. 360
D. 300

76. If n is an even natural number, what is the expression for the product of the previous even number and the next even number divided by n?

E. $\frac{(n-1)(n+1)}{n}$
F. $\frac{(n-2)(n+2)}{n}$
G. $\frac{n}{(n-1)(n+1)}$
H. $\frac{n}{(n-2)(n+2)}$

77. Using the definition of the absolute value of a number, what is the value of the expression below?

$$\left|(-3+(-1))\cdot 5-12\right|$$

A. 32
B. 2
C. −22
D. 22

78. Bugs Bunny ate 75 carrots during winter, which is 30% of all the carrots he had in stock. What is the total number of carrots he had in stock?

E. 750
F. 250
G. 500
H. 275

79. Rays BO and DO are angle bisectors of $\angle AOC$ and $\angle COE$. What is the measure of $\angle COD$?

A. 48°
B. 42°
C. 58°
D. 52°

80. If $a=-4,\ b=4$ and $c=-3$, what is the value of the expression $(b-a)\cdot c+(b+c)\cdot a$?

E. −4
F. −28
G. 20
H. 12

Questions 81 - 86

81. Given $\frac{a}{4} = b + 3$, $\frac{b}{5} = d + 1$, $d = 3c$, which variable has the greatest value if $c < -1$?

A. a
B. b
C. c
D. d

82. In the parallelogram ABCD, the diagonal BD is perpendicular to the side AB. If the angle BAD = 36°, what is the measure of the angle ABC?

B C
36°
A D

E. 90°
F. 126°
G. 54°
H. 144°

83. A recipe requires 4 eggs for 9 cookies. How many eggs are required to prepare 72 cookies?

A. 8
B. 16
C. 32
D. 64

84. Lisa has greater number of nickels than Tom has dimes. If together they have \$5.55, what is the smallest possible number of nickels Lisa could have?

E. 36
F. 37
G. 38
H. 39

85. A snail moves up the tree 32 cm each night and moves down the tree 7 cm each day. At which height the snail will be at the end of 6th day, if it starts moving from the ground 1st day during the night?

A. 125 cm
B. 132 cm
C. 118 cm
D. 150 cm

86. The ratio between girls and boys in 6th grade is 3 : 4 and the ratio between girls and boys in 7th grade is 7: 5. What is the number of children in 6th grade, if there are a total of 78 students in both grades and the number of all girls is the same as the number of all boys?

E. 36
F. 39
G. 42
H. 44

Questions 87 - 92

87. The table below shows the number of students that like or don't like sport. Based on this information, what is the probability that a randomly chosen student doesn't like sport?

	Gr 5	Gr 6	Gr 7
Like Sport	32	36	40
Don't like sport	24	18	12

A. $\frac{1}{3}$
B. $\frac{1}{2}$
C. $\frac{2}{3}$
D. $\frac{1}{4}$

88. What is the greatest common factor of 54, 72 and 180?

E. 18
F. 36
G. 9
H. 12

89. The average of 12 numbers is x and the average of 7 of them is y. What is the average of the remaining 5 numbers?

A. $\frac{12x+7y}{5}$
B. $\frac{7y-12x}{5}$
C. $\frac{7x+12y}{5}$
D. $\frac{12x-7y}{5}$

90. 25 students passed a math test with a score greater than 80 points, 36 students scored greater than 60 but less than 80 points and 39 students scored greater than 40 but less than 60 points. What is the probability that a student chosen at random has a score less than 80?

E. $\frac{1}{4}$
F. $\frac{1}{2}$
G. $\frac{9}{25}$
H. $\frac{3}{4}$

91. Two circles with radii 9 cm and 6 cm are tangents from the inside. What is the area of the shaded region?

A. $36\pi\ cm^2$
B. $45\pi\ cm^2$
C. $54\pi\ cm^2$
D. $9\pi\ cm^2$

92. The table below shows discounts offered on pens in a certain wholesale store. If the initial price of the pen is \$1.20, what is the price of 4,125 pens, taking into account the discounts offered?

No. of Pens	100	1,000	3,000
Discount	5%	10%	15%

E. \$4,207.50
F. \$4,950
G. \$4,284
H. \$4,168.50

Questions 93 - 98			
93.	How many positive even numbers satisfy the inequality below? $$29 < 4x + 5 \leq 93$$ A. 9 B. 8 C. 17 D. 16	96.	A family spends 15% of its income on food, 50% on children' education and 70% of the remaining on the house rent. What percent of the family's income is left? E. 31.5% F. 10.5% G. 19.5% H. 13.5%
94.	When 162 is divided by an unknown number x squared, the result obtained is six times the number x. What is the unknown number x? E. 3 F. 4 G. 6 H. 9	97.	Point M divides the segment $\overline{AB}$ on the number line in the ratio 3 : 4. If the position of the point B is 15 on the number line and the position of the point M is 7, what is the position of point A? A. -1 B. 0 C. 1 D. 2
95.	Two negative numbers a and b lie on the number line at a distance of 5 units. A positive number c lies twice as close to the number b than to the number a. Which of the following sets of numbers $a,$ b and c can be the correct ones? A. $a = -1,\ b = -6,\ c = 4$ B. $a = -1,\ b = -6,\ c = 3$ C. $a = -6,\ b = -1,\ c = 3$ D. $a = -6,\ b = -1,\ c = 4$	98.	The ratio of three numbers $a,$ b and c is 2 : 3 : 4. What is the ratio $\frac{a}{b}:\frac{b}{c}:\frac{c}{a}$? E. $2:3:4$ F. $8:9:24$ G. $3:4:2$ H. $4:6:12$

Questions 99 - 104			
99.	In the last exam, 3 students got an average score of 85 points, 7 students got an average score of 80 points and 15 students got an average score of 72 points. What is the average score of all the students? A. 74.6 B. 74.8 C. 75.8 D. 76.6	102.	The surface of a lake is covered with lotus flowers. It is known that the amount of lotus flowers doubles each day. If it takes 80 days to cover the lake's surface fully by the lotus flowers, how many days will it take to cover $\frac{1}{4}$ of the lake? E. 20 F. 40 G. 78 H. 79
100.	Romi draws the map of Italy, in which $1\ mm$ represents a distance of $15\ km$. If the distance between Rome and Florence is about $270\ km$, what is the length of the line connecting these cities on Romi's map? E. 1.7 cm F. 1.8 cm G. 17 cm H. 18 cm	103.	If $x + 1$ is an odd number, which of the following statements must be false? A. $8x + 5$ is an odd number B. $3x - 2$ is an even number C. $x + x + 1 + x + 2$ is an odd number D. $(x + 1)(x - 1)$ is an even number
101.	After 4 years, the brother will be three times as old as his sister was 3 years ago. What is the brother's age now, if 5 years ago he was twice as old as his sister was? A. 11 B. 10 C. 9 D. 8	104.	Three buses start travelling from point A and moves in three different directions B, C, and D. A bus goes towards direction B every 45 minutes, towards direction C each hour and towards direction D every 2 hours. After how many minutes will these three buses start their journey from point A at the same time? E. 360 minutes F. 240 minutes G. 180 minutes H. 120 minutes

Questions 105 - 110			
105.	Which expression is an equivalent of the expression given below? $(2-3x)7-3(x+4)$ A. $8(2-3x)$ B. $2(1-12x)$ C. $2(9x-13)$ D. $2(13-9x)$	108.	Jane interchanged places of the digits in a 2-digit number and get a new number that is 36 greater than the original number. Which of the following cannot be the original number? E. 59 F. 37 G. 48 H. 16
106.	Digits 1, 2, 3, 4 and 5 are written on 5 separate cards. How many different odd numbers can be formed using all these cards once? E. 120 F. 48 G. 96 H. 72	109.	In the rectangle ABCD, points K and N are midpoints of the sides AB and CD. What is the area of the shaded region, if the four quadrilaterals AKQP, KBLQ, MCNR and SRND are squares? B L M C K Q R N 6 4 A P S D A. 88 $units^2$ B. 112$units^2$ C. 64 $units^2$ D. 104 $units^2$
107.	If Dylan gives his brother 25% of his money, then his brother will have \$90. If Dylan's brother gives Dylan $\frac{1}{3}$ of his money, he had in the beginning, then Dylan will have \$118. What is the initial amount of money Dylan had? A. \$90 B. \$96 C. \$100 D. \$112	110.	A Custom office returns the tax fee at a rate of \$15 at every \$200 spent abroad. If a family presented a \$640 worth of shopping receipt at the customs office, what is expected amount of money to be returned to the family? E. \$45 F. \$48 G. \$52 H. \$55

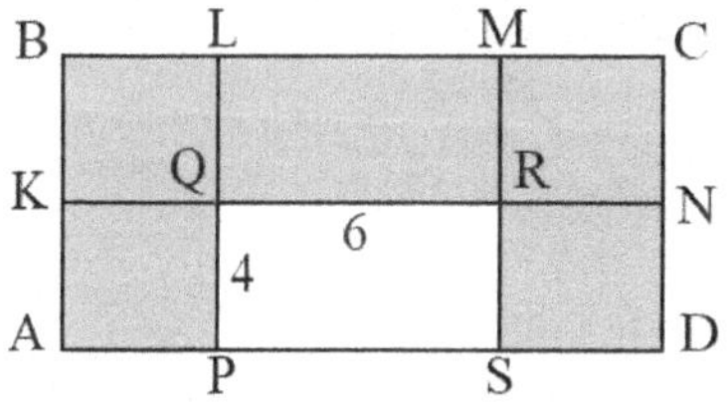

Questions 111 - 114			
111.	A girl is dressing up for a party. She has 4 different party dresses (Green, Pink, Violet and Black) and 10 pairs of shoes. In how many ways can she dress herself for a party, if the green dress only goes with one pair of her shoes? A. 41 B. 39 C. 31 D. 30	113.	A prism has all square shaped lateral faces. If the area of one lateral face of the prism is 36 $units^2$, what will be the volume of the prism? A. 144 $units^3$ B. 216 $units^3$ C. 180 $units^3$ D. 196 $units^3$
112.	In the below equation, what is the value of a? $1 - 2a = 3(a - 4)$ E. -2.6 F. -2.2 G. 2.2 H. 2.6	114.	At a distance of 560 meters, Achilles noticed a turtle that was moving at a rate of 1.2 km/h. How long did it take Achilles to catch the turtle, if his running speed was 18 km/h? E. 2 minutes F. 2 minutes 10 seconds G. 2 minutes 20 seconds H. 2 minutes 30 seconds

PRACTICE TEST 3

GRID-IN QUESTIONS			
Questions 58 - 62			
58.	The average age of Kevin, his mother and father is 28 years. The average of mother's and son's ages is 23 years and the average of father's and son's ages is 25 years. What is the son's age?	61.	The measuring cup contains 150 ml of liquid. How many measuring cups will be needed to fill in a 6-liter tank?
59.	Carlson ate $\frac{1}{4}$ of jam in the jar. Next day, he ate $\frac{1}{2}$ of the remaining jam in the jar. What percent of jam was left in the jar?	62.	A fair coin is thrown 5 times. What is the probability that the coin will land on heads more than 3 times?
60.	In the isosceles triangle ABC, $AB = BC = 9$ and $AC = 6$. If $AT : TB = 2 : 1$, what is the perimeter of the parallelogram ATOM? B T O A M C		

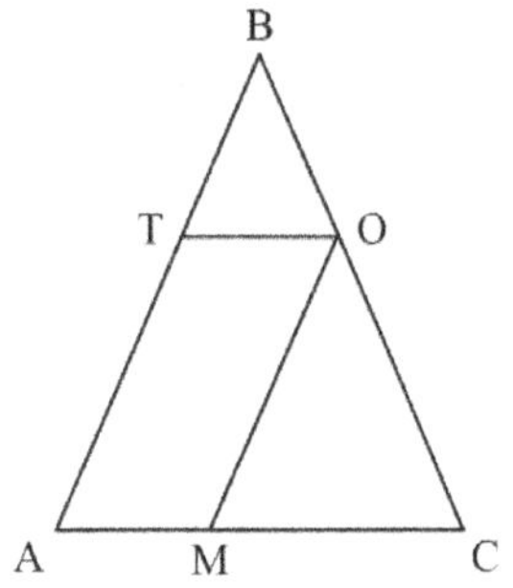

MULTIPLE CHOICE QUESTIONS			
Questions 63 - 68			
63.	In the 6th grade, 40% of students prefer to do homework with their parents and the other 24 students do it themselves. If one eighth of the students who do homework with their parents gets bad marks, then what is the number of students who do homework with their parents and get good marks? A. 12 B. 13 C. 14 D. 15	66.	The sum of two consecutive odd integers is 72. If both the odd numbers is written in reverse order such that the tens become ones and the ones become tens. What is the sum of the two new numbers obtained by interchanging their places? E. 27 F. 110 G. 72 H. 126
64.	If $b - c = c + a$ and $a = \frac{c}{2} + 1$, what is the expression for b in terms of c? E. $b = \frac{3c}{2} + 1$ F. $b = \frac{c}{2} + 1$ G. $b = \frac{5c}{2} + 1$ H. $b = \frac{3c}{2} - 1$	67.	Variable x takes its values from the set $\{-4, 2, 10\}$. Which of the following sets corresponds to the possible values of variable y, if $-\frac{x}{2} = y + 3$? A. $\{-8, -4, -1\}$ B. $\{-8, 4, 20\}$ C. $\{-11, 1, 17\}$ D. $\{-11, -4, 2\}$
65.	On the number line two points A and B have positions $-\frac{3}{4}$ and $1\frac{1}{2}$, respectively. Point C has positive position, lies between points A and B and is twice as close to point B as to point A. What is point C position? A B (number line) A. 0 B. $\frac{3}{4}$ C. $\frac{3}{2}$ D. 1	68.	Expression $(x + 1)(2x - 5) - (x - 3)(x + 1)$ is equivalent to expression E. $(x + 1)(x - 8)$ F. $(x + 1)(2x + 2)$ G. $2(x + 1)^2$ H. $(x + 1)(x - 2)$

Questions 69 - 74

69. The average of 6 numbers is 22 greater than the average of 4 of those numbers. What is the average of the two remaining numbers, if the sum of all 6 numbers is 180?

A. 74
B. 90
C. 79
D. 44

70. If Paolo gives one third of his coins to his brother, then both of them get the same numbers of coins. How many coins did two brothers had at the beginning?

E. 24 and 18
F. 24 and 12
G. 24 and 8
H. 24 and 6

71. The map scale coefficient is

$1\ mm : 25{,}000{,}000\ mm.$

If the distance between two cities is 525 kilometers, what is the distance between these cities on the map?

A. 21 cm
B. 2.1 cm
C. 0.21 cm
D. 210 cm

72. A parking service recorded the number of cars been parked during the last month. Find, what percent of cars used the parking service more than three times?

Number of parking times	1	2	3	4	>4
Number of cars	120	180	240	210	150

E. 40%
F. 50%
G. 60%
H. 75%

73. What is the area of the shaded region in a square with side length of 1 cm?

A. $1 - \pi\ cm^2$
B. $1 - \frac{\pi}{2}\ cm^2$
C. $1 - \frac{\pi}{4}\ cm^2$
D. $1 - 2\pi\ cm^2$

74. If you place the books on the shelf by groups of 3, 4 or 5 books, then one extra book will remain. If you place the books by groups of 7, then no extra book is left. What is the minimal number of books that can be placed on the shelf?

E. 210
F. 245
G. 280
H. 301

Questions 75 - 80

75. Three sides of a rectangular garden are bounded with a fence and one shorter side measuring 18 m is bounded by a river. The ratio of the width to the length of the garden is 6 : 11. What can be the total length of the fence?

A. 84 m
B. 69 m
C. 66 m
D. 54 m

76. Which of the following number lines represents the solution of the inequality $-3 < \frac{x}{3} \leq 6$?

E. -20 -10 0 10 20
F. -20 -10 0 10 20
G. -20 -10 0 10 20
H. -20 -10 0 10 20

77. Willy has at least four times as many coins as Anna has. If Willy gives 23 coins to Anna, they will have the same amount of coins. What is the greatest possible number of coins Anna can have in the beginning?

A. 13
B. 14
C. 15
D. 16

78. A bag contains red, green, and black balls. The probability of choosing the black ball from the bag is $\frac{1}{6}$ and the probability of choosing the red ball from the bag is $\frac{2}{5}$. What is the probability of choosing the green ball?

E. $\frac{13}{30}$
F. $\frac{3}{5}$
G. $\frac{5}{6}$
H. $\frac{17}{30}$

79. Three sisters decided to share $112 according to the ratio between their ages. If the sisters are 12, 10 and 6 years old, how many will each sister get?

A. $50, $37, $25
B. $52, $34, $26
C. $46, $43, $23
D. $48, $40, $24

80. In a trapezoid COLA, $OL = LH = HA$. The area of the trapezoid $COLA$ is $26\ units^2$ and the area of the triangle LHA is $8\ units^2$. What is the length of the base AC?

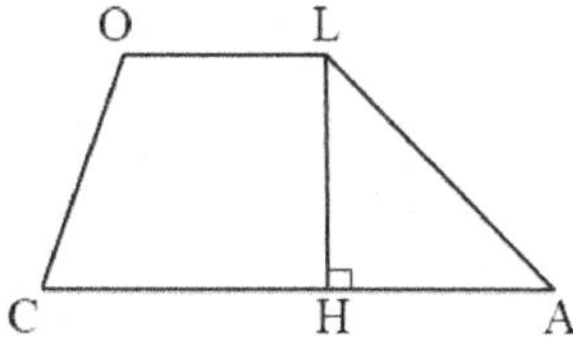

E. 8 $units$
F. 9 $units$
G. 10 $units$
H. 11 $units$

Questions 81 - 86

81. A travel agency surveyed 1,000 people to find out how many of them visited London and Paris. 310 people visited London, 222 people visited Paris and 118 people visited both cities. How many people visited none of these cities?

A. 414
B. 104
C. 192
D. 586

82. Mrs. Hudson bought apples and pears for the dinner. On the way back home, she realized that she forgot how much of each fruit she bought. Apples were sold by $1.35 per kg and pears were sold by $2.52 per kg. The weight of her purchase was 9 kg and the total cost was $18. How much apples did she buy?

E. 4 kg
F. 3 kg
G. 5 kg
H. 6 kg

83. 2 cards are chosen from a standard deck of cards. The first card is replaced before choosing the second card. What is the probability that they both will be aces?

A. $\frac{1}{169}$
B. $\frac{1}{156}$
C. $\frac{1}{663}$
D. $\frac{1}{221}$

84. In an ancient market the animals were exchanged by the rule:
1 sheep = 12 rabbits
2 pigs = 5 sheep
1 cow = 3 pigs.
How many rabbits could be exchanged for 4 cows?

E. 120
F. 180
G. 300
H. 360

85. The table below shows the speed of a particular mode of transport. If the average speed of all transport modes is 46 km/h, what is the value of x?

Transport	Bus	Car	Bicycle	Walk
Speed (km/h)	60	90	30	x

A. 3 km/h
B. 4 km/h
C. 5 km/h
D. 6 km/h

86. STUDENTS WHO LIKE MATH

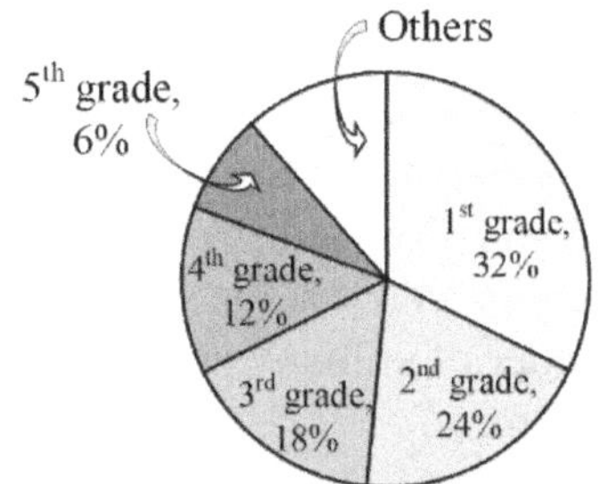

If total number of students in school is 1,200, how many other students like Math?

E. 96
F. 100
G. 104
H. 108

Questions 87 - 92

87. What is the value of the expression $3\frac{1}{2} + 5\frac{3}{4} + 7\frac{1}{8}$?

A. $15\frac{1}{8}$
B. $16\frac{1}{8}$
C. $15\frac{3}{8}$
D. $16\frac{3}{8}$

88. The large rectangle is dilated to the small rectangle using a scale factor $\frac{3}{4}$. What is the area of the shaded region, if the small rectangle is 3 units by 6 units?

E. 18 $units^2$
F. 14 $units^2$
G. 30 $units^2$
H. 24 $units^2$

89. Lily collected 48 roses, 56 lilies and 84 herbs. What is the maximal number of identical bouquets she can create using all these flowers?

A. 4
B. 6
C. 8
D. 10

90. If 20% of John's family are blue-eyed, 15% are green-eyed, 25% are grey-eyed and the rest are black-eyed. What is the probability that John's baby will be green-eyed or black-eyed?

E. $\frac{3}{5}$
F. $\frac{11}{20}$
G. $\frac{3}{4}$
H. $\frac{2}{5}$

91. The speed of the train is 120 km/h and 1 kilometer = 3,280 feet. Which of the following calculations would give the train's speed in feet per second?

A. $\frac{120 \times 3,280}{3,600}$
B. $\frac{120 \times 3,600}{3,280}$
C. $\frac{3,280 \times 60}{120}$
D. $\frac{3,280 \times 120}{60}$

92. The sum of the ages of Steve and Ali is three times the difference of their ages. What is the ratio of Ali's age to Steve's age if Ali is older?

E. 5: 1
F. 4: 1
G. 3: 1
H. 2: 1

Questions 93 - 98

93. What is the sum of all the numbers divisible by 6 between 13 and 85?

A. 534
B. 612
C. 480
D. 558

94. Numbers a, b, c and d are four consecutive odd numbers. Which statement must be true?

E. The sum $a + b + c + d$ is 12 greater than a
F. The sum $a + b + c + d$ is 6 greater than a
G. The differences $b - a$ and $d - c$ are always equal
H. The differences $c - b$ and $d - a$ are always equal

95. Jim is a waiter. He is paid $325 each week and gets tipped $22 on an average per day. How much will Jim earn in two-weeks period?

A. $958
B. $633
C. $804
D. $479

96. Three farmers rent a pasture together. The 1st farmer feeds 100 sheep for 6 months, the 2nd farmer feeds 120 sheep for 4 months and the 3rd farmer feeds 150 sheep for 2 months. If the rent of the pasture is $552, how much must the 3rd farmer pay as his share of the rent?

E. $120
F. $150
G. $160
H. $180

97. There are four different routes between cities S and T. How many ways can a round trip be made from city S to city T and back if it is desired to take a different route on the way back?

A. 12
B. 7
C. 8
D. 16

98. Which of the following fractions represents the repeating decimal $0.\overline{04}$?

E. $\frac{1}{33}$
F. $\frac{1}{22}$
G. $\frac{4}{99}$
H. $\frac{5}{121}$

Questions 99 - 104

99. Alice cuts a rectangular sheet of a color paper into identical squares of maximum size to create wrappings for gifts. How many wrappings can she create without wasting any piece of paper if the sheet of paper measures $120\ cm \times 96\ cm$?

A. 5
B. 24
C. 20
D. 480

100. A carpenter makes 42 wooden chairs in 28 minutes. Continuing his work at the same rate, how long it will take him to complete an order of 300 chairs?

E. 3 hours 4 minutes
F. 3 hours 8 minutes
G. 3 hours 10 minutes
H. 3 hours 20 minutes

101. If $\frac{x+y}{2y} = 5$, then $\frac{y}{x} =$?

A. $4\frac{1}{2}$
B. 9
C. $\frac{1}{9}$
D. $9\frac{1}{2}$

102. John has 3 quarters, 6 dimes, 14 nickels, and 17 pennies in his piggy bank. If John chooses 2 of the coins at random without replacement, what is the probability that none of the 2 coins that John chooses is a dime?

E. $\frac{187}{260}$
F. $\frac{289}{400}$
G. $\frac{16}{25}$
H. $\frac{68}{95}$

103. If a, b, c and d are positive integers and $\frac{a}{b} = \frac{2c}{d}$, which of statements given below is not true?

A. $\frac{d}{b} = \frac{2c}{a}$
B. $\frac{bc}{d} = 2a$
C. $\frac{d}{c} = \frac{2b}{a}$
D. $\frac{ad}{c} = 2b$

104. The length of the segment AB is 10 units. Point D lies between points A and B such that AD = 4 units. Point C lies to the right from point B and BC = 2 units. What is the length of the segment DC?

A B

E. 4 units
F. 6 units
G. 8 units
H. 9 units

Questions 105 - 110

105. n is an even natural number. Which statement is true?

A. $3n + 2$ is an odd number
B. $3n + 1$ is an odd number
C. $3n + 3$ is an even number
D. $3n + 5$ is an even number

106. A man standing in a queue is 37th from the beginning. A girl standing five positions in front of him is at 24th position from the end. How many people are standing in the queue?

E. 54
F. 55
G. 53
H. 56

107. What is the value of the expression $(2{,}019)^2 - (2{,}018)^2$?

A. 2,019
B. 4,037
C. 2,018
D. 4,036

108. Two fair dice are rolled. What is the probability of obtaining a sum of at least 7?

E. $\frac{1}{2}$
F. $\frac{5}{12}$
G. $\frac{7}{12}$
H. $\frac{3}{4}$

109. If $5b - 7a = 70$, what is a in terms of b?

A. $a = \frac{5}{7}b - 10$
B. $a = \frac{7}{5}b - 10$
C. $a = \frac{5}{7}b + 10$
D. $a = \frac{7}{5}b + 10$

110. 220 students were asked about their preferences about afterschool activities and the results are represented in the table below.

Activity	Chat Online	Play Sport	Visit Friend	Read Books	Walk with a dog
Number	75	54	42	33	

How many more students prefer chatting online than walking with a dog?

E. 16
F. 59
G. 24
H. 63

Questions 111 - 114

111. Maria is using 2.5-liter juice bottle to serve juice to her 25 friends invited at her birthday party. How many juice bottles will she need in order to serve 300 milliliters of juice to each of her friends?

A. 2
B. 3
C. 4
D. 5

112. After 5 years Denys will be as old as his sister is now. After 5 years Denys' sister will be twice as old as Denys is now. How old is Denys' sister now?

E. 8
F. 10
G. 12
H. 15

113. In a right triangle ABC, segment BD is perpendicular to the side AC, and BE is angle B bisector. What is the measure of $\angle BAE$, if $\angle DBE = 23°$?

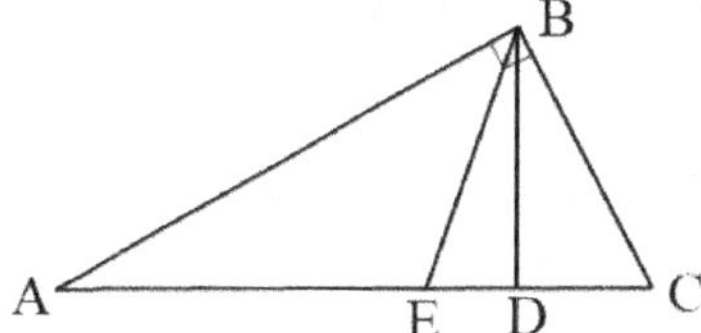

A. 22°
B. 23°
C. 24°
D. 25°

114. A bag contains 26 alphabet cards, one for each letter of the alphabet written on it. What is the probability that a randomly selected card is one of the first five alphabets or a vowel?

E. $\frac{5}{13}$
F. $\frac{7}{26}$
G. $\frac{4}{13}$
H. $\frac{9}{26}$

PRACTICE TEST
4

GRID-IN QUESTIONS

Questions 58 - 62

58. Three lines AB, CD and EF intersect at a point O. If $\angle AOC = 32°$ and $\angle BOF = 91°$, what is the measure of $\angle COE$?

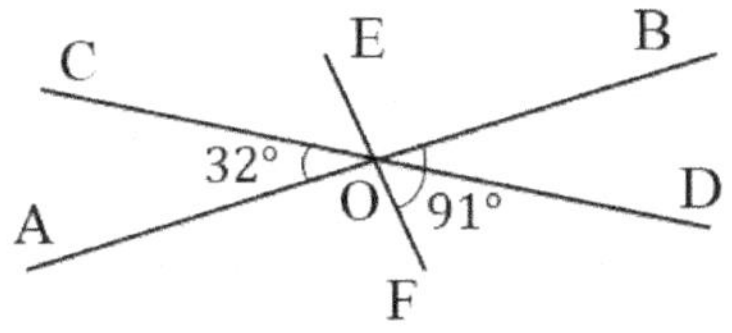

C E B 32° A O 91° D F

59. The ratio of sheep to geese on the farm is 7 : 4. If the animals on the farm have a total of 180 legs, what is the number of geese on the farm?

60. If $5a - 78 = 3a + 24$, what is the value of a?

61. Jim can go to school by bus, car, train or on foot. If he has to return through a different mode of transport, in how many different ways could he go to school and return back home?

62. Wendy has completed $\frac{9}{25}$ of her homework. Find the decimal representation of the homework she has to do yet?

MULTIPLE CHOICE QUESTIONS

Questions 63 - 68

63. The perimeter of the rectangle ROSE is 22 cm, the length of the broken line RAPS is 13 cm. If the points A and P bisect the sides OS and RE respectively, find the perimeter of the triangle RAP?

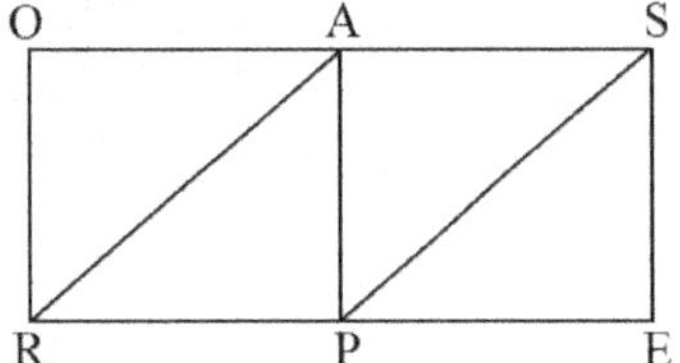

A. 16 cm
B. 14 cm
C. 12 cm
D. 10 cm

64. If $3a - \frac{b}{c} = \frac{c}{a} + 1$, what is the expression for b in terms of a and c?

E. $\frac{3a^2c - c^2 - ac}{a}$
F. $\frac{3a^2 - c - a}{ac}$
G. $\frac{3a^2 - c^2}{ac}$
H. $\frac{3ac - c^2 - a}{a}$

65. The age of Jacob's father is the same as that of the sum of Jacob's age and his mother's age. After 8 years Jacob's age will be $\frac{1}{3}$ times his father's age, if her mother is 26 years old, what is Jacob's age now?

A. 4 years
B. 5 years
C. 6 years
D. 7 years

66. Billy divided all his money among 3 of his friends Simon, Denys and Kallis. Simon got twice as much as the other two friends got together. Denys got one-third of the money Kallis got. If Kallis got $12, how much money does Billy had in the beginning?

E. $144
F. $96
G. $60
H. $48

67. If $12x = 64 - 3y$, then $y =$?

A. $y = \frac{64}{3} + 4x$
B. $y = 4x - \frac{64}{3}$
C. $y = \frac{64}{3} - 4x$
D. $y = -\frac{64}{3} - 4x$

68. What is the least common multiple of 15, 18 and 210?

E. 1050
F. 420
G. 840
H. 630

Questions 69 - 74

69. John, Romi and Sue can finish their work in 3 hours, if they work together. If John does the same work alone, he can finish it in 12 hours and Romi can finish it in 9 hours alone. How long will it take for Sue to finish the work alone?

    A. 7 hours 2 minutes
    B. 7 hours 12 minutes
    C. 7 hours 20 minutes
    D. 7 hours 30 minutes

70. Three consecutive even numbers have an average of 38. What is the smallest number in this set?

    E. 32
    F. 34
    G. 36
    H. 38

71. Die A has 4 black faces and 2 white faces. Die B has 2 black faces and 4 white faces. What is the probability that Die A will land on a black face and Die B will land on a white face?

    A. $\frac{4}{9}$
    B. $\frac{2}{9}$
    C. $\frac{1}{9}$
    D. $\frac{2}{3}$

72. If a square has the side length of 4 cm, what is the area of the shaded region?

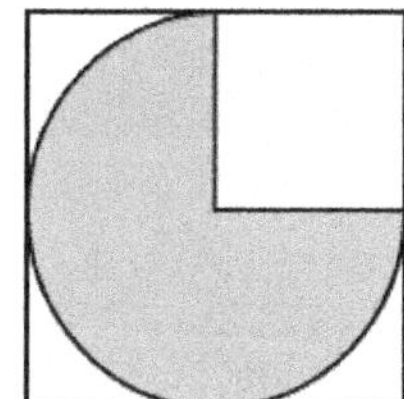

    E. 12π
    F. 4π
    G. 3π
    H. 16π

73. On the number line shown below, the position of point n is -2.5. If $|m-n| = 2$ and $|n-k| = 4$, what is the value of $m \times k$?

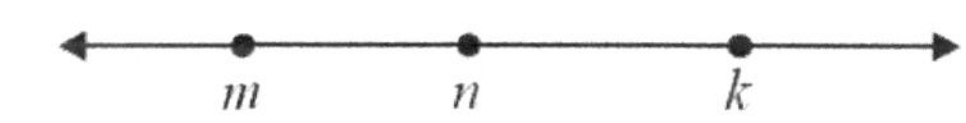

    A. -6.75
    B. 6.75
    C. -3.25
    D. 3.25

74. A supermarket announced a promotion: If you buy 5 units for \$$k$ each, then every additional unit will cost you \$$m$ less. Which expression represents the cost of n units, if $n > 5$?

    E. $5n + (n-5)m$
    F. $5k + nm$
    G. $nk - 5m$
    H. $5k + (n-5)(k-m)$

Questions 75 - 80

75. If $\frac{a+2b}{3} = \frac{2}{c}$, what is $\frac{4}{b}$?

A. $\frac{4}{b} = \frac{c}{12-2ac}$
B. $\frac{4}{b} = \frac{8c}{6-ac}$
C. $\frac{4}{b} = \frac{12-2ac}{c}$
D. $\frac{4}{b} = \frac{6-ac}{8c}$

76. A special nut mixture contains hazelnuts, almonds and walnuts in the ratio of 3 : 5 : 7. If a bag of this mixture contains 6 pounds of almonds, how many walnuts does it contain?

E. 3.6 pounds
F. 8.4 pounds
G. 4.5 pounds
H. 10.5 pounds

77. In summer, Brian bought new skies with a summer discount of 22%. What was the price of the skies before discount, if he paid $234?

A. $320
B. $310
C. $300
D. $290

78. The height of the house in a 3D sketch is 6.5 in. The scale used for the drawing is $2\ in = 7\ ft$. What is the actual height of the house?

E. 22.75 ft
F. 23 ft
G. 23.25 ft
H. 23.5 ft

79. In ΔBUS, V is midpoint of the side BS. If area of the ΔBVW is 4.5 $units^2$ and area of ΔBUV is 3 times the area of ΔBVW, what is the area of quadrilateral $SVWU$?

A. 27 $units^2$
B. 24 $units^2$
C. 23.5 $units^2$
D. 22.5 $units^2$

80. Among 200 book readers, 85 people like reading only historical novels, 12% likes reading historical novels and mystery novels and the rest of them like to read only mystery novels. How many people like reading only mystery novels?

E. 91
F. 115
G. 24
H. 109

Questions 81 - 86

81. From a set of numbered cards from 1 to 30, one card was picked at random. What is the probability that the card picked is a multiple of 3 or 5?

A. $\frac{1}{2}$
B. $\frac{8}{15}$
C. $\frac{7}{15}$
D. $\frac{13}{30}$

82. Variable x can take its value from the set $\{-4, -2, 0, 2, 4\}$. If $y = -\frac{x^2}{2} + 1$, what is the set of values for y?

E. $\{-7, -1, 1, 7\}$
F. $\{-7, -1, 1\}$
G. $\{-7, -1\}$
H. $\{-7, -1, 0, 1, 7\}$

83. The table below shows the distribution of time spent by mother and father. Which activity has the greatest difference in time spent?

	Chatting online	Watching TV	Cooking	Baby sitting
Mother	112 min	118 min	26 min	44 min
Father	44 min	33 min	68 min	155 min

A. Chatting online
B. Watching TV
C. Cooking
D. Babysitting

84. In an isosceles triangle ABC, the area of the shaded region is 16 $units^2$ and the area of the rectangle PLUS is 10 $units^2$. If the segment SU is half of the segment CB, what is the area of the pentagon APSUL?

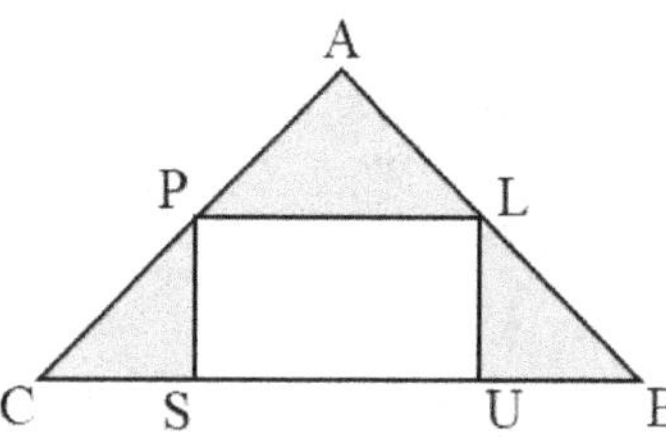

E. 16 $units^2$
F. 18 $units^2$
G. 20 $units^2$
H. 24 $units^2$

85. Which of the following fractions is not a repeating decimal?

A. $\frac{2}{33}$
B. $\frac{11}{99}$
C. $\frac{8}{125}$
D. $\frac{4}{99}$

86. What is $\frac{4}{216}$ of 3^7?

E. 121.5
F. 40.5
G. 13.5
H. 1.5

Questions 87 - 92

87. The wolf sees a rabbit from a distance of 800 meters. The rabbit is running away from the wolf at a speed of 2 m/s. If the wolf starts running towards the rabbit at a speed of 4 m/s, how far will the rabbit run before the wolf catches him?

A. 400 m
B. 600 m
C. 800 m
D. 1000 m

88. If $a = -2,\ b = 3$, what is the greatest number in the set $a + b^2,\ a^2 + b,\ a + b^3,\ a^3 + b$?

E. $a + b^2$
F. $a^2 + b$
G. $a + b^3$
H. $a^3 + b$

89. What is the sum of the first 10 terms in the pattern $-5,\ -1,\ 3,\ \ldots$?

A. 130
B. 126
C. 134
D. 122

90. In an exam, 1,200 boys and 800 girls appeared. 45% of the boys and 50% of the girls passed the exam. Find the percentage of the students who could not pass the exam?

E. 50%
F. 51%
G. 52%
H. 53%

91. For what value of x, the expression $\frac{x^2-16}{x^3+8}$ becomes undefined?

A. -8
B. 2
C. -2
D. 8

92. There are 50 green balls, 50 blue balls and 100 white balls in a box. 24% of the blue balls and 16% of the green balls are taken away. What is the percent of white balls in the box after taking away the green and blue balls?

E. nearly 51%
F. nearly 53%
G. nearly 56%
H. nearly 59%

Questions 93 - 98

93. In a quadrilateral $ABCD$, interior angles $\angle A$ and $\angle B$ measure $110°$ and $130°$, respectively. If an exterior angle $\angle C$ measures $80°$, what is the measure of the interior angle at vertex D?

A. $20°$
B. $10°$
C. $30°$
D. $40°$

94. If $a : b = 3 : 7$ and $b : c = 4 : 5$, what is the ratio $a : c$?

E. $14:35$
F. $12:35$
G. $21:40$
H. $7:40$

95. On a coordinate plane, the points $A(-3,1)$, $B(6,2)$ and $C(9,-3)$ represent the vertices of a triangle ABC. Find the coordinates of a point, where medians of triangle ABC intersect each other?

A. (3,1)
B. (3,0)
C. (4,1)
D. (4,0)

96. From a group of 6 men and 5 women, 4 people are selected to form a committee such that there are at least 3 men in the committee. How many different ways can it be done?

E. 125
F. 120
G. 115
H. 110

97. A solution of water and juice concentrate contains 15% of juice concentrate. How many liters of water must be added to 25 liters of the solution to make a new solution that contains 10% of juice concentrate?

A. 12.5 liters
B. 12 liters
C. 11.5 liters
D. 11 liters

98. Samantha has three times as many coins as Pamela has. If Samantha gets 2 coins and Pamela gets 3 coins from their mother every day, then Samantha will have twice as many coins as Pamela will have after 6 days. After how many days both of them will have equal number of coins?

E. 6
F. 12
G. 24
H. 48

Questions 99 - 104

99. In a rhombus $ABCD$, length of diagonals are $AC = 12$ and $BD = 8$. If the points K and L are the midpoints of sides AD and CD respectively, what is the area of the shaded region?

B
A C
K L
D

A. $12\ units^2$
B. $15\ units^2$
C. $18\ units^2$
D. $36\ units^2$

100. An ancient tribe used to do barter trade using the following exchange model:

32 mandarins = 114 olives
3 pineapples = 228 olives

How many mandarins can be exchanged for 18 pineapples?

E. 384
F. 366
G. 342
H. 396

101. Twice the area of a circle C is equal to 3 times the circumference of the same circle. What is the area of circle O, whose radius measures half as that of the radius of circle C?

A. π
B. 2π
C. 2.25π
D. 2.56π

102. Two fair dice are rolled. What is the probability of getting a 3 on the first die and not getting a 5 on the second die?

E. $\frac{1}{36}$
F. $\frac{7}{36}$
G. $\frac{11}{36}$
H. $\frac{5}{36}$

103. If $\frac{S}{M} = 12$ and $M < -4$, what could be the greatest possible value for S?

A. -46
B. -48
C. -49
D. -47

104. In the isosceles trapezoid $ABCD$, the diagonal AC is perpendicular to the side CD. If $\angle CAD = 30°$ and $CD = 4\ units$, what is the perimeter of the trapezoid $ABCD$?

B C
A 30° D

E. 16 units
F. 18 units
G. 20 units
H. 22 units

Questions 105 - 110

105. What is the average of the first ten prime numbers?

A. 12.9
B. 10.7
C. 10.1
D. 13.1

106. A fraction has a numerator 5 less than its denominator. When 8 is added to both its numerator and denominator, the new fraction becomes $\frac{3}{4}$. What was the initial fraction?

E. $\frac{5}{10}$
F. $\frac{24}{29}$
G. $\frac{7}{12}$
H. $\frac{9}{14}$

107. If n is an even number and m is an odd number, which statement must be true?

A. $3n + 2m + 1$ is an even number
B. $2n + 3m + 1$ is an even number
C. $5n + 2m + 2$ is an odd number
D. $2n + 5m + 1$ is an odd number

108. In a regular hexagon, the side length is $2\ cm$. What is the area of the shaded region?

E. $6\sqrt{3} - 3\pi\ cm^2$
F. $3\sqrt{3} - 3\pi\ cm^2$
G. $6\sqrt{3} - \pi\ cm^2$
H. $3\sqrt{3} - \pi\ cm^2$

109. Using the approximation, $\pi = \frac{22}{7}$, what is the circumference of a circle with a diameter of $21\ cm$?

A. 77 cm
B. 88 cm
C. 66 cm
D. 55 cm

110. In an infinite sequence, 1, 2, 3, 4, 5, 6, 1, 2, 3, 4, 5, 6, ..., Find the number at 2019th position in the sequence?

E. 5
F. 3
G. 4
H. 2

Questions 111 - 114			
111.	You have 10 coins in your pocket. 9 of them are ordinary coins with one tail and one head and the 10th coin has two heads. You randomly pick one coin from your pocket. What is the probability that this coin will land on head? A. 0.45 B. 0.48 C. 0.55 D. 0.52	113.	Which expression represents the following statement: 60% of a number is half the sum of the number and 4? A. $0.6n = \frac{1}{2}n + 4$ B. $0.6n = 2(n + 4)$ C. $0.6n = 2n + 4$ D. $0.6n = \frac{1}{2}n + 2$
112.	Points A, B and C divide the segment MN into four equal parts. If $MB = 12$ and $AN = 18$, what is possible length of the segment MN? E. 36 F. 48 G. 24 H. 28	114.	If $x = -2{,}020$ and $y = 2{,}019$, what is the value of the expression $x^2 - y^2$? E. 4,039 F. $-4{,}039$ G. 1 H. -1

PRACTICE TEST 5

GRID-IN QUESTIONS			
Questions 58 - 62			
58.	In the figure below, EB is perpendicular to AC. If $\angle DBE = 45°$, $\angle ABD = ?$ D, E, 45°, ?°, A, B, C	61.	On a trip to Florida, Tariq wants to visit New Jersey, Maryland, South Carolina, Washington, and Fayetteville. If he wants to visit these states in any order, how many different combinations are possible?
59.	If the ratio of students to teachers in Bobby-Tariq tutoring center is $4 : 1$ and there is a total of 400 people in the center including students and teachers, how many teachers are there?	62.	Bobby walked $4\frac{3}{20}$ km to go to his local library. Express the distance in decimal form.
60.	If $10x + 20 = 40$, then $x = ?$		

MULTIPLE CHOICE QUESTIONS

Questions 63 - 68

63. If $AH = 4\ cm$, what is the area of the square MATH given below?

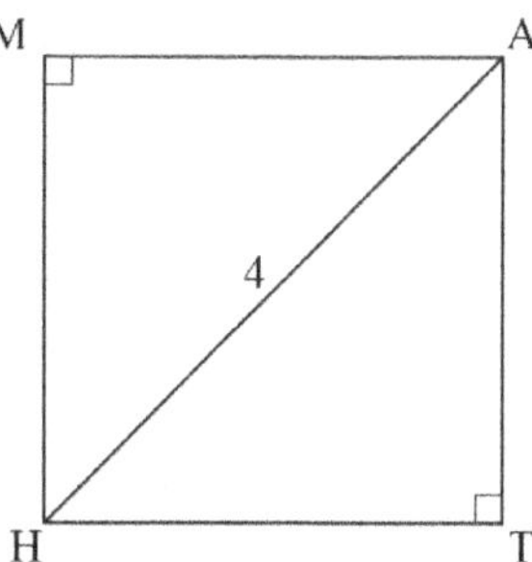

A. $16\ cm^2$
B. $12\ cm^2$
C. $8\ cm^2$
D. $4\ cm^2$

64. If $a = -3$, $b = -1$ and $c = 2$, what is the value of the expression below?
$a^2 - (b + c) + b$

E. 6
F. 7
G. 8
H. 9

65. Liam is 3 times as old as Noah. After 3 years, Liam will be 8 years more than two third of Noah's age. How old is Noah now?

A. 3
B. 4
C. 6
D. 8

66. Benjamin lent some money to his brother and two of his friends. His brother got $\frac{2}{3}$ of the total money and each of the friends got $\frac{1}{2}$ of the remaining amount Benjamin had.
If each friend received \$5,000 of his share, then what was the total amount of money Benjamin lent to his brother and the two friends?

E. \$20,000
F. \$30,000
G. \$40,000
H. \$50,000

67. If $10a + 5b = 20$, what is a in terms of b?

A. $2 - \frac{b}{2}$
B. $4 - \frac{5}{7}b$
C. $4 + \frac{b}{2}$
D. $10 - \frac{b}{4}$

68. There is a total of 9 students in a class. In order to assign a project, the teacher needs to make groups of three students each. How many different combinations of groups are possible?

E. 84
F. 39
G. 1,680
H. 3

Questions 69 - 74

69. What is the prime factorization of 600?

A. $2^3 \times 3 \times 5^2$
B. $2^5 \times 5^2$
C. $3^3 \times 5$
D. 6×10^2

70. John can finish a certain job in 3 hours. Bobby can finish the same job in 2 hours. If they work together, how long will it take for them to finish the job?

E. $5\ hours$
F. $1\frac{1}{5}\ hours$
G. $6\ hours$
H. $12\ hours$

71. The sum of three consecutive even integers is 1,206. If the least among them is k and the largest number among them
is y, what is the average of k and y?

A. 402
B. 404
C. 800
D. 804

72. A jar of coins contains 3 nickels, 5 dimes, 10 quarters and 7 pennies. If Ethan selects 2 coins at random without replacement in order to buy a pencil, what is the probability that the first coin is a quarter and the second coin is a dime?

E. $\frac{1}{12}$
F. $\frac{2}{25}$
G. $\frac{50}{73}$
H. $\frac{3}{25}$

73. If each side length of the square CAKE is 6, what is the area of shaded region?

A. $18\pi - 36$
B. $72\pi - 36$
C. $36\pi - 36$
D. $18\pi + 36$

74. In the number line above, the position of y is -1.5, $|y - z| = 10.5$ and $|x - z| =$ $= 30.5$ .What is the position of x?

E. -21.5
F. -20.5
G. -30.5
H. -40.5

Questions 75 - 80

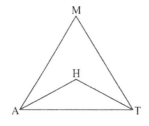

75.	A phone company charges k cents for the first 10 minutes and g cents for each additional minute of talking over the phone. What is the cost, in cents, for talking over the phone for m minutes, where m is greater than 10? A. $k+g$ B. $k+(m-10)g$ C. kmg D. $m+(k-10)g$	78.	Jackson bought a gift for his sister and paid \$68 after getting a discount of 15%. What was the original price of the gift before the discount? (Assuming that there is no sales tax). E. \$50 F. \$60 G. \$70 H. \$80
76.	If $\frac{k+g}{a}=\frac{4}{m}$, then what is $\frac{a}{6}$? E. $\frac{m(k+g)}{24}$ F. $\frac{k+g}{24m}$ G. $\frac{24}{m(k+g)}$ H. $\frac{24m}{k+g}$	79.	Grace draws a map of two villages for her history project using a scale, $\frac{3}{4}\ inch = 1{,}000\ km.$ Find the distance, in km, between two villages that are $1\frac{7}{8}$ inches apart from each other on the map? A. 2,400 B. 2,500 C. 2,600 D. 2,700
77.	Jacob is six times as old as Sofia and $2\frac{3}{4}$ times as old as Lucas. What fraction of Sofia's age is Lucas's age? A. $2\frac{2}{11}$ B. $4\frac{1}{11}$ C. $2\frac{3}{4}$ D. $11\frac{2}{3}$	80.	In the figure below, $AH = TH$, $AM = TM$ and $m\angle AHT$ is 120°. If the line segments AH and TH bisect $\angle MAT$ and $\angle MTA$ respectively, then what is the measure of $\angle AMT$? M H A T E. 30° F. 40° G. 60° H. 80°
Questions 81 - 86			

81. BLOOD TYPES OF 400 DONORS

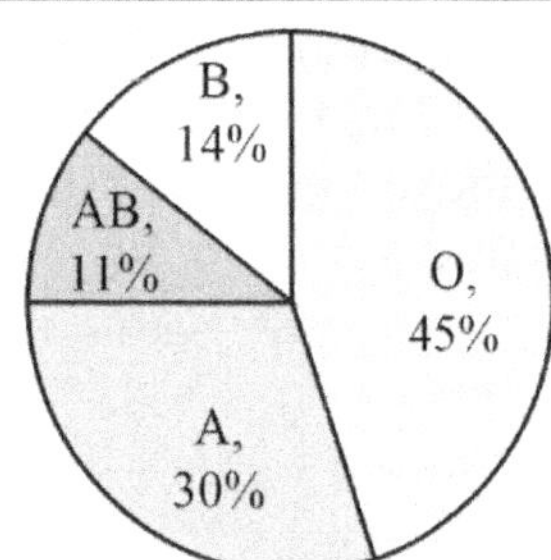

How many donors have type AB blood?

A. 34
B. 44
C. 160
D. 176

82. There are 2 jars, labeled A and B, on a shelf. Jar A contains 4 red marbles and 3 blue marbles whereas; Jar B contains 5 black marbles and 2 yellow marbles. Robin picks a marble randomly from jar A and places it into the jar B. Then he picks a marble randomly from jar B. What is the probability that the marble he picks from jar B is red?

E. $\frac{1}{7}$
F. $\frac{3}{14}$
G. $\frac{1}{14}$
H. $\frac{9}{17}$

83. If x is an even integer and

$$-2x + 4 > 12$$

What is the greatest possible value of x?

A. -6
B. -7
C. -8
D. 7

84. The table below shows the scores, David and Camilia, obtained in 6 different tests.

TEST SCORES

	Test 1	Test 2	Test 3	Test 4	Test 5	Test 6
David	70	85	90	88	97	89
Camilia	76	80	85	95	100	92

What is the difference between the average of David's and Camilia's test scores?

E. 1.0
F. 1.5
G. 2.5
H. 3.5

85. What is the area of the polygon above?

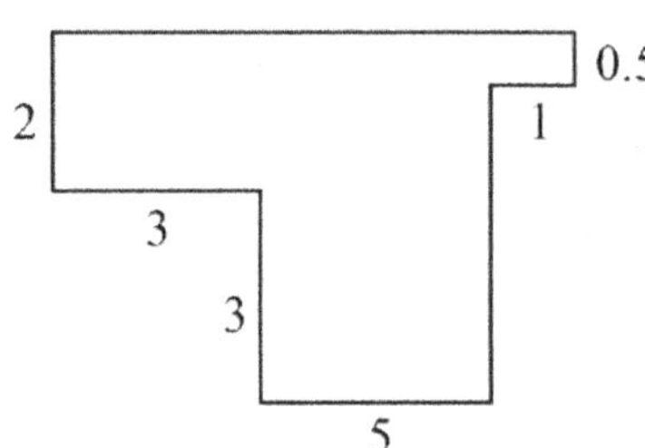

A. 43
B. 31.5
C. 23.5
D. 14

86. Which of the following fraction is equivalent to $1.\overline{4}$?

E. $1\frac{2}{5}$
F. $\frac{14}{10}$
G. $1\frac{4}{9}$
H. $1\frac{1}{2}$

Questions 87 - 92

87. What is $\frac{1}{4}$ of 2^{20}?

A. 4^2
B. 2^{19}
C. 2^{16}
D. 4^9

88. In a community, 250 people own Toyota cars and 275 people own BMW. Assuming that there is no other car brand in the community, if 20 people own both Toyota and BMW cars and 50 people don't have any car, then how many people live in the community?

E. 495
F. 505
G. 555
H. 575

89. If $x = -1$, what is the smallest number in the set $-4x^2$, $3x^3$, x, $\frac{x^3}{2}$, 1?

A. $-4x^2$
B. $3x^3$
C. $\frac{x^3}{2}$
D. x

90. How many multiples of 3 are between 1,040 and 3,060?

E. 640
F. 673
G. 674
H. 1,020

91. In a stadium, 30 people support team *A* and 40 people support team *B*. How many more supporters, does team *A* need in order to have 60% of the total supporters?

A. 70
B. 50
C. 30
D. 20

92. For what value of x, the expression $\frac{x-4}{x^3-27}$ is undefined?

E. 3
F. 4
G. 27
H. 4, 3

Questions 93 - 98

93. In 2016, there were 2,000 students in a certain school. In 2018, the number of students increased to 2,600. What was the percent of increase of students by 2018?

A. 12.6%
B. 20%
C. 23.07%
D. 30%

94. Jackson draws a regular pentadecagon (15-sided polygon) on a piece of paper. His math teacher wishes to know the measure of each interior angle of the pentadecagon. Which one of the following is the measure of each interior angle of the pentadecagon?

E. 108°
F. 156°
G. 180°
H. 200°

95. The diameter of a hydrogen atom is 10^{-10} m and the diameter of a red blood cell is 8×10^{-6} m. Find how many times, the diameter of a red blood cell is bigger than the diameter of a hydrogen atom?

A. 10^{-4}
B. 8×10^{-8}
C. 8×10^{8}
D. 8×10^{4}

96. On a coordinate grid, the coordinates of point A are $(-4, 3)$ and the coordinates of B are $(5, -1)$. If point C is the midpoint of points A and B, which of the following ordered pairs represents point C?

E. $(0.5, 1)$
F. $(1, 2)$
G. $(0.5, 2)$
H. $(2, 1)$

97. The triangles ABC and DEF, drawn below, are similar triangles. If $\angle A = 70°$ and angle $\angle F = 60°$, what is the measure of angle B?

A
70°
C B
D
60°
F E

A. 40°
B. 50°
C. 60°
D. 70°

98. In a community center, 14 people can sit on a bench. If there are 379 people in the community center and the benches have to be filled from left to right, how many people have to sit on the table that is farthest to the right?

E. 1
F. 5
G. 14
H. 27

Questions 99 - 104			
99.	Currently, Oliver has 500 marbles and Aria has 800 marbles. If Oliver receives 50 marbles per month from his father and Aria receives 20 marbles per month from her aunt, how many months will it take for both of them to have the same amount of marbles? A. 5 months B. 10 months C. 30 months D. 50 months	102.	The radius of a bicycle wheel is 14 inches. If the wheel makes 24 revolutions, how many feet will the bicycle travel? (Use the approximation $\frac{22}{7}$ for π) E. $88\,ft$ F. $176\,ft$ G. $220\,ft$ H. $2{,}112\,ft$
100.	In the diagram below, $FE = 3, AF = 5$, $DC = 3$ and ABDE is a square. What is the area of the trapezoid AFCB? 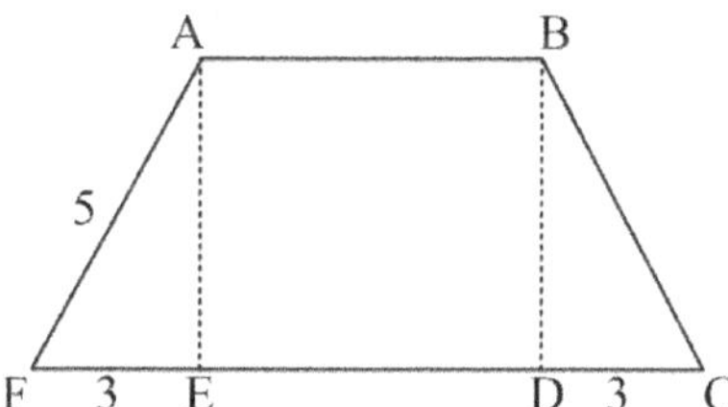 E. $30\ units^2$ F. $28\ units^2$ G. $40\ units^2$ H. $55\ units^2$	103.	A garden contains 10 red flowers and 5 white flowers. Three of the flowers are a mixture of both red and white colors. If one flower is plucked from the garden at random, what is the probability that it will be a white flower? A. $\frac{1}{3}$ B. $\frac{1}{6}$ C. $\frac{13}{18}$ D. $\frac{5}{18}$
101.	John wants to buy some fruits from his uncle's store. In the store, if 3 apples cost as much as 4 bananas and 3 bananas cost as much as 9 cherries, how many cherries can he buy at the cost of one apple? A. 4 B. 6 C. 8 D. 10	104.	In the figure below, each side length of the rhombus $MATH$ is $10\ cm$ and $OM = 6\ cm$. If MT and AH are the two diagonals of the rhombus, then what is the area of the rhombus? 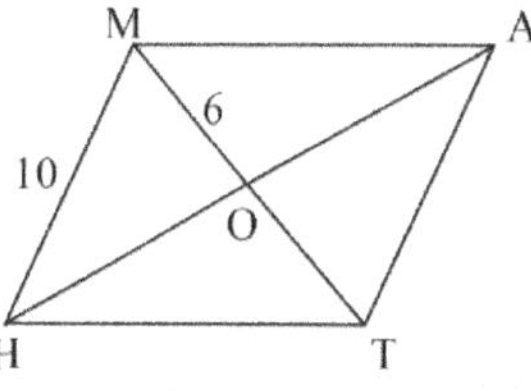 E. $192\ cm^2$ F. $100\ cm^2$ G. $96\ cm^2$ H. $48\ cm^2$

Questions 105 - 110

105. If $20 \div K = y$ and $y > 20$, then which of the following conclusion about K is true?

A. $K > 1$
B. $K < 1$
C. $-1 < K < 1$
D. $0 < K < 1$

106. Andy goes on a trip to his uncle's house. He drives at an average of 50 miles per hour during the first 10 hours. The next 5 hours, he drives a total of 300 miles. If his car covers 20 miles per gallon and each gallon costs \$3.20, how much will his entire trip cost?

E. \$320.00
F. \$230.00
G. \$178.00
H. \$128.00

107. In a garden of 100 flowers, the ratio of rose flowers to dahlia flowers is 3 : 2. In a flower shop, the ratio of rose flowers to dahlia flowers is 1: 4. When the flowers from the garden and the store are combined, the ratio of rose flowers to dahlia flowers is 1: 2. How many flowers are there in the flower shop? (Assume there are no other types of flowers in the garden and flower shop)

A. 100
B. 200
C. 150
D. 250

108. If $K + C = 10$ and $K - C = 20$, then $K^2 + 2C = ?$

E. 225
F. 215
G. 210
H. 200

109. In the figure below, ΔABC is an equilateral triangle and B is the center of the circle. If the radius $AB = 6$, what is the perimeter of the shaded region?

A. $6 + 8\pi$
B. $6 + 2\pi$
C. $12 + 2\pi$
D. $18 + 8\pi$

110. Dozens of Eggs Sold each Month by a Store

According to the graph above, by what percent does the sale of eggs, in dozens, increase from the month of April to May?

E. 75%
F. 150%
G. 175%
H. 200%

Questions 111 - 114			
111.	$0, 2, 4, A, B$ In how many different ways can the 3 digits and two letters, mentioned above, be arranged to make a password for a computer, if digit 0 cannot be on either end and each digit or character in the password doesn't repeat? A. 120 B. 98 C. 72 D. 64	113.	An art teacher took her students and their parents on a trip to an amusement park. The entry ticket to the park cost \$20 per adult and \$10 per child. If a total of 40 people, including the teacher went on the trip and paid a total of \$500 as entry ticket fee, how many children were on the trip? A. 25 B. 40 C. 20 D. 30
112.	If $3^a \times 7^b = 3087$, then $(a - b)^2 = ?$ E. 10 F. 5 G. 4 H. 1	114.	If the operation * is defined as $a * b = a^2 - b$, then what is the value of $(2 * 7) * 4$? E. 5 F. 6 G. 7 H. -9

PRACTICE TEST 6

GRID-IN QUESTIONS			
Questions 58 - 62			
58.	Tariq drives $8\frac{9}{20}$ kilometers to go to his tutoring appointment. What is the number expressed in decimal form?	61.	Bobby drives to his friend's house to borrow some books. He drives at an average of 60 miles per hour for the first half-hour and 40 miles an hour for the next $1\frac{1}{2}$ hours. What is the average speed of his entire trip to his friend's house in in miles per hour?
59.	For what value of a, the expression $\frac{a+3}{a-9}$ is undefined?	62.	Ted wants to set a four digit passcode on his laptop. If the passcode cannot start with a zero, how many different combinations of passcodes can he make?
60.	Jacob wants to sell some pencils, pens and books in his store. If 4 pencils cost as much as 2 pens and 5 pens cost as much as one book, how many pencils cost as much as one book?		

MULTIPLE CHOICE QUESTIONS

Questions 63 - 68

63. If $6k + 7m = 14$, what is m in terms of k?

A. $14 - 6k$
B. $2 - \frac{6}{7}k$
C. $14 - \frac{6}{7}k$
D. $7 - \frac{6}{2}k$

64. A jar contains 5 red marbles, 6 blue marbles, and 7 white marbles. If Daniel selects two marbles at random, without replacement, what is the probability that the first marble is blue and second marble is white?

E. $\frac{5}{51}$
F. 5
G. $\frac{7}{51}$
H. $\frac{17}{51}$

65. Alexander is three times as old as Jackson and five times as old as Grace. What percent of Jackson's age is Grace's age?

A. 30%
B. 40%
C. 50%
D. 60%

66. There are 2 boxes, labeled as X and Y, on a table. Box X contains 5 black and 6 blue crayons; box Y contains 8 red and 3 orange crayons. David picks a crayon randomly from box X and places it in box Y. What is the probability that the crayon he picks from box Y is a blue crayon?

E. $\frac{6}{121}$
F. $\frac{1}{22}$
G. $\frac{1}{121}$
H. $\frac{2}{7}$

67. What is $\frac{1}{8}$ of 2^{10}?

A. 2^7
B. 2^8
C. 2^{13}
D. 2^{15}

68. The triangles CAT and XYZ, drawn below, are similar triangles, with AC = 4 and YX = 6. If YZ = 10, what is the measure of the line segment AT?

C
60°
4
A
T
X
6
50°
70°
Y
10
Z

E. 15
F. $6\frac{2}{3}$
G. $20\frac{1}{2}$
H. 24

Questions 69 - 74

69. There are 200 employees in a coffee shop, where the ratio of male to female employees is 1 : 3. The ratio of male to female customers, who visit the coffee shop on Sunday is 1 : 5. When employees and customers are combined, the ratio of male to female is 1 : 4. How many customers visit the coffee shop on Sunday?

A. 100
B. 200
C. 300
D. 400

70. If $2^c \cdot 3^k = 1{,}728$, then $c + k =$?

E. 9
F. 10
G. 12
H. 14

71. If $m = -3$, $A = -2$, $T = 3$ and $H = -1$, then $(m + A)^2 - (T - H)^2 =$?

A. 6
B. 8
C. 9
D. 12

72. Sum of three consecutive odd integers is 1,437. If the least number among them is k and the greatest number among them is c, what is the value of $k + c$?

E. 477
F. 958
G. 956
H. 900

73. Saqib pays $97.20, including tax, for buying a book after receiving a discount of 10% on the original price. If he pays 8% tax on the discounted price, what is the original price of the book before the discount and the tax?

A. $100
B. $90
C. $85
D. $60

74. What is the area of the rectangle below in terms of x?

Rectangle ABCD with AB = $x+3$ and BC = $x+2$.

E. $x^2 + 6$
F. $6x + 6$
G. $x^2 + 6x + 3$
H. $x^2 + 5x + 6$

Questions 75 - 80

75. Jack has $50,000 and David has $60,000 in their bank accounts. At the end of each year, Jack and David deposit $1,500 and $500, respectively, in their accounts. After how many years, will Jack and David have the same amount of money in their bank accounts?

A. 15
B. 10
C. 5
D. 3

76. The movie tickets in a theater cost $20 for each adult and $10 for each child. On a Saturday night, the theater sold a total of 50 tickets for $700. How many adult tickets were sold?

E. 20
F. 30
G. 40
H. 50

77. Out of 80 people in a meeting, $\frac{1}{5}$ of them were unemployed. If $\frac{3}{8}$ of the employed people were Engineers, how many people in the meeting were neither unemployed nor Engineers?

A. 20
B. 25
C. 40
D. 45

78. A clothing store charges a total of x dollars for the first two shirts and y dollars for each additional shirt it sells. What is the cost, in dollars, of buying 20 shirts from the store?

E. $\$(x + 20y)$
F. $\$(2x + 18y)$
G. $\$(x + 18y)$
H. $\$(20xy)$

79. The table below shows the frequency distribution of the weights of 40 students in the class. What percent of the students weigh more than 150 pounds?

FREQUENCY DISTRIBUTION TABLE OF THE WEIGHTS OF 40 STUDENTS

Class Weight (in pound)	Number of students
121-130	5
131-140	12
141-150	11
151-160	7
161-170	5

A. 25%
B. 30%
C. 40%
D. 44%

80. In 2014, there were 400 employees in a certain office. In 2016, the number of employees decreased to 300. What was the percent decrease of the employees by 2016?

E. 25%
F. 27%
G. 30%
H. 35%

Questions 81 - 86

81. The diameter of a car's wheel is 28 inches. If the car travels 176 feet, how many revolutions of a wheel are needed to cover the distance?
(Use the approximation $\frac{22}{7}$ for π)

A. 20
B. 24
C. 34
D. 56

82. Tariq has four books, Math, Physics, Chemistry and Biology. In how many different combinations can the books be ordered, assuming that they are placed in a straight line?

E. 12
F. 15
G. 18
H. 24

83. Jacob is three times as old as Jackson. In four years, Jacob will be 14 years more than $\frac{1}{4}$ of Jackson's age. How old is Jackson now?

A. 4
B. 5
C. 8
D. 10

84. What is the prime factorization of 1,176?

E. $2^3 \times 3 \times 7^2$
F. $2^4 \times 5 \times 49$
G. $2^5 \times 3 \times 7$
H. $2^3 \times 3^2 \times 7$

85. In the figure below, the diagonal of the square MATH is $4\sqrt{2}$ units. What is the area of the shaded region?

M A
H T

A. $(4\pi - 16)\ units^2$
B. $4(4 - \pi)\ units^2$
C. $(16 + 4\pi)\ units^2$
D. $(6 - 2\pi)\ units^2$

86. Bobby is $1\frac{1}{5}$ times as old as David and $1\frac{1}{2}$ times as old as Rose. What fraction of David's age is Rose's age?

E. $1\frac{1}{4}$
F. $\frac{6}{7}$
G. $\frac{4}{5}$
H. $\frac{7}{10}$

Questions 87 - 92			
87.	STUDENTS WHO TAKE SCIENCE AND MATH CLASSES Chemistry, 12% Biology, 14% Algebra, 14% Physics, 35% Geometry, 25% If a total of 2,000 students take Science and Math classes, how many students take the algebra class? A. 28 students B. 280 students C. 600 students D. 4,000 students	90.	If each angle of a regular polygon is 144°, how many sides does this polygon have? E. 8 F. 9 G. 10 H. 12
88.	What is the area of an equilateral triangle that has the same perimeter as the square above? 3 E. 4.5 $units^2$ F. $4\sqrt{3}\,units^2$ G. $9\sqrt{3}\,units^2$ H. 72 $units^2$	91.	Express 563.18×10^3 in scientific notation. A. 5.6318×10^5 B. 0.56318×10^5 C. 56.318×10^4 D. 5.6318×10
89.	If $a = -2$ and $3a(5b - 5a) = 30$, what is the value of b? A. -10 B. 3 C. -4 D. -3	92.	If $J = 2^2 \times 3 \times 7^2, K = 2 \times 3^4 \times 7$, then what is the least common multiple of J and K? E. $2^4 \times 3^2 \times 7^4$ F. $2^3 \times 3^3 \times 7^3 \times 9$ G. $2^2 \times 3^4 \times 7^2$ H. $2^3 \times 3^5 \times 7^3$

Questions 93 - 98

93. Jacob is labeling his sharpies from letter A to P. What is the label of his 417th sharpie?

A. K
B. P
C. M
D. A

94. In the table below, find, during which of the following periods, the percent increase in the price of the book was greatest?

	YEAR					
	2003	2006	2009	2012	2015	2018
Price of a math book	\$4	\$8	\$15	\$22	\$40	\$70

E. 2003 – 2006
F. 2006 – 2009
G. 2012 – 2015
H. 2015 – 2018

95. In the figure below, four equilateral triangles have a common vertex. What is the average of angle a, b, c and d?

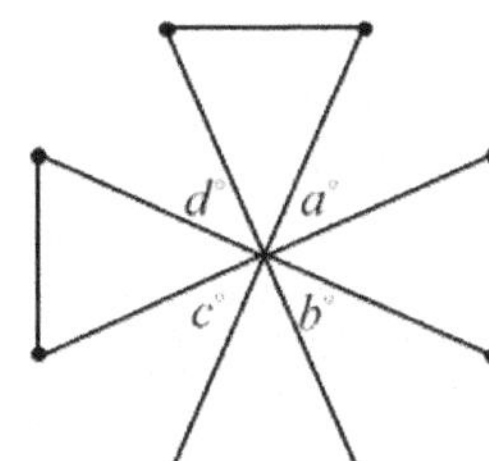

A. 120
B. 90
C. 60
D. 30

96. For any integer k, which of the following represents four consecutive multiples of 3?

E. $k,\ k+1,\ k+3,\ k+5$
F. $3k,\ 3k+3,\ 3k+6,\ 3k+9$
G. $k,\ k+3,\ k+6,\ k+9$
H. $k,\ k+3,\ k+3,\ k+6$

97. On a Sunday, Jason received a box full of chocolates from his father.
On Monday, he ate $\frac{1}{7}$ of the chocolates.
After he ate 16 more chocolates on Tuesday, $\frac{2}{3}$ of the original number of chocolates were left.
How many total chocolates were there in the box when Jason received it?

A. 28
B. 48
C. 84
D. 104

98. If the cost of k pencils is x dollars, what will be the cost of y pencils, in dollars, at the same rate?

E. $\frac{xy}{k}$
F. $\frac{kx}{y}$
G. $\frac{ky}{x}$
H. kxy

<table>
<tr><th colspan="4">Questions 99 - 104</th></tr>
<tr><td>99.</td><td>If $B * A = 2A - B$ and $A \Delta B = 3B$ then which of the following is equal to the expression $(3 * 2) * (2 \Delta 3)$?

A. 17
B. -1
C. 1
D. 27</td><td>102.</td><td>Solve the expression.
$\sqrt{(-8+1)^2 + (-5+4)^2} = ?$

E. $2\sqrt{2}$
F. $5\sqrt{2}$
G. $\sqrt{51}$
H. $7\sqrt{2}$</td></tr>
<tr><td>100.</td><td>A jar contains 5 nickels, 8 dimes and 9 quarters. If the coins are pulled out of the jar at random and not replaced, what is the minimum number of coins that must be pulled out of the jar to ensure that at least three of every kind of coin has been pulled out of the jar?

E. 12
F. 15
G. 17
H. 20</td><td>103.</td><td>One U.S. dollar worth 2.12 Fijian dollars. David gave 318 Fijian dollars as a gift to Jackson. Jackson wants to exchange his 318 Fijian dollars for U.S. dollars. How much money should Jackson receive in US dollars?

A. 150 USD
B. 318 USD
C. 674.16 USD
D. 800 USD</td></tr>
<tr><td>101.</td><td>What is the area of the triangle below?

y
8 7 6 5 4 3 2 1
(5, 7)
(3,3)
(6, 3)
x
0 1 2 3 4 5 6 7 8

A. $4\ units^2$
B. $6\ units^2$
C. $8\ units^2$
D. $10\ units^2$</td><td>104.</td><td>What is the average of the 5th and 7th terms of the following sequence?

$-4, \ -6, \ -10, \ -18, \ \_\_\_, -66, \ \_\_\_$

E. -34
F. -74
G. -82
H. -164</td></tr>
</table>

Questions 105 - 110

105. Jordan can clean a room in 45 minutes. Clara can clean the same room in 30 minutes. If Jordan and Clara work together, at the same time, how long will it take for them to clean the room together?

A. $18\ minutes$
B. $30\ minutes$
C. $37.5\ minutes$
D. $75\ minutes$

106. $5.\overline{3} + 6.\overline{6} = ?$

E. $\frac{9}{11}$
F. 15
G. $11.\overline{3}$
H. 12

107. Madeline spins the following spinning wheel twice. What is the probability that she will get a number divisible by 4 in the first spin and an odd number in the second spin?

A. $\frac{1}{36}$
B. $\frac{1}{3}$
C. $\frac{1}{12}$
D. $\frac{11}{36}$

108. David works in a pizza store during his summer vacations. He got a salary of \$2,170 for the month of July, which has 31 days. The store owner pays \$80 per day to every other employee. If David takes a day off without pay and his friend Ruby is paid to work during his shift, how much more does the store owner had to pay Ruby instead of David for that day?

E. \$10
F. \$15
G. \$20
H. \$25

109. What is $a + b + c + d + e + f = ?$

A. $120°$
B. $360°$
C. $720°$
D. $1440°$

110. If 200% of a number is $4n$, what is the 50% of that number in terms of n?

E. $\frac{n}{4}$
F. $\frac{n}{2}$
G. $\frac{4n}{3}$
H. n

Questions 111 - 114			
111.	Simplify the expression. $\left(\frac{a+b}{b-a}\right)\cdot\left(\frac{a-b}{a+b}\right)\cdot(-7) = ?$ A. -7 B. 7 C. $7a^2+7b^2$ D. $7a-7b$	113.	Jack buys a cylindrical water tank for his house. The height of the tank is 10 feet. If the volume of the tank is 1,540 cubic feet, what is the radius of the tank? (Assume $\pi = \frac{22}{7}$) A. 9 B. 7 C. 6 D. 4
112.	Cooper goes on a trip with his friend for 5 days. He drives 50 miles on the first day, 70 miles on the second day, 75 miles on the third day, and 85 miles on the fourth day. If he covers an average of 72 miles per day during the 5-day journey, how many miles does he drive on the fifth day? E. 80 miles F. 90 miles G. 95 miles H. 100 miles	114.	What is the average of all the integers from 50 to 110? E. 50 F. 55 G. 70 H. 80

ALL ANSWER KEYS & EXPLANATIONS

- **TOPIC BY TOPIC EXERCISE**

&

- **6 PRACTICE TESTS**

EXERCISE 1: RATIO & PROPORTION (EXPLANATIONS)

---

1. A

Solution: There are a total of 13 playing cards

A, K, Q, J, 2, 3, 4, 5, 6, 7, 8, 9, 10

Out of these 13 cards, 4 are odd-numbered (3, 5, 7 and 9). There are $13 - 4 = 9$ other cards. Therefore, the ratio of the odd-numbered cards to the other cards is $4 : 9$.

---

2. B

Solution: The number of students obtaining 3A's was 4. The number of students with 4 A's was 2. The total number of students obtaining 3 or more A's was $4 + 2 = 6$.
The number of students obtaining 1 A was 9 and the number of students getting 2 A's was 6. The total number of students getting fewer than 3 A's was $9 + 6 = 15$.
The ratio of students obtaining 3 or more A's to the number of students obtaining fewer than 3 A's was therefore 6:15 or 2:5.

---

3. D

Solution: Out of 24 students, 3 out of 8 are left-handed.

The number of left-handed students $= \frac{3}{8} \times 24 = 9$.

The number of right-handed students in the class is therefore $24 - 9 = 15$

---

4. B

Solution: There are a total of 16 small triangles inside the large triangle.

Out of these, 6 small triangles are shaded.

The fraction of the largest triangle that is shaded is $\frac{6}{16} = \frac{3}{8}$

---

5. B

Solution: There are a total of 9 shapes. 4 of these are stars and 5 are other shapes.

The ratio of stars to other shapes is $4 : 5$.

---

6. D

Solution:

Color	Number of Horses
Brown	7
Black	9
White	4

There are 9 black horses and 4 white horses. The ratio of black horses to white horses is therefore $9 : 4$.

7. C

Solution: Divide both sides of each ratio in the answer choices by the number of liters of the additive to convert it to the format $1\!:n$. In option C, the given ratio is 2.5: 25; dividing both sides by 2.5 gives the desired ratio of $1 : 10$.

8. C

Solution: The total number of students is 50. The number of students who chose Spanish is 27. The number of students who chose German is 5. The number of students who chose French must therefore be $50 - 27 - 5 = 18$. The ratio of students who chose Spanish to the students who picked French is $27 : 18$. Dividing both sides by 9 gives the ratio $2 : 3$ or $\frac{2}{3}$.

9. A

Solution: The total number of people wearing a jacket is 28. The number of people wearing a jacket but not a hat must be $28 - 7 = 21$. The number of people wearing a hat but not a jacket must be $21 - 7 = 14$. The ratio of people wearing only a hat to people wearing only a jacket is $14 : 21$. Divide both sides by 7 to simplify it to $2 : 3$ or $\frac{2}{3}$.

10. D

Solution: Write the ratio $7 : 2$ as a fraction $\frac{7}{2}$. Multiply both the numerator and the denominator by 3 to get $\frac{7\times3}{2\times3} = \frac{21}{6}$.

---

11. B

Solution: Count the number of small squares at the edge of the pond to find the area of the pond. The pond is 2 units wide and 2 units long. The area of the pond is $2 \times 2 = 4$ un^2. Count the tiles around the pond; there are a total of 12 tiles which gives an area of 12 un^2. The ratio of the area of the pond to the area of the tiles is $4 : 12$ or $1 : 3$.

---

12. D

Solution: The largest share in the ratio $2 : 5 : 7$ is 7. The total of the three shares is $2 + 5 + 7 = 14$.

Divide the largest share by the total of the three shares to find the fraction for the largest share $\frac{7}{14}$. Multiply the fraction by the total amount to find the largest share $\frac{7}{14} \times \$70 = \$35$.

---

13. D

Solution: The ratio of flour to butter is $3 : 1$; this can be written as $\frac{\text{flour}}{\text{butter}} = \frac{3}{1}$.

Similarly we can write $\frac{\text{butter}}{\text{milk}} = \frac{2}{5}$

The ratio flour : milk is equal to $\frac{\text{flour}}{\text{milk}} = \frac{\text{flour}}{\text{butter}} \times \frac{\text{butter}}{\text{milk}} = \frac{3}{1} \times \frac{2}{5} = \frac{6}{5}$

The fraction $\frac{6}{5}$ can be written as a ratio $6 : 5$.

---

14. A

Solution: The length of the cube is 6 cm. The ratio of the length to the height is $3 : 1$. The height of the cube must therefore be $6 \times \frac{1}{3} = 2$ cm. The ratio of the width to the height is therefore 5 cm : 2 cm or simply $5 : 2$.

---

15. A

Solution: The salaries of Allan and Bob are in the ratio $3 : 5$; multiply both sides of the ratio by 3 to express it as $9 : 15$. The salaries of Bob and Charles are in the ratio $3 : 7$; multiply both sides of the ratio by 5 to get the equivalent ratio $15 : 35$. Since the same number (15) in both ratios represents Bob's salary now, we can combine the two ratios as $9 : 15 : 35$ to get the ratio of the salaries of Allan, Bob and Charles.

---

16. C

Solution: The total height of the hill is 400 ft. The rate of climbing is 5 ft per minute. The time required to climb the hill is $\frac{400}{5} = 80$ minutes. Converting this to hours and minutes gives a time of 1 hour and 20 minutes.

---

17. B

Solution: Let x be the distance covered by Bryan

Divide the distance covered by Allison by the distance covered by Bryan to set up a proportion $\frac{5}{2} = \frac{340}{x}$

Multiply both sides by x to get: $\frac{5x}{2} = 340$

Multiply both sides by $\frac{2}{5}$ to get: $x = 340 \times \frac{2}{5} = 136$

---

18. C

Solution: Let x be the number of flowering plants.

Express the given information as a ratio of the number of flowering and non-flowering plants, to set up a proportion $\frac{4}{9} = \frac{x}{2754}$

Multiply both sides of the equation by 2,754 to get: $x = \frac{4}{9} \times 2{,}754 = 1{,}224$

---

19. C

Solution: Let n be the number of boats that can be produced in 2 years.

Convert 2 years to months $2 \times 12 = 24$ months

Set up the proportion using the given information $\frac{3}{4} = \frac{n}{24}$

Multiply both sides by 24 to get: $n = \frac{3}{4} \times 24 = 18$ boats

---

20. D

Solution: Let n be the number of cans that can be filled in 2 hours.

Convert 1 hour to minutes $1 \times 60 = 60$ minutes

Set up a proportion using the ratio of the number of cans to time $\frac{250}{3} = \frac{n}{60}$

Multiply both sides by 60 to get: $n = \frac{250}{3} \times 60 = 2500$ cans

---

21. B

Solution: Calculate the total time in minutes, Murielle has available for baking:
Convert 8 hours to minutes and subtract the 40-minute break $(8 \times 60) - 40 = 440$ minutes
Let p be the number of pots she bakes during this time
Equate the ratio of the number of pots baked in 20 minutes to the number of pots baked in 440 minutes: $\frac{11}{20} = \frac{p}{440}$
Multiply both sides by 440 to calculate $p = \frac{11}{20} \times 440 = 242$

---

22. D

Solution: Let x be the number of USD that CAD 630 is worth

Equate the ratio of USD 3 and CAD 4 to the ratio of x USD and CAD 630

$$\frac{3}{4} = \frac{x}{630}$$

Multiply both sides by 630 to get $x = \frac{3}{4} \times 630 = 472.5$

---

23. C

<u>Solution:</u> Let w be the number of white sheep.

Setup a proportion for the number of white sheep to the number of black sheep

$$\frac{13}{3} = \frac{x}{39}$$

Multiply both sides by 39 to get $x = \frac{13}{3} \times 39 = 169$

There are 169 white sheep. The size of the herd is the number of black sheep plus the number of white sheep $= 39 + 169 = 208$

24. D

<u>Solution:</u> Let m be the number of months after which Carlton will have \$300 in his bank account.

Set up a proportion for the number of months to the money in the bank $\frac{2}{45} = \frac{m}{300}$

Multiply both sides by 300 to get $m = \frac{2}{45} \times 300 = 13\frac{1}{3}$

Since Carlton deposits the money after every two months, the minimum number of months required is 14.

25. A

<u>Solution:</u> For each school, calculate the teacher to student ratio

School	Students	Teachers	Teacher/Student Ratio
X	440	40	$\frac{40}{440} = \frac{1}{11}$
Y	480	60	$\frac{60}{480} = \frac{1}{8}$
Z	210	30	$\frac{30}{210} = \frac{1}{7}$

The teacher to student ratio for school X is the smallest (largest denominator) followed by School Y and School Z.

---

26. D

Solution: The number of chocolates left $16 - 7 = 9$.

The percentage of chocolates left $= \frac{9}{16} \times 100 = 56.25\%$

---

27. B

Solution: The discount on the dress is 45%.

Calculate the dollar amount of the discount by multiplying 45% by the regular price:

$$\frac{45}{100} \times 140 = 63$$

Subtract the discount from the regular price to find the new discounted price

$$\$140 - \$63 = \$77$$

---

28. B

Solution: Find the percentage of students who participate in swimming by subtracting the percentage of students playing football and basketball from 100

$$100 - 12.5 - 25 = 67.5$$

Divide the percentage of students playing basketball by the percentage of students in swimming $\frac{25}{67.5}$.

Divide both the numerator and denominator by 12.5 to get $\frac{2}{5}$. This fraction is equivalent to the ratio 2 : 5.

---

29. A

Solution: The percentage of download remaining is $100 - 35 = 65$

Let t be the number of minutes required to download the remaining 65%

Set up a proportion using the fact that 3 minutes are required to download 5% of the file

$$\frac{3}{5} = \frac{t}{65}$$

Multiply both sides by 65 and simplify: $t = \frac{3}{5} \times 65 = 39$ minutes

---

30. C

<u>Solution:</u> Total points scored by Jane = $26 + 37 = 63$

Total maximum points = $40 + 50 = 90$

Combined percentage for the two tests = $\frac{63}{90} \times 100 = 70\%$

EXERCISE 2: NUMBER SYSTEM (EXPLANATIONS)

Solution: $-2(3-2)+3(1-2)$

$= -2(1) + 3(-1)$ [Combine the terms inside the parentheses]

$= -2 - 3$ [Remove the parentheses and multiply the terns]

$= -5$

---

1. C

Solution: $ab - bc$

$b(a-c)$ [Factor out b]

$3(-2-(-5))$ [Substitute $a=-2, b=3$ and $c=-5$]

$= 3(-2+5)$ [Negative times negative is positive]

$= 3(3) = 9$ [Simplify]

---

2. C

Solution: The depth of the submarine and the height of the target are both given with reference to the sea level. If we take the sea level to be 0, then the starting point of the missile was -35 meters and the height of the target was $+127$ meters. To find the total height, subtract the initial value from the final value

$= 127 - (-35)$

$= 127 + 35 = 162$

---

3. B

Solution: Add the changes in temperature to the starting temperature to find the new temperature.

$$-2 + (2 - 7 + 3 - 4)$$

$$-2 + (-6) = -8°C$$

---

4. D

Solution:

$-182.96 - (-195.79)$ [Subtract the two temperatures]

$= 182.96 + 195.79 = 12.83$ [Drop the negative sign (if any) to calculate the absolute value]

---

5. D

Solution: Calculate the difference between successive expressions:

$$(x+1)-(x-1) = x+1-x+1 = 2$$

The difference between the first two terms should always be 2. Similarly, the difference between the 2nd and the 3rd terms works out to 4 and the difference between the 3rd and 4th terms must be 8. The difference between the 3rd and 4th terms in option D) is 7 instead of 8.

---

6. A

Solution: The sum of a and b is $(a+b)$
The difference of a and b is $(a-b)$
"*The sum of two numbers a and b is twice their difference*"
We can write this as $a+b=2(a-b)$
$a+b=2a-2b$
$b+2b=2a-a$
$3b=a$

---

7. D

Solution: If the product of two numbers is positive then, either both numbers must be positive or both must be negative. Since the expression $ab \geq 0$ also allows the product to have the value 0, either or both a and b can be 0.Therefore, b cannot be negative if a is positive.

---

8. C

Solution: $t-3(t-8)+6(3t+4)$
Apply the distributive property
$$=t-3t+24+18t+24$$
Rearrange to write the like terms together
$$=t-3t+18t+24+24$$
Combine the like terms
$$=16t+48$$

---

9. D

Solution: $5^2 \times (55 \div 550) \times (12 \div 60) \div 1^5$
Rewrite the contents of the parentheses as fractions. Also note that $1^5 = 1$
$$=25 \times \frac{55}{550} \times \frac{12}{60} \div 1$$
Reduce the fractions to lowest terms
$$=25 \times \frac{1}{10} \times \frac{1}{5}$$
$$=\frac{5}{10}=\frac{1}{2}$$

---

10. C

Solution: When $x > \frac{1}{x}$:

Since $x > 0$, we can multiply both sides by x without changing the inequality sign.

$$x^2 > 1$$

Take the positive square root.

$$x > 1$$

When $x < \frac{1}{x}$:

Since $x > 0$, we can multiply both sides by x without changing the inequality sign.

$$x^2 < 1$$

Take the positive square root: $x < 1$

---

11. B

Solution: Point x is located at the position -2.5 on the number line. The point y can be 4 units to the left or right of x. To find the position on the left, subtract 4 and to find the position on the right add 4 to -2.5. The two values are $-2.5 - 4 = -6.5$ and $-2.5 + 4 = 1.5$

---

12. A

Solution: In option A), removing the parentheses requires the negative sign outside to be multiplied with each term inside. Since negative times a negative is a positive we get:

$-(-15.5 - 27.8) = 15.5 + 27.8$

Option B: $-(-15.5 + 27.8) = 15.5 - 27.8$

Option C: $-15.5 - 27.8 = -(15.5 + 27.8)$

Option D: $-15.5(-27.8) = 15.5 \times 27.8$

---

13. B

Solution: Convert the fraction $\frac{77}{15}$ to decimal. The decimal value is $5.1333333...$

3 is the only repeating digit in the value and therefore the vinculum must only be on top of this digit.

---

14. A

Solution: The given expression is negative when $3 - x < 0$.

Add x to both sides to get $3 < x$

This can be rewritten as $x > 3$

---

15. B

Solution: Convert the fraction $\frac{1}{32}$ to the decimal form using long division. The decimal value is 0.03125 The decimal value does not have any repeating digits and terminates after 5 decimal places.

---

16. C

Solution: Receiving an allowance adds to his saving; therefore, the amount received must be added to the initial balance. Spending money reduces his savings and therefore the money spent should be subtracted from his savings.

$$\$19.40 + \$12.50 - \$6.90 = \$25.00$$

---

17. C

Solution: Tom is 3 years old.

Jerry is thrice as old as tom. His age must therefore be $3(3) = 9$

Elmer is aged two years less than twice Jerry's age so he must be aged $2(9) - 2 = 16$

The sum of their ages is $3 + 9 + 16 = 28$

---

18. A

Solution:

$\left(-\frac{12}{7}\right) \times \left(3\frac{2}{3}\right) \div \left(-\frac{6}{7}\right)$ [The given expression]

$= \left(-\frac{12}{7}\right) \times \left(\frac{11}{3}\right) \times \left(-\frac{7}{6}\right)$ [Change division to multiplication and invert the fraction]

$= \left(-\frac{12}{7}\right) \times \left(-\frac{77}{18}\right)$ [Multiply the last two fractions]

$= \frac{12}{7} \times \frac{77}{18} = \frac{2}{1} \times \frac{11}{3}$ [Simplify, remembering that negative times negative is positive]

$= \frac{22}{3} = 7\frac{1}{3}$ [Convert the answer to mixed fraction]

---

19. B

Solution: Subtract the amount of money already collected (\$283.50) from \$500. Also, subtract 3 times the amount each student will contribute (\$25). Add the amount of expenses (\$19.70), which they must also collect, to find the answer.

$$\$500.00 - \$283.50 - 3(\$25.00) + \$19.70$$
$$= \$161.20$$

---

20. D

21.

Solution: Consider the paces in the North-South direction and the East-West direction separately. Take the North and West Directions to be positive and the South and East directions to be negative.

North-South direction: $+20 - 11 = 9$

Since we took North to be positive and the answer is also positive, Jim must be 9 paces North of the starting point.

East-West direction: $-9 + 5 = -4$

Since we took West to be positive and the answer is negative, Jim must be 4 paces East of the starting point.

---

22. D

Solution: Multiply the decimal by $\frac{1000}{1000}$ to remove the decimal point and convert the number to a fraction. Simplify by dividing both the numerator and denominator by common factors.

$$5.125 \times \frac{1000}{1000} = \frac{5125}{1000}$$

$$\frac{5125}{1000} = \frac{1025}{200}$$

$$= \frac{205}{40} = \frac{41}{8}$$

---

23. B

Solution: Since deposits add to the bank balance and withdrawals must be subtracted from the bank balance, we can take deposits to be positive numbers and withdrawals to be negative numbers. Combine all the deposits and withdrawals using the appropriate sign.

$$\$158 + \$95 - \$203 - \$275 + \$50 = -\$175$$

Divide by the number of transactions to calculate the average.

$$\frac{-\$175}{5} = -\$35$$

Since the average is negative and we specified deposits to be positive and withdrawals to be negative, the average transaction is a withdrawal of \$35 per day.

---

24. C

Solution: Let the initial amount of sales be s

Sales after a 10% increase $= s\left(1 + \frac{10}{100}\right) = 1.1s$

Sales after a 10% decrease, applied to the increased sales $= 1.1s\left(1 - \frac{10}{100}\right)$

$$= 1.1s \times 0.9s = 0.99s$$

The initial sales s and the final sales $0.99s$ means there was a change of $s - 0.99s = 0.01s$

---

25. C

Solution: Buttercup scored 69 points.

Bubbles scored $\left(\frac{2}{3}\right)^{rd}$ of the points scored by Buttercup $= \frac{2}{3} \times 69 = 46$

Blossom scored 11 more points than Bubbles $= 46 + 11 = 57$

Total points

$$= 69 + 46 + 57 = 172$$

---

26. B

Solution: $3(-2.9) - 3.1 -$ _____ $= 0$.

Substitute x for the blank in the equation and solve

$3(-2.9) - 3.1 - x = 0$

$-8.7 - 3.1 - x = 0$

$-11.8 - x = 0$

$x = -11.8$

The expression that makes the equation true must have a value of -11.8

Option B: $2(-2.3 - 3.6) = 2(-5.9) = -11.8$

---

27. A

Solution: To find the increase, subtract the initial temperature from the final temperature:

Increase in temperature $= y - (-x) = y + x$

---

28. D

Solution: Number of matchsticks used to make triangles $= 3(36)$

Number of matchsticks used to make squares $= 4(24)$

Number of sticks left$= 279 - 3(36) - 4(24)$

Number of Pentagons$= [279 - 3(36) - 4(24)] \div 5$

---

29. D

Solution: If the average length of 5 fish is $4\frac{1}{4}$ then the sum of their length must be $5 \times 4\frac{1}{4}$

$$= 5 \times \frac{17}{4} = \frac{85}{4}$$

The length of the fifth fish can be obtained by subtracting the total length of 4 fishes from the total. Length of fifth fish:

$$= \frac{85}{4} - \left(3\frac{1}{4} + 4\frac{1}{8} + 5 + 4\frac{1}{2}\right)$$

$$= \frac{85}{4} - \left(\frac{13}{4} + \frac{33}{8} + 5 + \frac{9}{2}\right)$$

$$= \frac{85}{4} - \left(\frac{26 + 33 + 40 + 36}{8}\right)$$

$$= \frac{170 - 26 - 33 - 40 - 36}{8}$$

$$= \frac{35}{8} = 4\frac{3}{8}$$

30. B

Solution: To compare the numbers, we must convert all of them to the decimal form or convert all of them to fractions with a common denominator.

$$\frac{15}{32}, \frac{31}{64}, 0.5, \frac{3}{4}$$

Rewrite 0.5 as a fraction $\frac{1}{2}$

$$\frac{15}{32}, \frac{31}{64}, \frac{1}{2}, \frac{3}{4}$$

Convert the denominator of each fraction to 64 by multiply the numerator and the denominator by the same number

$$\frac{15}{32} \times \frac{2}{2}, \frac{31}{64}, \frac{1}{2} \times \frac{32}{32}, \frac{3}{4} \times \frac{16}{16}$$

$$\frac{30}{64}, \frac{31}{64}, \frac{32}{64}, \frac{48}{64}$$

When the denominators are equal, the value of the numerators can be used to arrange the fractions in an ascending order.

EXERCISE 3: EXPRESSIONS & EQUATIONS (EXPLANATIONS)

1. A

Solution: $7 + 2(3 - 9)$
$= 7 + 2(-6)$
$= 7 - 12 = -5$

---

2. D

Solution: Factor out 3 from the expression $9x - 15$
$= 3(3x - 5)$.

The factor outside the parenthesis now matches the factor on the right hand side of the equation. The expression inside makes the two sides equivalent for all values of x.

---

3. B

Solution:

$$\frac{3}{y-3} = -\frac{5}{x+2}$$

Cross-multiply to get $3(x + 2) = -5(y - 3)$
Add $5(y - 3)$ to both sides to get $3(x + 2) + 5(y - 3) = 0$

---

4. B

Solution: Let the number of required packs be e
The total number of eggs required is $45 \times 3 = 135$
The total number of eggs after purchasing e packs will be $28 + 12e$ which must be greater than 135:

$$28 + 12e \geq 135$$
$$12e \geq 135 - 28$$
$$e \geq \frac{107}{12}$$
$$e \geq 8.92$$

The minimum number of packs required is therefore 9.

---

5. C

Solution:

$$\frac{2}{3}(2x+1)-\frac{1}{6}(2x+9)$$

$=\frac{4}{3}x+\frac{2}{3}-\frac{2}{6}x-\frac{9}{6}$

$=\frac{4}{3}x-\frac{2}{6}x+\frac{2}{3}-\frac{9}{6}$

$=\frac{8x-2x+4-9}{6}$

$=\frac{(6x-5)}{6}$

$=x-\frac{5}{6}$

---

6. C

Solution: Let x be the price of the jacket before the discount.
Apply the 35% discount to the price x and set it equal to the discounted price p

$$\left(1-\frac{35}{100}\right)\times x=p$$

$$(\frac{100-35}{100})x=p$$

$$\frac{65}{100}x=p$$

$$x=\frac{100p}{65}$$

---

7. A

Solution:

$$-5\left(\frac{2}{3}+h\right)+\frac{11}{3}h$$

$$=-\frac{10}{3}-5h+\frac{11}{3}h$$

$$= \frac{-10 - 15h + 11h}{3} = \frac{-10 - 4h}{3}$$

$$\frac{-2(5 + 2h)}{3} = -\frac{2}{3}(5 + 2h)$$

---

8. D

Solution: When a strip of width w is cut away along the length y, the new rectangle will have the width $(x - w)$ and the length y.
The perimeter of the new rectangle is two times the width plus two times the length

$$2(x - w) + 2y$$
$$= 2(x - w + y)$$
$$= 2(x + y - w)$$

---

9. C

Solution: The average is the sum of the wealth divided by 3

$$\frac{(3.3x - 5y) + (2.9y - 2.8z) + (3.7z - 2.1x)}{3}$$

Rearrange to write the like terms together and simplify

$$= \frac{3.3x - 2.1x - 5y + 2.9y + 3.7z - 2.8z}{3}$$

$$= \frac{1.2x - 2.1y + 0.9z}{3}$$

$$= 0.4x - 0.7y + 0.3z$$

---

10. B

Solution: Let the number of oranges be x. Write and expression for the total cost of a apples and x oranges and set it equal to the given value.

$$0.25a + 0.20x = 3.40$$

$$0.20x = 3.40 - 0.25a$$

$$x = \frac{3.40 - 0.25a}{0.20}$$

---

11. C

Solution: Option C has a sign error.
Multiplying both sides of the given equation by 3 and subtracting $2x$ from both sides gives the equation in option A.
Multiplying both sides of the given equation by 6 gives the equation in option B.
Subtracting 1 from both sides of the given equation and multiplying both sides by $\frac{3}{2}$, gives the equation in option D.

---

12. A

Solution: The price after the 35% discount is given by $\left(1-\frac{35}{100}\right)p = (0.65)p$
The price after the additional 10% discount is $\left(1-\frac{10}{100}\right)(0.65)p = (0.90)(0.65)p$

---

13. B

Solution:

$$\begin{aligned}\frac{2.3-9.2}{3}+\frac{0.25(11.9+4.1)}{-2} \\ &= \frac{-6.9}{3}+\frac{0.25(16)}{-2} \\ &= -2.3-\frac{4}{2} \\ &= -2.3-2 = -4.3\end{aligned}$$

---

14. D

Solution: Distance covered during the first hour: x
Distance covered during the second hour was 25% less: $\left(1-\frac{25}{100}\right)x = 0.75x$
Distance covered during the third hour was 80% of the distance covered during the second hour:

$$\frac{80}{100}\times 0.75x = 0.6x$$

Total distance covered in three hours was: $x + 0.75x + 0.6x = 2.35x$

---

15. B

Solution:

The given expression: $6\pi - (-72)$
Remove parenthesis and combine the signs (negative-negative is positive): $= 6\pi + 72$
Factor out 6 to get: $6(\pi + 12)$

---

16. C

Solution: The volume of water poured by Tom is equal to the number of jugs he poured times the capacity of his jug $18(1.5)$. Subtracting this value from the capacity of the bucket (32 liters) gives the volume of water poured in by Jerry $32 - 18(1.5)$. Dividing the volume poured in by Jerry, by the volume of his jug gives the number of jugs he poured.

$$(32 - 18(1.5)) \div 0.5$$

---

17. B

Solution: A value can be increased by $x\%$ by multiplying it with a multiplier equal to $\left(1 + \frac{x}{100}\right)$.
A value can be decreased by $x\%$ by multiplying it with a multiplier equal to $\left(1 - \frac{x}{100}\right)$.
For the purpose of making a quick estimation, we can round 21% to 20% and 9.6% to 10%.
The multiplier for an *increase* of 20% is 1.2 and the multiplier for a *decrease* of 10% is 0.9.
The estimate for the July rainfall is therefore $3.5(1.2)$.
The estimate for the August rainfall is $3.5(1.2)(0.9)$.

---

18. D

Solution:

$j + 3 - (0.91j + 1.32) \cdot 2$

$$= j + 3 - 2(0.91j + 1.32)$$

Expand the parentheses taking into account the negative sign outside

$$= j + 3 - 1.82j - 2.64$$

Rearrange to write like terms together

$$= j - 1.82j + 3 - 2.64$$

Combine like terms

$$= -0.82j + 0.36$$

---

19. A

Solution:

$$\frac{3}{5}(3a + 10b) - \frac{4}{7}(7a + 14b)$$

$= \frac{9}{5}a + 6b - 4a - 8b$
$= \frac{9}{5}a - 4a + 6b - 8b$
$= \frac{9a - 20a}{5} - 2b$
$= -\frac{11}{5}a - 2b$
$= -(\frac{11}{5}a + 2b)$

---

20. D

Solution: Since the objective is to collect 180 points with the *minimum* number of throws, Carol must hit the 25 point region with all her throws to minimize the number of throws. Carol has already scored 45 points. After x throws, she can have a maximum of $45 + 25x$ points. Set this expression to greater than 180 to write the inequality.

$$45 + 25x \geq 180$$

Rearrange to get

$$180 \leq 25x + 45$$

---

21. D

Solution: The original price of the sneakers is s. A discount of 40% equals $\frac{40}{100}s = 0.4s$. Subtracting the discount from the original price gives $s - 0.4s$. Subtracting 5, from the discounted price, gives the price which Donald must pay $s - 0.4s - 5$.

---

22. C

Solution: The first game lasted 1 hour (60 minutes). The cost of the first games was \$5.00 plus 3 times \$1.75 fee as the game went 30 minutes over the allotted time and \$1.75 for 10 minutes must be charged 3 times.
Cost of first game $= 5 + 3(1.75) = 10.25$

The maximum number of additional games will be achieved if all other x games are completed within 30 minutes and cost only \$5 each. The total cost of x games will be $5x$.
The total amount George spends equals $10.25 + 5x$.
This amount must be less than or equal to the total amount that George has $10.25 + 5x \leq 52$

---

23. A

Solution: The number of beads used to make 12 necklaces is equal to the total number of beads minus the beads remaining at the end: $255 - 27$.
Divide the number of beads used $(255 - 27)$ by the number of necklaces made (12) to find the number of beads in each necklace: $(255 - 27) \div 12$.
Note: It is necessary to enclose $(255 - 27)$ in parenthesis to ensure that the subtraction is carried out before the division.

---

24. B

Solution: The amount of batter left after using 1.5 kg for the large cake is: $5 - 1.5$
The medium cake uses $\frac{2}{7}$ of the remainder; this means that $\left(1 - \frac{2}{7}\right) = \frac{5}{7}$ of $(5 - 1.5)$ is left over

$$= (5 - 1.5) \times \frac{5}{7}$$

Divide this remaining batter by 10 to find the weight of batter used for each cake

$$= (5 - 1.5) \times \frac{5}{7} \div 10$$

---

25. B

Solution: The altitudes are given with respect to the sea level. The height above sea level is positive and the height below sea level is negative. Therefore the altitude of Altimus is $+251$ and the altitude of Lowplains is -27. The question asks for the height of Altimus above Lowplains, we must therefore subtract the altitude of Lowplains from that of Altimus

$$= 251 - (-27)$$

---

26. C

Solution: The length of the joined stick is equal to the sum of the two individual lengths $(x + y)$ minus the length of the overlap region (w):

$$x + y - w$$

---

27. B

Solution: The temperature change between two successive days is calculated by subtracting the temperature of the previous day from the following day. The changes in temperature between successive days were as follows

Day 1 and 2: $3 - 1 = 2$
Day 2 and 3: $0 - 3 = -3$
Day 3 and 4: $-7 - 0 = -7$
Day 4 and 5: $-9 - (-7) = -2$
Day 5 and 6: $-11 - (-9) = -2$
Day 6 and 7: $-5 - (-11) = \mathbf{6}$
The greatest positive difference gives the highest temperature rise.

---

28. C

Solution: The multiplication operation must be carried out before the addition and subtractions.

$$2 + 5 \cdot 8 - 3$$
$$= 2 + 40 - 3$$
$$= 39$$

---

29. D

Solution: Use the first equation $x \div 3 = a$ to write x in terms of a

$$\frac{x}{3} = a$$

Multiplying both sides by 3 gives $x = 3a$.
Substitute this expression for x in the second equation

$$x \div \frac{1}{3} = b$$
$$3a \div \frac{1}{3} = b \Rightarrow 3a \times \frac{3}{1} = b$$
$$9a = b$$

---

30. C

Solution: A positive number can result from the multiplication of two positive numbers or from the multiplication of two negative numbers. A positive number multiplied by a negative number will always give a negative answer.

EXERCISE 4: GEOMETRY (EXPLANATIONS)

1. C

Solution: The radius of the table is half of its diameter. $r = \frac{d}{2} = \frac{70}{2} = 35$

The area of a circle is given by $A = \pi r^2$

$$A = 3.14 \times 35^2 = 3{,}846.5 \approx 3{,}850 \text{ cm}^2$$

---

2. B

Solution: The circumference of a circle is given by $C = \pi d$

Substitute the value of the circumference and isolate the diameter on one side.

$$107 = 3.14d$$

$$d = \frac{107}{3.14} \approx 34 \text{ cm}$$

---

3. C

Solution: The circumference of a merry-go-round is given by

$$C = \pi d = 3.14(25)$$
$$= 78.5 \text{ ft}$$

20 revolutions of the merry-go-round means that a point on the outer edge will move

$$20 \times 78.5 = 1{,}570 \text{ feet}$$

Use the formula Speed $= \frac{\text{Distance}}{\text{Time}}$ to calculate the time taken to move a distance of 1,570 feet at a speed of 4 feet/sec

$$4 = \frac{1570}{t}$$

$$t = \frac{1570}{4} = 392.5 \text{ Seconds}$$

---

4. D

Solution: Find the circumference of the wheel.

$$C = 2\pi r = 2(3.14)(40)$$
$$= 251.2 \text{ cm}$$

Convert the circumference into meters and divide the distance covered by the circumference.

$$C = \frac{251.2 \text{ cm}}{100} = 2.512 \text{ m}$$

$$\text{Number of revolutions} = \frac{100}{2.512} \approx 40$$

---

5. A

Solution: Use the circumference to calculate the radius of the plate.

$$C = 2\pi r$$
$$80 = 2(3.14)r$$
$$r = \frac{80}{2(3.14)} \approx 12.74$$

Use the value of the radius in the area formula to calculate the area

$$A = \pi r^2$$
$$= 3.14(12.74)^2$$
$$\approx 510 \text{ cm}^2$$

---

6. C

Solution: The figure shows that the building has the same width from left to right. Only options C) and D) show a uniform width. When viewed from the top the building should show 3 sections; one for the tower in the middle and one for the mall on either side.

---

7. B

Solution: The side length of the square is equal to the diameter of the circle. Points A and D are diagonally opposite corners of the square in which the circle lies. The diagonal of a square is greater than the length of the side.

---

8. B

Solution: The section of a cone parallel to its base and perpendicular to its vertical axis is a circle. The section shown in the figure is at an angle to the base and is therefore an elongated "circle" called an ellipse.

---

9. B

Solution: Find the circumference of a circle with a diameter of 12 inches

$$C = \pi d$$
$$= 3.14(12) = 37.68 \text{ inches}$$

Divide the circumference by 8 to find the length of the curved edge of each slice.

$$= \frac{37.68}{8} = 4.71 \text{ inches}$$

---

10. D

Solution: Every point on the edge of a circle has the same distance from the center, which is equal to the radius of the circle. If the teacher is standing at the center then all the students can be 10 feet away from her by standing on the edge of a circle with radius 10 feet. This circle will have a diameter that is twice the radius. $d = 2r = 2 \times 10 = 20$ feet.

11. C

Solution: The string around the 4 cans can be divided into 4 circular arcs, one at each corner, which are together equal to the circumference of a circle with a diameter of 10 cm. The 4 straight parts are each equal to the length of a diameter as shown in the figure below. The total length of the string is equal to the circumference plus 4 times the diameter.

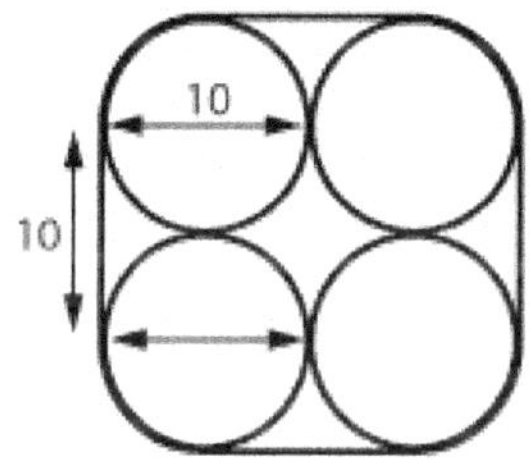

$$\begin{aligned}\text{String length} &= C + 4d \\ &= \pi d + 4d \\ &= d(\pi + 4) \\ &= 10(3.14 + 4) \\ &= 71.4\end{aligned}$$

10

10

12. C

Solution: The formula for the area of a rectangle is given by

$$\begin{aligned}\text{Area} &= \text{length} \times \text{width} \\ &= y \times x \\ &= yx\end{aligned}$$

The formula for the area of a parallelogram is given by

$$\text{Area} = \text{base} \times \text{height}$$

The base of the parallelogram is y

The height of the parallelogram is x since the rectangle and the parallelogram are between parallel lines and the perpendicular distance between parallel lines is constant.

Therefore, the area of the parallelogram is

$$\begin{aligned}\text{Area} &= y \times x \\ &= yx\end{aligned}$$

The area of the rectangle is equal to the area of the parallelogram.

13. A

Solution: The length $\overline{AC}$ is the diameter of the circle and must equal twice the length of $\overline{OD}$ which is the radius. Therefore, $\overline{AC} = 2 \times 2.5 = 5$.
Add the lengths of the three sides of the triangle to find the perimeter:

$$\overline{AB} + \overline{BC} + \overline{AC}$$
$$= 3 + 4 + 5$$
$$= 12$$

14. D

Solution: The area of a rectangle is given by the formula $A = l \times w$. Use the formula to find the width of the rectangle using the given values of length and the area.

$$143 = 13 \times w$$
$$w = \frac{143}{13} = 11 \text{ cm}$$

The perimeter of a rectangle is given by the formula $P = 2(l + w)$

$$= 2(11 + 13) = 48$$

15. C

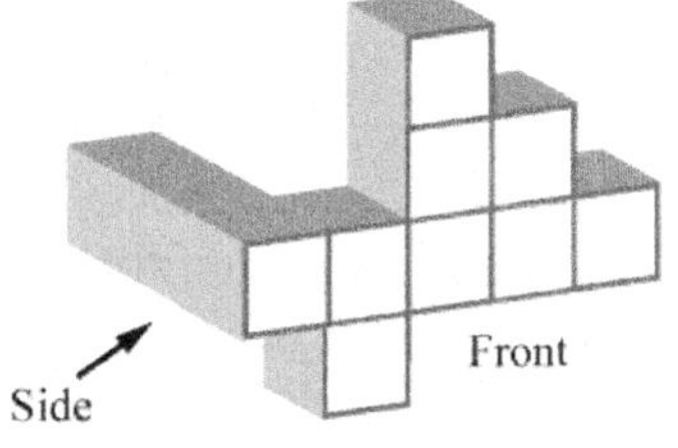

Solution: When viewed from the side the object must be 4 blocks high and have a 3 block width in the 2nd layer from the bottom.

16. B

Solution: Use a ruler to measure the lengths of w and h as indicated in the diagram. The height of the window in the figure is 1.2 cm and the width of the house in the figure is 7.2 cm. The ratio of the drawing length to the actual length for the width of the house and the height of the window must be equal.

$$\frac{\textit{Actual window height}}{\textit{Drawing window height}} = \frac{\textit{Actual house width}}{\textit{Drawing house width}}$$
$$\frac{3}{1.2} = \frac{w}{7.2}$$
$$w = \frac{3 \times 7.2}{1.2} = 18 \text{ feet}$$

---

17. B

Solution: Measure the length and wingspan of the aircraft in the figure. The length of the aircraft is 4.5 cm and the wingspan is 3.6 cm. Substitute the values in the following formula to calculate the actual wingspan

$$\frac{Actual\ length}{Drawing\ length} = \frac{Actual\ wingspan}{Drawing\ wingspan}$$

$$\frac{120}{4.5} = \frac{w}{3.6}$$

$$w = \frac{120 \times 3.6}{4.5} = 96 \text{ feet}$$

---

18. A

Solution: If the level of water is 3 cm below the top of the aquarium then the height of water in the aquarium is $30 - 3 = 27$ cm.

The volume of a cuboid is given by the formula

$$V = \text{length} \times \text{width} \times \text{height}$$

$$= 60 \times 25 \times 27 = 40{,}500 \text{ cm}^3$$

Divide the volume in cm^3 by 1,000 to find the volume in liters:

$$V = \frac{40{,}500}{1000} = 40.5 \text{ liters}$$

---

19. C

Solution: Find the ratio of the scales of the two drawings. The first drawing has a scale of 1:120 which can be written as $\frac{1}{120}$. The second drawing has a scale of 1:25 or $\frac{1}{25}$

Divide the second scale by the first to find the ratio

$$\frac{1}{25} \div \frac{1}{120}$$

$$= \frac{1}{25} \times \frac{120}{1}$$

$$= 4.8$$

Multiply the length on the 1:120 scale drawing with the above ratio to find the length on the 1:25 scale drawing

$$= 4.8 \times 5 = 24 \text{ cm}$$

---

20. B

Solution: On a scaled drawing, the areas are scaled down by the square of the linear scale.

Therefore, the area shown on the drawing is scaled down by $\left(\frac{1}{40}\right)^2 = \frac{1}{1600}$

Divide the given area by this factor to find the actual area

$$36 \div \frac{1}{1600} = 36 \times 1600 = 57{,}600 \text{ cm}^2$$

Convert the area in cm^2 to m^2

$$1 \text{ m} = 100 \text{ cm}$$
$$1 \text{ m}^2 = (100)^2 \text{ cm}^2$$
$$1 \text{ m}^2 = 10{,}000 \text{ cm}^2$$
$$57{,}600 \text{ cm}^2 = \frac{57{,}600}{10{,}000} \text{ m}^2 = 5.76 \text{ m}^2$$

21. D

Solution: In any triangle, the sum of the lengths of any two sides must be greater than the length of the third side. In option D) $12 + 18 < 31$ which violates this condition.

22. D

Solution:

Option A gives the three sides of a triangle (SSS) which is sufficient to define a unique triangle.
Option B gives two sides and the angle between them (SAS) which defines a unique triangle.
Option C gives two angles and the side between them (ASA) which defines a unique triangle.
Option D gives three angles which does not define a unique triangle. An infinite number of similar triangles with varying side lengths can be drawn with these angles.

23. A

Solution: The line l is parallel to the side of the pyramid and does not pass through the apex of the pyramid. The planar section will therefore be a trapezoid with two sloping sides and two parallel sides.

---

24. B

Solution: Since the plane slicing the prism was perpendicular to the base, the resulting face will have the same height as the prism itself (6 cm). The length of the intersection of the plane with the prism is given as 8 cm, which becomes the width of the resulting face. The dimensions of the face are, therefore, 8 cm × 6 cm.

---

25. A

Solution: The angles $4x$ and 40° are complementary. Add the measures of the two angles and set the sum equal to 90°.

$$4x + 40° = 90°$$
$$4x = 90 - 40°$$
$$x = \frac{50}{4} = 12.5°$$

---

26. D

Solution: The sum of angles on a straight line is 180°. Add the given angles and set the sum equal to 180°.

$$60° + 3x + 2x = 180°$$
$$5x = 180° - 60°$$
$$x = \frac{120°}{5} = 24°$$

.

---

27. B

Solution: $\angle AOB$ and $\angle BOC$ are adjacent angles.
Therefore $\angle AOC = \angle AOB + \angle BOC$

$$68° = 35° + \angle BOC$$
$$\angle BOC = 68° - 35°$$
$$\angle BOC = 33°$$

---

28. C

Solution: Calculate the surface area of the entire cuboid, before the piece was cut away and subtract the area of two small squares measuring 3×3 at the top and bottom.
The surface area of a cuboid is given by the formula

$$S = 2(lh + wh + lw)$$

where l is the length, w is the width, and h is the height.

$$\begin{aligned} S &= 2(12 \times 7 + 8 \times 7 + 12 \times 8) \\ &= 2(84 + 56 + 96) \\ &= 472 \end{aligned}$$

The area of the missing squares at the top and bottom is $2(3 \times 3) = 18$
Area of the object $= 472 - 18 = 454$
The sides of the piece that was cut away do not need to be subtracted as two more equal sides were created in the remaining piece.

---

29. C

Solution: The volume of the cuboid at the bottom is given by

$$\begin{aligned} V &= \text{length} \times \text{width} \times \text{height} \\ &= 6 \times 5 \times 2 = 60 \text{ m}^3 \end{aligned}$$

The triangle, which forms the prism, has a base of 5 m and a height of 1.5 m

$$\text{Area of the triangle} = \frac{1}{2}bh = \frac{1}{2} \times 5 \times 1.5 = 3.75$$

The volume of the triangular prism is given by $V = \text{base area} \times \text{height}$, where 'base area' is the area of the triangle and 'height' is the length perpendicular to the base

$$\text{Volume of Prism} = 3.75 \times 6 = 22.5 \text{ m}^3$$

$$\begin{aligned} \text{Total volume} &= \text{Volume of the Cuboid } + \text{Volume of the Prism} \\ &= 60 + 22.5 = 82.5 \text{ m}^3 \end{aligned}$$

---

30. D

Solution: The shape consists of a semicircle and three straight sides. The length of the wire needed for the semi-circle is equal to half the circumference of a circle with diameter 28 cm.
The circumference of a circle with diameter 28 cm is given by

$$C = \pi d = \frac{22}{7} \times 28 = 88 \text{ cm}$$

Half the circumference $= \frac{88}{2} = 44$ cm
The total length of wire needed for one shape $= 44 + 35 + 35 + 28 = 142$ cm
The total length of wire George must buy to make 18 such pieces $= 18 \times 142 = 2{,}556$ cm.

EXERCISE 5: STATISTICS & PROBABILITY (EXPLANATIONS)

1. D

Solution: Calculate the total number of chocolates in the box by adding the quantities of each type. Total quantity= $5 + 7 + 4 + 8 = 24$

The number chocolates with a filling $= 5 + 7 + 4 = 16$

$$\text{Probability} = \frac{\text{Number of outcomes of interest}}{\text{Total number of possible outcomes}}$$

$$= \frac{16}{24} = \frac{2}{3}$$

---

2. B

Solution: The player with the highest probability is the most likely to score. Convert the probabilities to a decimal format or into equivalent fractions with a common denominator to compare.

- Scottie: $\frac{1}{3} = \frac{20}{60}$
- Michael: $\frac{2}{5} = \frac{24}{60}$
- Shaquille: $\frac{7}{20} = \frac{21}{60}$
- Kobe: $\frac{3}{10} = \frac{18}{60}$

Michael is the most likely to score from a three-pointer.

---

3. C

Solution: There were 20 slips with each topic at the start.

Since 13 students have already drawn Topic I there are $20 - 13 = 7$ slips of Topic I left in the jar.

The number of Topic II slips left in the jar is $20 - 9 = 11$

The total number of slips in the jar is $7 + 11 = 18$

The probability of the next student drawing Topic II is therefore $\frac{11}{18}$.

---

4. D

Solution: For survey results to be meaningful, the sample must be randomly chosen. Examine each option to see if the selection method used gives every resident of Pasadena the same chance of being selected.

Option A is incorrect because it only includes people who shop at large supermarkets and ignores other who may be shopping at smaller grocery stores.

Option B is incorrect because it selects people from the entire state of California instead of the city of Pasadena.

Option C is incorrect because it focuses on car owners and people who attend sporting events.

Option D is correct as it is random and gives every resident the same chance of being selected.

---

5. B

Solution: The numbers divisible by 3, in the range 2-10, are 3, 6, and 9.
There are a total of 9 + 4 =13 cards

$$\text{Probability} = \frac{\text{Number of outcomes of interest}}{\text{Total number of possible outcomes}}$$

The probability of drawing a numbered card divisible by 3 is $\frac{3}{13}$.

---

6. C

Solution: 8 shots were directed towards the top-right corner and 5 shots were directed towards the bottom right corner. The total shots directed towards the right were $8 + 4 = 12$
The probability of a chance event is its long-run relative frequency. The probability of the next shot being directed to the right is therefore given by

$$\text{Probability} = \frac{\text{Number of Shots to the right}}{\text{Total number of Shots}} = \frac{12}{30} = \frac{2}{5}$$

---

7. A

Solution: The probability of rolling each number 1-6 is $\frac{1}{6}$
The number of times each number will show up in 30 rolls of the dice is $\frac{1}{6} \times 30 = 5$
It is likely that there will be 5 days when John rolls a 1 and puts $1 \times 25¢ = 25¢$ in the box, 5 days when he rolls a 2 and puts $2 \times 25¢ = 50¢$ in the box and so on
The total amount is given by:

$$5 \times 25¢ + 5 \times 50¢ + 5 \times 75¢ + 5 \times 100¢ + 5 \times 125¢ + 5 \times 150¢$$
$$= 2625¢$$
$$= \$26.25$$

---

8. B

Solution: The proportion of people who wear glasses is given by $\frac{1{,}500}{10{,}000} = \frac{3}{20}$
The proportion of the people at the fair who are wearing glasses is likely to be the same as it is a sample of the population. Therefore the number of people wearing glasses is given by

$$\frac{3}{20} \times 500 = 75$$

---

9. A

Solution: Use the results of the sample of 80 sweets to estimate the proportion of Lemon flavored sweets in the bag. 18 sweets from the sample of 80 sweets were lemon flavored. Therefore, the estimate for the proportion of lemon flavored sweets in the bag is

$$\frac{18}{80} = \frac{9}{40}$$

The probability that the next sweet drawn is lemon flavored is equal to the proportion of lemon flavored sweets in the bag.

---

10. C

Solution: Notice that the given list of weights is not in ascending order

$$34, 37, 45, 35, 39, 36, 42, 36, 38, 48$$

Sort the list and rewrite it in ascending order

$$34, 35, 36, 36, \mathbf{37}, \mathbf{38}, 39, 42, 45, 48$$

The median term is the $\left(\frac{n+1}{2}\right)^{th}$ term

$$\frac{n+1}{2} = \frac{10+1}{2} = 5.5$$

This means that the median is the average of the 5th and 6th weights

$$\text{Median} = \frac{37+38}{2} = 37.5$$

---

11. D

Solution: The oldest child to visit him was 11 years old. This is shown by the end of the whisker on the right and not by the right edge of the box. The line inside the box shows the median and the edges of the box show the range in which 50% of the data lies.

---

12. D

Solution: The proportion of the number of times the spinner pointed to blue is given by

$$\frac{80}{250} = \frac{8}{25}$$

The proportion of the spinner pointing to Blue is likely to remain the same in the second season. Therefore, the number of times the spinner will point to Blue in 400 spins is given by

$$\frac{8}{25} \times 400 = 128$$

---

13. C

Solution: If it is very unlikely that the asteroid will collide with earth, then the probability of the asteroid colliding must be very small. The probability of an event not happening is one minus the probability of the event occurring. Therefore, the probability of the asteroid NOT colliding must be very close to 1. The probability of the asteroid missing Earth cannot be 1 because the scientists said it was very *unlikely* that the asteroid would collide with earth but they did not say that it was impossible.

14. B

Solution: Since all the scores lie between 30 and 100, the whiskers from the box should extend to 30 to the left and 100 to the right. The line inside the box shows the median and must therefore be at the median score of 70.

15. B

Solution: Add the numbers in each column and divide by 4 to find the average. Runner 2 has the smallest average of 62 seconds and is therefore running the fastest average lap. The question can also be solved without actually computing the averages of the 4 columns. Notice, that most of the numbers for Runner 1 are close the value 70, for Runner 2 the values are close to 60 for Runner 3 the values are centered around 65 and for runner 4 the values are centered around the number 75. Runner 2 must therefore have the lowest average.

16. B

Solution: The figure shows a total of 10 shapes as follows:

Shapes	**`Quantity**
Triangles	3
Squares	3
Pentagons	3
Hexagons	1

The probability of selecting a pentagon is

$$\text{Probability} = \frac{\text{Number of outcomes of interest}}{\text{Total number of possible outcomes}} = \frac{3}{10}$$

The number of pentagons likely to be selected in 80 tries is given by

$$\frac{3}{10} \times 80 = 24$$

17. D

Solution: Since the samples were representative of the population of the two cities, we can extend the results of the survey to the population of the two cities.

In Rochester, $\frac{100}{250} = \frac{2}{5} = 40\%$ population prefers basketball and the remaining 60% prefer football.

In Buffalo, $\frac{90}{150} = \frac{3}{5} = 60\%$ population prefers basketball and the remaining 40% prefer football.

Therefore, we can say that residents of Rochester prefer football whereas residents of Buffalo prefer basketball.

---

18. D

Solution: Arrange the given numbers in ascending order:

$$21, 23, 24, 27, \mathbf{27}, \mathbf{28}, 29, 31, 32, 35$$

Since there are a total of 10 terms, the median is the $\frac{n+1}{2} = \frac{10+1}{2} = 5.5^{th}$ term or the average of the 5th and 6th terms. The median is $\frac{27+28}{2} = 27.5$

When one of the numbers, 27 is replaced by the number 22 the new ordered set becomes

$$21, 22, 23, 24, \mathbf{27}, \mathbf{28}, 29, 31, 32, 35$$

The 5th and 6th terms in this new set are still 27 and 28 and the median is therefore unchanged.

---

19. A

Solution: The probability of drawing a black ball is given by

$$\text{Probability} = \frac{\text{Number of outcomes of interest}}{\text{Total number of possible outcomes}} = \frac{7}{15}$$

The probability of not drawing a black ball is 1 minus the probability of drawing a black ball

$$= 1 - \frac{7}{15} = \frac{15 - 7}{15} = \frac{8}{15}$$

---

20. C

Solution: The line inside the box of a box plot shows the median. The box plot for the group that was fed a diet without supplement shows a median lifespan of 8 months. The group which was given the supplement shows a median lifespan of 9 months. Therefore, the median lifespan for the groups which was fed the supplement was 1 month greater.

---

21. D

Solution: Count the number of sections for each number

Number	Number of Sections
1	1
2	3
3	2
4	2

Since all sections are equal, the probability of a number being selected is proportional to the number of sections on the spinner which contain that number. There are two sections each for numbers 3 and 4 and therefore both have the same probability of being selected.

---

22. B

Solution: Since the dice has six faces, and it is *fair*, each face is equally likely to land up. The probability of rolling a 6 is therefore $\frac{1}{6}$. The outcome of the previous rolls does not affect the probability of the number on the next roll.

---

23. C

Solution: The figure shows that the distribution for the Lions peaks at 3 stars while the distribution for the Tigers peaks at 4 stars. The number of students who scored 1-3 stars is smaller for the Tigers while the number of students who received 4-5 stars is greater for the Tigers. Therefore, the average rating of the Tigers must be greater than the lions.

---

24. C

Solution: If Brenda pays \$1 for each game played, she will pay a total of $\$1 \times 54 = \$54$
The probability of the player hitting the middle hole is $\frac{1}{9}$ as there are nine holes and each hole is equally likely to be hit. In 54 games, the player is likely to hit the middle hole $\frac{1}{9} \times 54 = 6$ times.
Brenda will win \$5 each time the middle hole is hit and is likely to win $\$5 \times 6 = \$30$.
Therefore, the amount of money she is likely to lose is $\$54 - \$30 = \$24$.

---

25. B

Solution: The probability of picking a black sheep is given by

$$\frac{\text{Number of black sheep}}{\text{Total number of sheep}}$$

Since we know that the probability of picking a black sheep is $\frac{1}{19}$, we can write

$$\frac{\text{Number of black sheep}}{\text{Total number of sheep}} = \frac{1}{19}$$

Substituting, number of black sheep $= 12$, and cross-multiplying, we can write

$$\text{Total Number of sheep} = 12 \times 19 = 228$$

$$\text{Number of white sheep} = \text{Total number of sheep} - \text{Number of black sheep}$$
$$= 228 - 12 = 216$$

---

26. D

Solution: Make a table for the sample space of the possible totals of the two dice. There are a total of 36 different combinations and 10 different ways in which the numbers on the two dice can combine to give a number greater than or equal to 9 (9, 10, 11 or 12). Therefore, the probability of the total on the two dice being greater than or equal to 9 is given by $\frac{10}{36} = \frac{5}{18}$

Dice 2 \ Dice 1	1	2	3	4	5	6
6	7	8	9	10	11	12
5	6	7	8	9	10	11
4	5	6	7	8	9	10
3	4	5	6	7	8	9
2	3	4	5	6	7	8
1	2	3	4	5	6	7

---

27. C

Solution: Since there are 2 types of cheese and 3 types of crusts, the total number of cheese-crust combinations is $2 \times 3 = 6$. Each of these combinations can be further combined with 1 of 6 types of toppings. The total number of combinations is therefore $2 \times 3 \times 6 = 36$ combinations.

---

28. A

Solution: The probability of hitting a home run is 0.15. We can write this as

$$0.15 = \frac{15}{100} = \frac{3}{20}$$

If red marbles represent a home run then there should be 3 red marbles. The denominator 20, represents the total number of marbles. Therefore the number of black marbles must be

$$20 - 3 = 17$$

---

29. B

Solution: The probability of drawing an ace from the deck of cards is given by $\frac{4}{52} = \frac{1}{13}$

Since there are 5 red marbles already in the bag we can obtain a useful equivalent fraction by multiplying both the numerator and the denominator by 5

$$= \frac{1}{13} \times \frac{5}{5} = \frac{5}{65}$$

The bag already has 5 red marbles and we only need to add enough blue marbles to make the total number of marbles equal to 65.

The number of blue marbles that need to added $= 65 - 50 - 5 = 10$

---

30. C

Solution: Make a table for the sample space of the possible combinations of the two rolls of the dice. There are a total of 36 different combinations. The first number shows the outcome of the first roll and the second number shows the outcome of the second roll. There are a total of **15 different ways** in which the number on the second roll can exceed the number on the first roll shown in the table. The probability of this happening is given by $\frac{15}{36} = \frac{5}{12}$.

Roll 2						
6	**(1, 6)**	**(2, 6)**	**(3, 6)**	**(4, 6)**	**(5, 6)**	(6, 6)
5	**(1, 5)**	**(2, 5)**	**(3, 5)**	**(4, 5)**	(5, 5)	(6, 5)
4	**(1, 4)**	**(2, 4)**	**(3, 4)**	(4, 4)	(5, 4)	(6, 4)
3	**(1, 3)**	**(2, 3)**	(3, 3)	(4, 3)	(5, 3)	(6, 3)
2	**(1, 2)**	(2, 2)	(3, 2)	(4, 2)	(5, 2)	(6, 2)
1	(1, 1)	(2, 1)	(3, 1)	(4, 1)	(5, 1)	(6, 1)
	1	**2**	**3**	**4**	**5**	**6**

Roll 1

TEST 1: ANSWER KEYS

Q #	Answer
58	60
59	330
60	3
61	120
62	1.16
63	C
64	G
65	A
66	G
67	B
68	H
69	C
70	E
71	D
72	F
73	A
74	H
75	B
76	E
77	D

Q #	Answer
78	F
79	A
80	H
81	D
82	G
83	C
84	E
85	C
86	F
87	D
88	E
89	C
90	G
91	A
92	E
93	D
94	F
95	D
96	G
97	D

Q #	Answer
98	F
99	D
100	E
101	B
102	F
103	D
104	E
105	B
106	F
107	C
108	G
109	B
110	F
111	C
112	E
113	D
114	F

Practice Test 1: Answers & Explanations

<table>
<tr><td colspan="4">GRID-IN QUESTIONS</td></tr>
<tr><td colspan="4">Questions 58 – 62</td></tr>
<tr><td>58.</td><td>Since $\overrightarrow{BD} \perp \overrightarrow{BE}$, we have $\angle DBE = 90°$.
Also $\angle ABD = 30°$ (Given).
We know that angles formed at a straight line always add up to 180°. Therefore,
$\angle ABD + \angle DBE + \angle CBE = 180°$
Plugging the values, we get
$30° + 90° + \angle CBE = 180°$
$120° + \angle CBE = 180°$
$\angle CBE = 180° - 120° = 60°$

Answer: 60°</td><td>61.</td><td>There are 5 different subjects.
The 1st subject can be chosen in 5 ways,
the 2nd – in 4 ways,
the 3rd – in 3 ways,
the 4th – in 2 ways and
the 5th – in 1 way.
Therefore, there are
$5 \cdot 4 \cdot 3 \cdot 2 \cdot 1 = 120$ possible combinations of the schedule.

Answer: 120</td></tr>
<tr><td>59.</td><td>Ratio of the girls to boys = 5 : 6
Then,
Number of girls $= 5x$
Number of boys $= 6x$
Since number of girls in the school is 150, then,
$5x = 150$
$x = \frac{150}{5} = 30$
Now, we can find the number of boys in the school as:
Number of boys $= 6x = 6(30) = 180$
Total number of students $= 150 + 180$
$= 330$

Answer: 330</td><td>62.</td><td>$1\frac{4}{25} = 1 + \frac{4}{25}$

Multiply the numerator and the denominator of the fraction by 4 to make the denominator equal to 100, as:
$= 1 + \frac{4(4)}{25(4)}$
$= 1 + \frac{16}{100}$
$= 1 + 0.16$
$= 1.16$

Answer: 1.16</td></tr>
<tr><td>60.</td><td>If $4x + 18 = 30$, then
$4x = 30 - 18$
$4x = 12$
$x = \frac{12}{4} = 3$

Answer: 3</td><td></td><td></td></tr>
</table>

MULTIPLE CHOICE QUESTIONS			
Questions 63 – 70			
63.	The hypotenuse of the right triangle inscribed in the circle is the diameter of the circle. The hypotenuse of the triangle can be calculated as: $Hypotenuse = \sqrt{(leg1)^2 + (leg2)^2}$ $= \sqrt{6^2 + 8^2} = \sqrt{36 + 64} = \sqrt{100} = 10$ Therefore, Diameter $= D =$ 10 units Perimeter of semi-circle $= \frac{\pi D}{2}$ $= \frac{\pi(10)}{2} = 5\pi$ Hence, perimeter of the shaded region is $5\pi + 6 + 8 = 14 + 5\pi$ units. **Answer:** C	66.	Since operation $*$ converts the pair of natural numbers n and m to $2^{\lvert n-m \rvert}$, therefore, $5 * 3 = 2^{\lvert 5-3 \rvert} = 2^2 = 4$, then $(5 * 3) * 1 = 4 * 1 = 2^{\lvert 4-1 \rvert} = 2^3 = 8$. **Answer:** G
64.	Percent decrease/increase can be calculated as: $\frac{Amount\ of\ Change}{Original\ Value} \times 100\%$ Kerry's score $=$ 60 Terry's score $=$ 80, then percent value of Kerry's score decrease from Terry's score is: $\frac{80 - 60}{80} \times 100\% = \frac{20}{80} \times 100\% = 25\%$ **Answer:** G	67.	Consider right triangle MON. In this triangle, by the Pythagorean theorem, $(ON)^2 = (MN)^2 - (OM)^2$ $(ON)^2 = 5^2 - 4^2$, $(ON)^2 = 25 - 16 = 9$ $ON = 3$ units $RN = RO + ON$ $RN = 12 + 3 = 15$ units $BC = RN = 15$ units Area of square $= (length\ of\ side)^2$ $= (15)^2 = 225$ square units. **Answer:** B
65.	Let x be the number of sheep and y be the number of geese a farmer sold. Then, $x + y = 60 \quad (i)$ Since, each sheep costs \$32 and each goose costs \$3.50, then $32x + 3.5y = 609 \quad (ii)$ From eq. (i), $x = 60 - y$. Plug it in eq. (ii), $32(60 - y) + 3.5y = 609$ $1920 - 32y + 3.5y = 609$ $-28.5y = 609 - 1920$ $28.5y = 1311, y = \frac{1311}{28.5} = 46$ Substitute $y = 46$ in eq. (i) to find x, $x = 60 - 46 = 14$ Therefore, 14 sheep were sold. **Answer:** A	68.	$(b \cdot (a - c) + 2)^2$ Substitute $a = 5$, $b = -2$ and $c = -3$ in the expression above. $= (-2 \cdot (5 - (-3)) + 2)^2$ $= (-2 \cdot (5 + 3) + 2)^2$ $= (-2(8) + 2)^2$ $= (-16 + 2)^2$ $= (-14)^2$ $= 196$ **Answer:** H

69.	Let x be the daughter's age and y be the sum of her parents' ages. Therefore, $x = \frac{1}{12}y \quad (i)$ After 4 years, daughter's age is $x + 4$ and the sum of parents' ages is $y + 8$. Thus, $x + 4 = \frac{1}{8}(y + 8) \quad (ii)$ Plugin $x = \frac{1}{12}y$ in eq. (ii), $\frac{1}{12}y + 4 = \frac{1}{8}(y + 8)$ $24 \cdot \left(\frac{1}{12}y + 4\right) = 24 \cdot \frac{1}{8}(y + 8)$, $2y + 96 = 3(y + 8)$, $2y + 96 = 3y + 24$ $y = 96 - 24 = 72$ Plugin $y = 72$ in eq. (i) to find x, $x = \frac{1}{12}(72) = 6$ years Daughter's age after 4 years $= x + 4 = 10$ years. **Answer:** C	72.	$a^2 - b^2 = 200 \quad (i)$ $a^2 + b^2 = 1258 \quad (ii)$, Adding eq. (i) and (ii), $a^2 - b^2 + a^2 + b^2 = 200 + 1258$ $2a^2 = 1458$ $a^2 = 729$ $a = 27$ Plugin $a = 27$ in eq. (i) to find b, $(27)^2 - b^2 = 200$ $729 - b^2 = 200$ $b^2 = 729 - 200 = 529$ $b = 23$ Now, find $\frac{a+b}{a-b}$ by plugging in the values of a and b. $\frac{a+b}{a-b} = \frac{27+23}{27-23} = \frac{50}{4} = 12.5$ **Answer:** F
70.	If three friends made a cash contribution of 3 : 5 : 8, then the 1st friend gave $\$3x$, the 2nd - $\$5x$ and the 3rd - $\$8x$. Thus, $3x + 5x + 8x = 96$ $16x = 96 \Rightarrow x = \frac{96}{16} = 6$ 1st friend invested $= 3x = 3(6) = \$18$ 2nd friend invested $= 5x = 5(6) = \$30$ 3rd friend invested $= 8x = 8(6) = \$48$ If they had invested the same amount of money, then each of them should give $\frac{96}{3} = \$32$. Thus, the 1st friend will return $32 - 18 = \$14$ 2nd will return $= 32 - 30 = \$2$ Hence, the ratio is $14 : 2 = 7 : 1$. **Answer:** E	73.	The 1st symbol in the password can be placed in 4 different ways because 0 cannot be at the first place, the 2nd – in 4 ways, the 3rd – in 3 ways, the 4th – in 2 ways and the last one in 1 way. Therefore, there are $4 \cdot 4 \cdot 3 \cdot 2 \cdot 1 = 96$ different ways of a password combination that doesn't start with 0. If this password differs from the car number, then there are $96 - 1 = 95$ different combinations John can attempt. **Answer:** A
71.	If the ratio of juice and water is 4 : 1, then $4x + x = 120 \Longrightarrow 5x = 120 \Rightarrow x = 24\ l$ Amount of juice $= 24(4) = 96\ l$ To make the ratio 1 : 4, amount of water should be 4 times amount of juice i.e. $96(4) = 384\ l$ Water to be added $= 384 - 24 = 360\ l$ **Answer:** D	74.	Since, $2^x \cdot 3^y = 6912 \quad (i)$, we can also write 6912 as: $6912 = 2^8 \cdot 3^3 \quad (ii)$. Comparing eq. (i) and (ii), we get, $x = 8$ and $y = 3$. Therefore, $\frac{x+y}{x-y} = \frac{8+3}{8-3} = \frac{11}{5} = 2.2$. **Answer:** H

75.	In order to choose 5 basketball players from all 12 players, the coach should count the number of combinations as: $C_5^{12} = \frac{12!}{5!\cdot(12-5)!}$ $= \frac{12!}{5!\cdot 7!} = \frac{12\cdot 11\cdot 10\cdot 9\cdot 8\cdot 7!}{5\cdot 4\cdot 3\cdot 2\cdot 1\cdot 7!}$ $= 11\cdot 9\cdot 8 = 792$ **Answer:** B	79.	Let numbers $x,\ x+1,\ x+2$ be 3 consecutive integers. Then, $Average = \frac{Sum\ of\ quantities}{Number\ of\ quantities}$ Average $= \frac{x+x+1+x+2}{3} = \frac{3x+3}{3} = x+1$ $396 = x+1.$ $x = 395$ (Smallest integer) Largest integer $= x+2 = 397.$ Sum of the largest and the smallest integer is: $395 + 397 = 792.$ **Answer:** A
76.	$2x - 6y = 11$ Solve for y by isolating y at one side of the equation as: $6y = 2x - 11$ $y = \frac{2}{6}x - \frac{11}{6}$ [Divided by 6] $y = \frac{1}{3}x - \frac{11}{6}.$ **Answer:** E	80.	Total balls $= 3+4+5+6 = 18$ $P(Red) = \frac{Number\ of\ red\ balls}{Total\ balls} = \frac{4}{18}$ After selecting red ball without replacement, there are 17 balls left. $P(Green) = \frac{Number\ of\ green\ balls}{Total\ balls}$ $= \frac{6}{17}$ By the product rule, the probability that the 1st ball will be red and the 2nd ball will be green is $\frac{4}{18}\cdot\frac{6}{17} = \frac{4}{51}$ **Answer:** H
77.	Prime factorization of 240 is $240 = 2\cdot 2\cdot 2\cdot 2\cdot 3\cdot 5$ $= 2^4\cdot 3\cdot 5.$ **Answer:** D	81.	Area of square $= 10\cdot 10 = 100\ units^2$ Diameter of circle = 10 units Radius = 5 units Area of the circle is $= \pi r^2$ $= \pi\cdot 5^2 = 25\pi\ units^2$ The area of the shaded region is: $100 - 25\pi\ units^2$ **Answer:** D
78.	James eats jar of jam in 6 minutes. In 1 minute James eats $= \frac{1}{6}$ of the jar His father eats twice as fast, hence, In 1 minute his father eats $= 2\cdot\frac{1}{6}$ $= \frac{1}{3}$ of the jar Together they eat in 1 minute $= \frac{1}{6} + \frac{1}{3}$ $= \frac{1}{2}$ of the jar Therefore, together they need 2 minutes to eat the whole jar of jam. **Answer:** F	82.	$c = 2.5$ $a\cdot c = -8.5$, then $a(2.5) = -8.5$ $a = -\frac{8.5}{2.5} = -3.4$ Also, $a\cdot b = -4.08$ Plugging in $a = -3.4$, we get, $(-3.4)b = -4.08$ $b = \frac{-4.08}{-3.4} = 1.2.$ **Answer:** G

83.	Each unit cost = $\$v$ Total cost of w units = $\$wv$ Since, each next unit after third will cost you $\$u$ less, then, Amount you save = $\$(w-3)u$ Amount to be paid= $\$(wv-(w-3)u)$ **Answer:** C	87.	If 1 cm = 864 km on the map, then $\frac{5}{6}$ cm = $\frac{5}{6}(864) = 720$ km. The distance between the cities is $720\ km$. **Answer:** D
84.	$\frac{a+2b}{c} = \frac{c}{2a}$ By cross multiplication, we can write: $2a(a+2b) = c(c)$ By distributive property, $2a^2 + 4ab = c^2$ $4ab = c^2 - 2a^2$ $b = \frac{c^2 - 2a^2}{4a}$ $b = \frac{c^2}{4a} - \frac{a}{2}$ **Answer:** E	88.	BO is the bisector of $\angle B$, which means that $\angle ABO = \angle CBO$. CO is the bisector of $\angle C$, which means $\angle BCO = \angle DCO$. Since, ABCD is an isosceles trapezoid, $\angle B = \angle C$. Hence, $\angle ABO = \angle CBO = \angle BCO = \angle DCO$. Also, $\angle BCO = \angle DOC$ and $\angle CBO = \angle AOB$, because they are alternate interior angles. Thus, in the trapezoid ABCD, there are 6 congruent angles: $\angle ABO,\ \angle CBO,\ \angle BCO,\ \angle DCO,\ \angle AOB$ and $\angle DOC$. Making 3 congruent equilateral triangles $\Delta ABO, \Delta BCO$ and ΔDCO with side length 6 cm, so the perimeter of ABCD is $5 \cdot 6 = 30\ cm$. **Answer:** E
85.	If Sofia has x coins, then Steve has $\frac{x}{5}$ coins and Tom has $\frac{x}{3}$ coins. Therefore, the fraction of Steve's number of coins to Tom's number of coins is $\frac{\frac{x}{5}}{\frac{x}{3}} = \frac{x}{5} \times \frac{3}{x} = \frac{3}{5}$ **Answer:** C	89.	Children having 2 pets = 26% Children having > 2 pets = 8% Total percent of children having 2 or more pets = 26% + 8% = 34% Number of children having 2 or more pets = 600 × 34% = 600 × 0.34 = 204 **Answer:** C
86.	Let Kallie scored x points, then Anna scored $x+33$ points. If $x+33$ is 155% of x, then $x + 33 = (155\%)x$ $x + 33 = 1.55x \Rightarrow\ 1.55x - x = 33$ $0.55x = 33 \Rightarrow\ x = 60$ (Kallie's score) Anna's score = $x + 33 = 93$ **Answer:** F	90.	$48 - 7x < 5$ $-7x < 5 - 48$ $-7x < -43$ $7x > 43$ $x > \frac{43}{7} \Rightarrow x > 6\frac{1}{7}$ The least even integer number that satisfies the inequality is 8. **Answer:** G

91.	Each of the boxes contains 9 balls. Dylan picks a ball randomly from the 2nd box and places it in the 1st box. Now, 1st box will have 5 red balls, 4 black balls and one ball could be pink or blue, (chosen from 2nd box); a total of 10 balls. The probability that the ball he picks from the 1st box will be red $= \frac{5}{10} = \frac{1}{2}$. **Answer:** A	95.	Note that, $\frac{1}{625} = \frac{1}{5 \times 5 \times 5 \times 5} = \frac{1}{5^4}$ Then $\frac{1}{625}$ of 5^{10} is: $\frac{1}{625} \times 5^{10} = \frac{1}{5^4} \times 5^{10}$ $= 5^{10-4} = 5^6$ $= (5^2)^3 = 25^3$ **Answer:** D
92.	Average $= \frac{Sum\ of\ quantities}{Number\ of\ quantities}$ The average price in 1st supermarket is $\frac{35+36+38+37+36+35+35}{7} = \frac{252}{7} = \$36.$ The average price in 2nd supermarket is $\frac{37+36+34+34+33+35+36}{7} = \frac{245}{7} = \$35.$ The difference between the average prices in both supermarkets is $36 - 35 = \$1$. **Answer:** E	96.	If 17 students learn French, 18 students learn German, 6 students learn both languages, then $17 + 18 - 6 = 29$ students learn French or German. Therefore, Japanese is learnt by $36 - 29 = 7$ students. **Answer:** G
93.	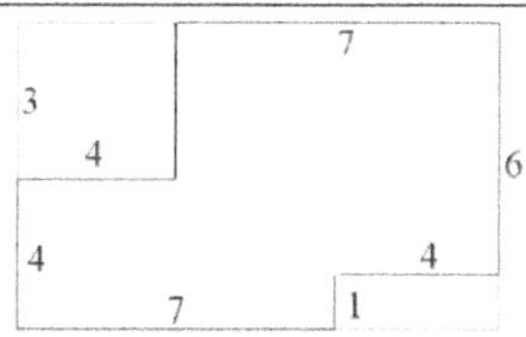 Consider the bigger rectangle with the side lengths 7 and 11 units. Area of bigger rectangle $= 7(11)$ $= 77\ units^2$ Area of small upper rectangle $= 4(3)$ $= 12\ units^2$ Area of small lower rectangle $= 4(1)$ $= 4\ units^2$ Area of the given figure $= 77 - 12 - 4$ $= 61\ units^2$ **Answer:** D	97.	$a = -2, b = 3$ Now, we will find the values of all the expressions in the list by plugging in the values of a and b, to see which one is the smallest. $ab = -2(3) = -6,$ $a^2b = (-2)^2(3) = 4(3) = 12,$ $ab^2 = (-2)(3)^2 = (-2)(9) = -18,$ $a^3b = (-2)^3(3) = (-8)(3) = -24,$ $ab^3 = (-2)(3)^3 = (-2)(27) = -54.$ The smallest number is -54, therefore, ab^3 is the smallest in the list. **Answer:** D
94.	We can calculate by long division method, that $\frac{4}{9} = 0.\bar{4}$. Thus, the fraction $2\frac{4}{9}$ is equivalent to $2.\bar{4}$. or $2\frac{4}{9} = \frac{22}{9} = 2.44444 \ldots. = 2.\bar{4}$ **Answer:** F	98.	The 1st multiple of 4 greater than 105 is 108, the last multiple of 4 less than 357 is 356. All multiples of 4 form an arithmetic sequence with a common difference 4, therefore, $a_n = a_1 + (n-1)d$ $356 = 108 + (n-1) \cdot 4$ $248 = 4(n-1)$ $n - 1 = 62 \Rightarrow n = 63$ 63 multiples of 4 between 105 and 357. **Answer:** F

99.	We know that, the number of apples is 20% of the number of pears. Let the number of pears $= x$ Number of apples $(20\%)(x) = 0.2x$ Find the number of pears is what percent of the number of apples: $\frac{x}{0.2x} \times 100\% = \frac{10}{2} \times 100\% = 500\%$ **Answer:** D	103.	Number of times Mars is closer to the Sun than Neptune $= \frac{4.459\times10^9}{2.297\times10^8}$ $= 1.941 \times 10^{9-8}$ $= 1.941 \times 10$ $= 19.41$ **Answer:** D
100.	The expression $\frac{x^2-4}{(x-2)^3}$ contains $(x-2)^3$ in the denominator. A rational expression is undefined when its denominator is zero. Therefore, $x - 2 = 0 \Rightarrow x = 2$ The expression is undefined when $x = 2$. **Answer:** E	104.	When a line segment is divided in the ratio $k_1 : k_2$, the coordinates of the point dividing the segment can be calculated as $\left(\frac{k_2x_1+k_1x_2}{k_1+k_2}, \frac{k_2y_1+k_1y_2}{k_1+k_2}\right)$. Using this formula, we can find coordinates of C: $\left(\frac{-2(3)+(-10)1}{3+1}, \frac{8(3)+(-4)1}{3+1}\right)$. $= \left(\frac{-6-10}{4}, \frac{24-4}{4}\right) = (-4, 5)$. **Answer:** E
101.	Let the price of the petrol $= \$x$ 20% increase $(20\%)x = \frac{20}{100}(x) = 0.2x$ Price after 20% increase $= x + 0.2x$ $= 1.2x$ 20% decrease $= (20\%)(1.2x)$ $= \left(\frac{20}{100}\right)(1.2x) = 0.24x$ Price after 20% decrease$= 1.2x - 0.24x$ $= 0.96x$ Original price was x, the final price $0.96x$ is $0.04x$ less than the original price, i.e. 4% less. It means that the final price decreases from the initial price by 4%. **Answer:** B	105.	Position of man from the end $=$ 17 Number of people standing behind him $= 16$ Position of man from the beginning $=$ 35 Number of people standing in front of him $= 34$ Total people standing in front of the man and behind him $= 16 + 34 = 50$ Total number of persons in the queue including the man himself $= 50 + 1$ $= 51$ **Answer:** B
102.	First, we will find the number of sides of the polygon by using the formula: $(n-2)180° = \mathit{Interior\ angles\ sum}$ $(n-2) \cdot 180° = 1980°$ $n - 2 = \frac{1980}{180}$ $n - 2 = 11 \Rightarrow n = 13$. The number of diagonals in a 13-sided polygon can be calculated as: $\frac{n(n-3)}{2} = \frac{13(13-3)}{2} = 65$ **Answer:** F	106.	Triangles are similar, therefore, the constant of proportionality k can be calculated by dividing the corresponding sides lengths of both triangles as: $k = \frac{28}{4} = 7$. To find LN, we can write: $\frac{BC}{LN} = k \Rightarrow \frac{21}{LN} = 7 \Rightarrow LN = \frac{21}{7} = 3$ units Perimeter of the triangle KLN $= KL + LN + NK = 4 + 5 + 3 =$ 12 units. **Answer:** F

107.	Let the speeds of the planes be x and $x+80$ mph. Since, the planes are flying towards each other, then $(x+x+80) = 2x+80$ mph is the speed at which, they are approaching towards each other. They pass each other after 6 hours, then using formula $S = vt$, we can write: $3000 = (2x+80)\times 6$ $2x+80 = 500 \Rightarrow x = 210$ mph Hence, speed of the plane moving at a higher rate $= x+80 = 290$ mph **Answer:** C	111.	A student can choose 1 bun in 5 different ways, 1 drink in 4 different ways and 1 cake in 6 different ways. Thus, he can choose $5\times 4\times 6 = 120$ different combinations. **Answer:** C
108.	C B D H A Consider the right triangle ABH. In this triangle, by the Pythagorean theorem, $BH^2 = AB^2 - AH^2$, $BH^2 = 13^2 - 5^2 = 169 - 25 = 144$ $BH = 12$ units. Now, $\overline{AD} = \overline{AH} + \overline{HD} = 5 + 12 = 17$ $\overline{BC} = 12$ Area of trapezoid $\left(\frac{BC+AD}{2}\right)\times BH$ $= \left(\frac{12+17}{2}\right)\times 12 = 174\, units^2$ **Answer:** G	112.	If $\frac{A}{120} = B \quad (i)$ $B < -2 \quad (ii)$ By eq. (i) and ineq. (ii), we can write: $\frac{A}{120} < -2$ $A < 120(-2)$ $A < -240.$ **Answer:** E
109.	You made 1st mistake when answering 34th question, so you earn $33\times 2 = 66$ points. You made 2nd mistake when answering 39th question, then you get $(38-34)\cdot 1 = 4$ additional points. In total, you earn $66+4 = 70$ points. **Answer:** B	113.	Rhombus ABCD consists of two equilateral triangles with the side length of 8 units. Area of equilateral triangle= $\frac{\sqrt{3}}{4}a^2$ Therefore the area of the rhombus is: $2\left(\frac{\sqrt{3}}{4}\times 8^2\right) = 32\sqrt{3}\, units^2$ **Answer:** D
110.	Speed of train $= 1km\ 500\ m\ per\ min$ $= \frac{1500}{60} m/sec = 25m/sec$ The train passes by a pole in 9 seconds, i.e. $t = 9\ sec$ Use $S = vt$ to find the length of train as: $S = 25\times 9 = 225$ m **Answer:** F	114.	Distance covered in first 6 hours: $S = vt = 60\times 6 = 360\ miles$ Next 6 hours he drove = 400 miles Total = 360 + 400 = 760 miles. 19 miles consume = 1 gallon 760 miles consume= $\frac{760}{19}$ = 40 gallons Cost of trip = \$3.25 × 40 = \$130 **Answer:** F

TEST 2: ANSWER KEYS

Q #	Answer
58	7/26
59	40
60	5.5
61	92
62	18
63	A
64	F
65	C
66	H
67	D
68	E
69	C
70	E
71	C
72	E
73	C
74	G
75	B
76	F
77	A

Q #	Answer
78	F
79	A
80	F
81	C
82	H
83	C
84	H
85	C
86	G
87	A
88	E
89	D
90	H
91	B
92	G
93	B
94	E
95	D
96	F
97	C

Q #	Answer
98	F
99	C
100	F
101	A
102	G
103	D
104	E
105	B
106	H
107	B
108	H
109	A
110	F
111	C
112	H
113	B
114	E

Practice Test 2: Answers & Explanations

GRID-IN QUESTIONS

Questions 58 - 62

58.

Face cards in the deck = 12
Black aces = 2
Cards to be selected = $12 + 2 = 14$
Total cards in the deck = 52
Probability that a card selected at random is face card or black ace is:
$= \frac{Number\ of\ Cards\ to\ be\ selected}{Total\ Number\ of\ Cards}$
$= \frac{14}{52} = \frac{7}{26}$

Answer: $\frac{7}{26}$

59.

Since, 3 pears = 2 apples
$\Rightarrow$ 6 pears = 4 apples (i)
Since, 1 apple = 4 Lego cubes
Plugging in eq. (i):
6 pears = 4 (4 Lego cubes)
6 pears = 16 Lego cubes (ii)
Since, 2 Lego cubes = 5 matches
Plugging in eq. (ii):
6 pears = 8 (2 Lego cubes)
6 pears = 8 (5 matches)
6 pears = 40 matches

Answer: 40 matches

60.

$\angle PVS \cong \angle VSM$ because they are alternate interior angles.
Also, $\angle PSV \cong \angle VSM$ by the definition of angle bisector.
Therefore, $\angle PSV \cong \angle PVS$, therefore ΔPSV is an isosceles triangle. Thus,
$PS = PV = 5\ cm$ and
$VA = 8 - 5 = 3\ cm.$
The length of the midline of the trapezoid can be calculated as:
$\frac{1}{2}(Sum\ of\ lengths\ of\ parallel\ sides)$
$= \frac{VA+SM}{2} = \frac{8+3}{2} = 5.5$ cm.

Answer: 5.5 cm.

61.

Let $2n$ and $2n + 2$ be two consecutive even integers, then
$2n + 2n + 2 = -46$
$4n = -46 - 2$
$4n = -48 \Rightarrow n = -12$
Consecutive even integers are:
$2n = 2(-12) = -24$ and
$2n + 2 = 2(-12) + 2 = -22$
The difference of the squares is:
$|(-24)^2 - (-22)^2|$
$= |576 - 484| = 92$

Answer: 92

62.

Total period = 28 days
Days spent on swimming = $\frac{2}{7}$ of 28 days
$= \frac{2}{7} \times 28 = 8$ days
Rest from trainings = $\frac{1}{14}$ of 28 days
$= \frac{1}{14} \times 28 = 2$ days
Days spent on gym = $28 - 8 - 2$
$= 18$ days.

Answer: 18 days.

MULTIPLE CHOICE QUESTIONS			
Questions 63 - 68			
63.	Expected profit = $\$4{,}450$ Profit earned = $\$4{,}450 \times 76\%$ $= \$4{,}450 \times \frac{76}{100}$ $= \$3{,}382$ **Answer:** A	66.	People who cannot sleep when the temperature is too high= $1{,}800$ People who cannot sleep when the temperature is too low= $2{,}400$ 600 people cannot sleep in both cases. Thus, People who cannot sleep when the temperature is too high or too low = $1{,}800 + 2{,}400 - 600 = 3{,}600$ People whose sleep is not affected by the temperature = $4{,}000 - 3{,}600 = 400$ **Answer:** H
64.	Oil flow rate = 2.6 gallons per minute Time taken to fill a tub having 221 gallons capacity = $\frac{221}{2.6} = 85$ minutes **Answer:** F	67.	In the word "laptop", there are 5 different letters. In a 3-letter word the 1st letter can be chosen in 5 ways, the 2nd letter – in 4 ways, the 3rd letter – in 3 ways. The total number of 3-letter words is $5 \times 4 \times 3 = 60$ **Answer:** D
65.	$Average = \frac{Sum\ of\ quantities}{Number\ of\ quantities}$ $190 = \frac{192 + x + 188 + 190 + 186}{5}$ $(190)5 = 756 + x$ $950 = 756 + x$ $x = 950 - 756 = 194$ cm **Answer:** C	68.	$\frac{k + 2m}{a - 4} = \frac{2k - m}{4}$ $4(k + 2m) = (a - 4)(2k - m)$ $(a - 4) = \frac{4(k + 2m)}{(2k - m)}$ $a = 4 + \frac{4k + 8m}{2k - m}$ $a = \frac{4(2k - m) + 4k + 8m}{2k - m}$ $a = \frac{8k - 4m + 4k + 8m}{2k - m}$ $a = \frac{12k + 4m}{2k - m}$ $a = \frac{4(3k + m)}{2k - m}$ **Answer:** E

Questions 69 - 74

69. The solution set on the number line is $[-3, 3.5)$.
Solve the inequalities one by one: Let's check option A first:
$\begin{cases} 2x - 7 < 0 \\ 4x + 12 \le 0 \end{cases} \Rightarrow \begin{cases} 2x < 7 \\ 4x \le -12 \end{cases} \Rightarrow \begin{cases} x < 3.5 \\ x \le -3 \end{cases}$
(Not correct)
Now check option B:
$\begin{cases} 2x - 7 \ge 0 \\ 4x + 12 < 0 \end{cases} \Rightarrow \begin{cases} 2x \ge 7 \\ 4x < -12 \end{cases} \Rightarrow \begin{cases} x \ge 3.5 \\ x < -3 \end{cases}$
(Not Correct)
$\begin{cases} 2x - 7 < 0 \\ 4x + 12 \ge 0 \end{cases} \Rightarrow \begin{cases} 2x < 7 \\ 4x \ge -12 \end{cases} \Rightarrow \begin{cases} x < 3.5 \\ x \ge -3 \end{cases}$'
which is represented by the number line.

Answer: C

70. The area of the right triangle TOU is
$= \frac{1}{2}(base)(height) = \frac{1}{2}(OU)(OT)$
$= \frac{1}{2}(10)(5) = 25\ units^2$.
The area of the right triangle SOV is
$= \frac{1}{2}(base)(height) = \frac{1}{2}(OV)(OS)$
$= \frac{1}{2}(8)(4) = 16\ units^2$.
The area of trapezoid STUV
$= 25 - 16 = 9\ units^2$.
Answer: E

71. The number of all possible outcomes is $6 \times 6 = 36$.
The outcomes with both odd number will be: $(1,1), (1,3), (1,5), (3,1), (3,3), (3,5), (5,1), (5,3), (5,5)$
Now choose only with sum greater than 7: $(3,5), (5,3), (5,5)$
Therefore, there are only 3 favorable outcomes.
Thus, the probability is $\frac{3}{36} = \frac{1}{12}$.

Answer: C

72. The fraction $\frac{47}{x}$ is equal to 2.9375, therefore, we can write it as:
$\frac{47}{x} = 2.9375$
$x = \frac{47}{2.9375}$
$x = 16$

Answer: E

73. The diameter of the circle is the midline of the triangle SAD. By the triangle midline theorem, the mid line is half the length of the parallel side.
Since the diameter of the circle is the midline of the triangle SAD, therefore,
$diameter = \frac{24}{2} = 12\ cm$
Radius $= \frac{diameter}{2} = \frac{12}{2} = 6\ cm$
Area of the semicircle $= \frac{1}{2}\pi r^2$
$= \frac{1}{2}(6)^2\pi = \frac{36}{2}\pi = 18\pi\ cm^2$

Answer: C

74. If point M divides segment AB in the ratio 3 : 4, then $AM = 3x,\ MB = 4x$.
If points K and L are midpoints of the segments AM and MB, then
$AK = KM = \frac{3x}{2} = 1.5x$ and
$ML = LB = \frac{4x}{2} = 2x$.
Hence,
$KB = KM + MB = 1.5x + 4x = 5.5x$
The ratio $AK : KB$ can be calculated as:
$\frac{AK}{KB} = \frac{1.5x}{5.5x} = \frac{15}{55} = \frac{3}{11} \Rightarrow 3 : 11$

Answer: G

Questions 75 - 80			
75.	6-digit number cannot start with 0, then there are 5 different ways to choose the 1st digit of the number. After choosing the 1st digit only 5 digits are left and the 2nd digit of the number can be chosen in 5 ways. Then 4 digits are left and the 3rd digit of the number can be chosen in 4 ways, the 4th digit – in 3 ways, the 5th digit – in 2 ways and the 6th – in 1 way. Thus, the total number of ways to create 6-digit number is $5 \times 5 \times 4 \times 3 \times 2 \times 1 = 600$ **Answer:** B	78.	Let n be the number of carrots Bugs Bunny had in stock. Then $n \times 30\% = 75$ $n \times \frac{30}{100} = 75$ $n = 75 \times \frac{100}{30}$ $n = 250$ Therefore, Bugs Bunny had 250 carrots in stock. **Answer:** F
76.	If n is an even natural number, then the previous even natural number is $n - 2$ and the next even natural number is $n + 2$. The product of the previous even natural number and the next even natural number is $(n-2)(n+2)$. Therefore, the product of the previous even natural number and the next even natural number divided by n is $\frac{(n-2)(n+2)}{n}$. **Answer:** F	79.	If BO is angle bisector of $\angle AOC$, then $\angle AOB = \angle BOC = 42°$ $\Rightarrow \angle AOC = 2(42°) = 84°$ $\angle AOC$ and $\angle COE$ together form 180°, $\angle AOC + \angle COE = 180°$ $84° + \angle COE = 180°$ $\angle COE = 180° - 84° = 96°$ Since, DO is $\angle COE$ bisector, then $\angle COD = \angle DOE = \frac{96°}{2} = 48°$ **Answer:** A
77.	Let's calculate the value of the expression: $\lvert(-3 + (-1)) \cdot 5 - 12\rvert$ $= \lvert(-4) \cdot 5 - 12\rvert$ $= \lvert-20 - 12\rvert$ $= \lvert-32\rvert = 32$ **Answer:** A	80.	If $a = -4$, $b = 4$ and $c = -3$, then the expression $(b - a) \cdot c + (b + c) \cdot a$ is $(4 - (-4)) \cdot (-3) + (4 + (-3)) \cdot (-4)$ $= (4 + 4) \cdot (-3) + (4 - 3) \cdot (-4)$ $= (8)(-3) + (1)(-4)$ $= -24 - 4 = -28$. **Answer:** F

Questions 81 - 86

81.	$d = 3c \quad (i)$ $\frac{b}{5} = d + 1 \Rightarrow \frac{b}{5} = 3c + 1$ $b = 5(3c + 1) = 15c + 5 \quad (ii)$ $\frac{a}{4} = b + 3 \Rightarrow \frac{a}{4} = 15c + 5 + 3$ $\frac{a}{4} = 15c + 8 \Rightarrow a = 4(15c + 8)$ $a = 60c + 32 \quad (iii)$ If $c < 0$, then c will have the greatest value because all other numbers a, b and c will have lesser value than that of c. **Answer:** C	84.	Let x be the number of nickels Lisa has and y be the number of dimes Tom has. Then $5x + 10y = 555$ $x + 2y = 111$ $x = 111 - 2y$. Since Lisa has more nickels than Tom has dimes, then $x > y$. Thus, $111 - 2y > y$ $111 > 3y$ $3y < 111 \Rightarrow y < 37$ Lisa has smallest number of nickels when Tom has greatest number of dimes i.e. 36. When $y = 36,\ x = 111 - 2(36) = 39$ **Answer:** H
82.	Since the sum of interior angles of a triangle is 180°, then in right triangle ABD, $\angle BDA + \angle BAD + \angle ABD = 180°$ $\angle BDA = 180° - \angle BAD - \angle ABD$ $\angle BDA = 180° - 36° - 90° = 54°$. $\angle BDA = \angle DBC$ because they are alternate interior angles, then $\angle ABC = \angle ABD + \angle DBC$ $\angle ABC = 90° + 54° = 144°$. **Answer:** H	85.	If the snail starts moving from the ground 1st day during the night and finishes moving at the end of 6th day, then it moves 6 days and 5 nights. Thus, the height is $5(32) - 6(7)$ $160 - 42 = 118$ cm. **Answer:** C
83.	4 eggs – 9 cookies, x eggs – 72 cookies. Then $\frac{4}{x} = \frac{9}{72}$ $4(72) = 9x$ $x = \frac{4(72)}{9}$ $x = 4(8) = 32$. Therefore, 32 eggs are required for 72 cookies. **Answer:** C	86.	If the ratio between girls and boys in 6th grade is 3 : 4, then the number of girls is $3x$ and the number of boys is $4x$. If the ratio between girls and boys in 7th grade is 7 : 5, then the number of girls is $7y$ and the number of boys is $5y$. Thus, $\begin{cases} 3x + 4x + 7y + 5y = 78 \\ 3x + 7y = 4x + 5y \end{cases}, \begin{cases} 7x + 12y = 78 \\ x = 2y \end{cases}$ Substitute $x = 2y$ in $7x + 12y = 78$, $7(2y) + 12y = 78 \Rightarrow 14y + 12y = 78$ $26y = 78 \Rightarrow y = 3$ $x = 2y = 6$. Total students in 6th grade $= 3x + 4x = 7x = 7(6) = 42$. **Answer:** G

Questions 87 - 92

87.

	Gr 5	Gr 6	Gr 7	Total
Like Sport	32	36	40	108
Don't like sport	24	18	12	54
Total				162

Total Children $= 162$
Children who don't like sport $= 54$
The probability that a randomly chosen student doesn't like sport $= \frac{54}{162} = \frac{1}{3}$.

Answer: A

88. Let's first write the numbers as a product of their prime factors:
$54 = 2 \cdot 3^3$
$72 = 2^3 \cdot 3^2$
$180 = 2^2 \cdot 3^2 \cdot 5$

Common factors $= 2 \cdot 3^2$
$GCF(54,72,180) = 2 \cdot 3^2 = 18.$

Answer: E

89. If the average of 12 numbers is x,
$Average = \frac{Sum}{n}$
$x = \frac{Sum\ of\ 12\ numbers}{12}$
$Sum\ of\ 12\ numbers = 12x$

If the average of 7 of them is y, then the sum of these 7 numbers is $7y$.

The sum of the remaining 5 numbers is $12x - 7y$.
Therefore, average of remaining 5 numbers $= \frac{12x-7y}{5}$.

Answer: D

90. Total students $= 25 + 36 + 39 = 100$
Students who scored less than 80 points $= 36 + 39 = 75$

Probability $= \frac{Favorable\ Outcomes}{Total\ Outcomes}$

The probability that a student chosen at random has score less than 80 $= \frac{75}{100} = \frac{3}{4}$

Answer: H

91. We know that,
$Area\ of\ circle = \pi r^2$
Therefore,
The area of large circle
$= 9^2 \cdot \pi = 81\pi\ cm^2$
The area of small circle
$= 6^2 \cdot \pi = 36\pi\ cm^2$
The area of the shaded region is:
$= 81\pi - 36\pi = 45\pi\ cm^2$

Answer: B

92. Price of 4,125 pens $= \$1.20 \times 4{,}125$
$= \$4{,}950$

We can write 4,125 as:
$4{,}125 = 3{,}000 + 1{,}000 + 100 + 25$
The discount offered on 4,125 pens can be calculated as:

$= \$1.20(3{,}000 \times 15\% + 1{,}000 \times 10\% + 100 \times 5\%)$
$= \$1.20(3{,}000 \times 0.15 + 1{,}000 \times 0.10 + 100 \times 0.05)$
$= \$1.20(580) = \$666$
Cost of 4,125 pens after discount
$= \$4{,}950 - \$666 = \$4{,}284.$

Answer: G

Questions 93 - 98			
93.	$29 < 4x + 5 \leq 93$ $29 - 5 < 4x \leq 93 - 5$ $24 < 4x \leq 88,$ $6 < x \leq 22.$ The number interval (6,22] contains 8 even numbers. **Answer:** B	96.	A family spends 15% of its income on food and 50% on children' education, then Remaining income will be: $= 100\% - 15\% - 50\% = 35\%$ If they spend 70% of the remaining on the house rent, then 30% of the remaining left. 30% of the remaining can be calculated as: $30\% \times Remaining\ income$ $= 30\% \times 35\% = 0.3 \times 35\% = 10.5\%.$ **Answer:** F
94.	The statement "When 162 is divided by an unknown number x squared, the result obtained is six times the number x" can be written mathematically as: $\frac{162}{x^2} = 6x$ $162 = 6x^3$ $x^3 = 27$ Taking cube root: $x = 3.$ **Answer:** E	97.	The distance between points B and M is $15 - 7 = 8$. If point M divides the segment $\overline{AB}$ in the ratio 3 : 4, then the length of the segment $\overline{AM}$ is $3x$ and the length of the segment $\overline{MB}$ is $4x$. Hence $4x = 8 \Rightarrow x = 2$ then $\overline{AM} = 3x = 3(2) = 6$ Point A lies to the left of the point M, then its position is $7 - 6 = 1$. **Answer:** C
95.	If a positive number c lies twice closer to the number b than to the number a, then a is the smallest number and c is the greatest number. If the distance between numbers a and b is 5, then the distance between numbers b and c is 5 too. Thus, option D is correct. **Answer:** D	98.	If the ratio of the numbers a, b, c is $2:3:4$, then $a = 2x,\ b = 3x,\ c = 4x$. Therefore, $\frac{a}{b}:\frac{b}{c}:\frac{c}{a} = \frac{2x}{3x}:\frac{3x}{4x}:\frac{4x}{2x}$ $\frac{a}{b}:\frac{b}{c}:\frac{c}{a} = \frac{2}{3}:\frac{3}{4}:\frac{4}{2}$ $\frac{a}{b}:\frac{b}{c}:\frac{c}{a} = \frac{8}{12}:\frac{9}{12}:\frac{24}{12}$ This gives us the ratio 8 : 9 : 24. **Answer:** F

Questions 99 - 104			
99.	To find an average score of all the students, we need to find the weighted average using formula: $Average = \frac{W_1X_1 + W_2X_2 + W_3X_3}{W_1 + W_2 + W_3}$ $Average = \frac{3(85) + 7(80) + 15(72)}{3 + 7 + 15}$ $Average = \frac{255 + 560 + 1080}{25}$ $Average = \frac{1895}{25} = 75.8$ **Answer:** C	102.	We know that the amount of lotus flowers doubles each day. The lake's surface is fully covered in 80 days. $\frac{1}{2}$ covered in 79 days. $\frac{1}{4}$ covered in 78 days. **Answer:** G
100.	$1\ mm - 15\ km$ $x\ mm - 270\ km$ $\frac{1}{x} = \frac{15}{270}$ $270 = 15x$ $x = \frac{270}{15} = 18\ mm$ Convert mm to cm: $1\ mm = 0.1\ cm$ $18\ mm = 1.8\ cm$ **Answer:** F	103.	If $x + 1$ is an odd number, then x is an even number and $x - 1$ is an odd number again. Then the product $(x - 1)(x + 1)$ is also an odd number. Option D is false. **Answer:** D
101.	Let "x" years be the brother's age and "y" years be his sister's age. After 4 years, the brother will be 3 times as old as his sister was 3 years ago, then $x + 4 = 3(y - 3)$ $x + 4 = 3y - 9$ $x = 3y - 9 - 4$ $x = 3y - 13 \quad (i)$ If 5 years ago he was twice as old as his sister was, then: $x - 5 = 2(y - 5)$ $x - 5 = 2y - 10$ $x = 2y - 10 + 5$ $x = 2y - 5 \quad (ii)$ Solving eq. (i) and (ii), we get: $3y - 13 = 2y - 5$ $3y - 2y = -5 + 13$ $y = 8$ Plugin $y = 8$ in eq. (ii), to get x: $x = 2y - 5 = 2(8) - 5 = 11$ years **Answer:** A	104.	A bus goes towards direction B every 45 minutes, towards direction C each hour and towards direction D every 2 hours. We know that, 1 hour = 60 minutes 2 hours = 120 minutes. Therefore to find, after how many minutes will these three buses start their journey from point A at the same time, we need to find LCM of 45, 60 and 120 minutes. $45 = 3^2 \cdot 5$ $60 = 2^2 \cdot 3 \cdot 5$ $120 = 2^3 \cdot 3 \cdot 5$, then $LCM = 5 \cdot 3 \cdot 2^2 \cdot 3 \cdot 2 = 360$ Therefore, after 360 minutes all three buses start their journey from point A at the same time. **Answer:** E

Questions 105 - 110			
105.	Simplifying the expression $(2 - 3x)7 - 3(x + 4)$ We get, $= 14 - 21x - 3x - 12$ $= 2 - 24x$ $= 2(1 - 12x)$. **Answer:** B	108.	Let the original 2 digit number has "a" at its units place and "b" at its tens place, then Original number = $a + 10b$ After interchanging the digits, New number = $10a + b$ According to the question statement: $10a + b - (a + 10b) = 36$ $10a + b - a - 10b = 36$ $9a - 9b = 36 \Rightarrow a - b = 4$ Only option H contains a number that has a difference of 5 and not 4 between its digits. **Answer:** H
106.	An odd number should end with an odd digit. There are 3 odd digits 1, 3, 5. Thus, the last 5th digit of a 5-digit number can be chosen in 3 different ways. The 1st digit can be chosen in 4 ways, the 2nd digit – in 3 ways, the 3rd digit – in 2 ways and the 4th digit – in 1 way. The total number of different combinations is $4 \times 3 \times 2 \times 1 \times 3 = 72$ **Answer:** H	109.	$Area\ of\ Rectangle = length \times width$ Length = $BC = BL + LM + MC$ Length = $BC = 4 + 6 + 4 = 14$ Width= $AB = AK + KB = 4 + 4 = 8$ Area of rectangle $ABCD = BC \times AB$ $= 14 \times 8 = 112\ units^2$ Area of rectangle $PQRS = PQ \times QR$ $= 4 \times 6 = 24\ units^2$ Area of shaded region = $112 - 24$ $= 88\ units^2$ **Answer:** A
107.	Let $\$x$ be the amount of money Dylan has and $\$y$ be the amount of money his brother has. If Dylan gives his brother 25% of his money, then his brother will have \$90. We can write it as: $y + 0.25x = 90 \quad (i)$ If Dylan's brother gives Dylan $\frac{1}{3}$ of his money, he initially had, then Dylan will have \$118. We can write it as: $x + \frac{1}{3}y = 118 \Rightarrow \frac{1}{3}y = 118 - x$ $y = 354 - 3x \quad (ii)$ Substitute it in eq. (i), we get: $354 - 3x + 0.25x = 90$ $2.75x = 264$ $x = 96$ **Answer:** B	110.	$\$200\ spent - \$15\ return$ $\$640\ spent - \$x\ return$ Then, we can write it as: $\frac{200}{640} = \frac{15}{x}$ $200x = 15 \times 640$ $x = \frac{15 \times 640}{200}$ $x = \$48$ **Answer:** F

Questions 111 - 114			
111.	For the green dress the girl has only one choice of shoes. For the 3 remaining dresses she can choose 9 different remaining pairs of shoes. Then she can dress up herself for the party in $C_1^3 \cdot C_1^{10} + 1 = 3(10) + 1 = 31\ ways.$ **Answer:** C	113.	Area of one square lateral face is $36\ units^2$. We know that: $Area\ of\ square = (Length\ of\ side)^2$ $36 = (Length\ of\ side)^2$ $Length\ of\ side = 6\ units$ We know that: $Volume\ of\ prism =$ $Length\ \times Width \times Height$ Since, all lateral faces of the prism are squares; therefore, length, width and height are all the same. Hence, Volume of the prism $= 6 \times 6 \times 6$ $= 216\ units^3$. **Answer:** B
112.	$1 - 2a = 3(a - 4)$ Simplifying, $1 - 2a = 3a - 12$ $1 + 12 = 3a + 2a$ $5a = 13$ $a = \frac{13}{5} = 2.6$ **Answer:** H	114.	Let "x" meters be the distance the turtle runs. Then Achilles runs $(560 + x)$ meters to catch the turtle. Convert both speeds into meters/min: $1.2\frac{km}{h} = \frac{1{,}200}{60}\frac{m}{min} = 20\frac{m}{min}$ $18\frac{km}{h} = \frac{18{,}000}{60}\frac{m}{min} = 300\frac{m}{min}$ Thus, x meters $- 20\ m/min$ $(560 + x)$ meters $- 300\ m/min$ We can write the proportion as: $\frac{x}{560 + x} = \frac{20}{300}$ $\frac{x}{560 + x} = \frac{1}{15}$ $15x = 560 + x \Rightarrow 14x = 560$ $x = \frac{560}{14} = 40$ It means turtles covered a distance of 40 meters before being caught. Total distance of turtle from Achilles is: $560 + 40 = 600\ m$ Time taken to catch the turtle= $\frac{distance}{speed}$ $= \frac{600}{300} = 2\ minutes$ **Answer:** E

TEST 3: ANSWER KEYS

Q #	Answer
58	12
59	37.5
60	16
61	40
62	3/16
63	C
64	G
65	B
66	H
67	A
68	H
69	A
70	G
71	B
72	E
73	C
74	H
75	A
76	F
77	C

Q #	Answer
78	E
79	D
80	F
81	D
82	E
83	A
84	H
85	B
86	E
87	D
88	F
89	A
90	F
91	A
92	H
93	B
94	G
95	A
96	E
97	A

Q #	Answer
98	G
99	C
100	H
101	C
102	E
103	B
104	G
105	B
106	F
107	B
108	G
109	A
110	F
111	B
112	H
113	A
114	G

Practice Test 3: Answers & Explanations

GRID-IN QUESTIONS			
Questions 58 - 62			
58.	Let, Mother's age $= m$ years Father's age $= f$ years Kevin's age $= s$ years Then average of all of them is 28 years, $\frac{m+f+s}{3} = 28 \Rightarrow m+f+s = 84 \quad (i)$ Average of mother's and son's age is 23: $\frac{m+s}{2} = 23 \Rightarrow m+s = 46 \quad (ii)$ Average of father's and son's age is 25: $\frac{f+s}{2} = 25 \Rightarrow f+s = 50 \quad (iii)$ Plugging $f+s = 50$ in eq. (i), we get: $m + 50 = 84 \Rightarrow m = 34$ Plugging $m = 34$ in eq. (ii), find s: $34 + s = 46 \Rightarrow s = 46 - 34 = 12$ Therefore, Kevin is 12 years old. **Answer:** 12 years	61.	We know that, 1 liter = 1,000 ml Therefore, 6 liters = 6,000 ml 1 cup = $150\ ml$ x cups = $6{,}000\ ml$ Then, we can write it as: $\frac{x}{1} = \frac{6{,}000}{150}$ $x = 40\ cups$ **Answer:** 40 cups
59.	Carlson ate $\frac{1}{4}$ of the jar of jam, therefore, $\frac{3}{4}$ of the jar of jam left. Next day, he ate $\frac{1}{2}$ of the remaining jam, $\frac{1}{2}$ of $\frac{3}{4} = \frac{1}{2} \times \frac{3}{4} = \frac{3}{8}$ Since he ate half and left half of the remaining. It means he left $\frac{3}{8}$ of the jam in the jar. To find the percentage $\frac{3}{8} \times 100\% = 37.5\%$ **Answer:** 37.5%	62.	The probability that the coin will land on head more than 3 times is the sum of the probability that the coin will land on head exactly 4 times and the probability that the coin will land on head exactly 5 times. $\Pr(4\ times) = \frac{C_4^5}{2^5} = \frac{5}{32}$ and $\Pr(5\ times) = \frac{C_5^5}{2^5} = \frac{1}{32}$. Then $\Pr(> 3\ times) = \frac{5}{32} + \frac{1}{32} = \frac{6}{32} = \frac{3}{16}$. **Answer:** $\frac{3}{16}$
60.	If $AT:TB = 2:1$, then $AT = 2x$ and $TB = x$. Since $AB = 9$ units and $AB = AT + TB$, then $9 = 2x + x \Rightarrow 3x = 9 \Rightarrow x = 3$ units. So, $AT = 2x = 2(3) = 6$ units and $TB = x = 3$ units. Triangles BTO and BAC are similar with coefficient of similarity $\frac{BT}{BA} = \frac{3}{9} = \frac{1}{3}$, then $\frac{TO}{AC} = \frac{TO}{6} = \frac{1}{3} \Rightarrow TO = \frac{6}{3} = 2$ units. The perimeter of the parallelogram ATOM is $P = 2(AT + TO) = 2(6+2) = 16$ units. **Answer:** 16 units		

MULTIPLE CHOICE QUESTIONS			
Questions 63 - 68			
63.	Let total students $= x$ Students who do homework with parents $= 40\%$ Students who do homework themselves $= 24$ i.e. 60% of total students We can write it as: $60\% \times x = 24$ $0.6 \times x = 24 \Rightarrow x = 40$ Therefore, total students $= 40$ No. of students who do homework with parents $= 40\% \times 40 = 0.4 \times 40 = 16$ If $\frac{1}{8}$ of the students who do homework with their parents get bad marks, then $\frac{7}{8}$ got good marks, their number will be: $\frac{7}{8} \times 16 = 14$ **Answer:** C	66.	Let the first odd integer $= n$ Second odd integer $= n + 2$ The sum of two consecutive odd integers is 72, therefore, $n + n + 2 = 72$ $2n + 2 = 72$ $2n = 70$ $n = 35$ (First odd integer) Second odd integer $= n + 2 = 37$. Two new numbers written in reverse order are 53 and 73 and their sum is $53 + 73 = 126$ **Answer:** H

64.	If $b - c = c + a$, then
	$b = c + a + c$
	$b = 2c + a$
	If $a = \frac{c}{2} + 1$, then
	$b = 2c + \frac{c}{2} + 1$
	$b = \frac{5c}{2} + 1$.
	
	Answer: G
		67.	$-\frac{x}{2} = y + 3 \Rightarrow y = -\frac{x}{2} - 3$
			When $x = -4$,
			$y = -\frac{-4}{2} - 3 = 2 - 3 = -1$
			When $x = 2$,
			$y = -\frac{2}{2} - 3 = -1 - 3 = -4$
			When $x = 10$,
			$y = -\frac{10}{2} - 3 = -5 - 3 = -8$
			$y \in \{-8, -4, -1\}$
			
			Answer: A

65.	Since point C is twice as close to point B as to point A. It means point B is diving the line segment AB in the ratio $AC:CB = 2:1$, The location of a point dividing a line segment AB in the ratio $k_1:k_2$ can be calculated using formula $\frac{kB+lA}{k_1+k_2}$. $\frac{2\left(\frac{3}{2}\right) + \left(-\frac{3}{4}\right)}{2+1} = \frac{3 - \frac{3}{4}}{3} = \frac{9}{4(3)} = \frac{3}{4}$ **Answer:** B	68.	$(x + 1)(2x - 5) - (x - 3)(x + 1)$ Factor our $(x + 1)$, we get: $= (x + 1)(2x - 5 - (x - 3))$ $= (x + 1)(2x - 5 - x + 3)$ $= (x + 1)(2x - x - 5 + 3)$ $= (x + 1)(x - 2)$ **Answer:** H

Questions 69 - 74

69. We know that,

$$Average = \frac{Sum\ of\ quantities}{Number\ of\ quantities}$$

Let $x_1, x_2, x_3, x_4, x_5, x_6$ be these 6 numbers. Then

$$\frac{x_1+x_2+x_3+x_4+x_5+x_6}{6} = \frac{x_1+x_2+x_3+x_4}{4} + 22$$

and $x_1 + x_2 + x_3 + x_4 + x_5 + x_6 = 180$

Substitute sum of 6 numbers in first equation:

$$\frac{180}{6} = \frac{x_1 + x_2 + x_3 + x_4}{4} + 22$$

$$\frac{x_1 + x_2 + x_3 + x_4}{4} = 8$$

$x_1 + x_2 + x_3 + x_4 = 32.$

Then $x_5 + x_6 = 180 - 32 = 148$ and

Average of two remaining numbers will be: $\frac{x_5+x_6}{2} = \frac{148}{2} = 74$

Answer: A

70. Let number of coins Paolo had $= x$

Number of coins his brother had $= y$

Number of coins Paolo gives to his brother $= \frac{1}{3}x$

Coins left to Paolo $= x - \frac{1}{3}x = \frac{2}{3}x$

Total coins his brother had $= y + \frac{1}{3}x$

After getting one third of Paolo's coins, they had the same number of coins.

$\frac{2}{3}x = y + \frac{1}{3}x \Rightarrow y = \frac{1}{3}x$. The only possible option is C, 24 and 8 coins.

Answer: G

71. We know that, $1\ km = 1{,}000{,}000\ mm$

Then,

$525\ km\ = 525{,}000{,}000\ mm$

The scale on map is

$1 - 25{,}000{,}000$ mm

$x - 525{,}000{,}000$ mm

We can write the proportion as:

$$\frac{x}{1} = \frac{525{,}000{,}000}{25{,}000{,}000} \Rightarrow x = 21\ mm$$

$$21\ mm = \frac{21}{10}\ cm = 2.1\ cm$$

Answer: B

72. The total number of cars is

$120 + 180 + 240 + 210 + 150 = 900.$

The number of cars that used the parking more than three times is

$210 + 150 = 360.$

Then, the percent of cars that used the parking service more than three times can be calculated as:

$$\frac{360 \cdot 100}{900} = 40\%$$

Answer: E

73. We know that, $Area\ of\ square = l^2$

Since, length of side of square is 1cm,

$Area\ of\ square = (1)^2 = 1\ cm^2$

Two semicircles together form a circle with the radius of $\frac{1}{2}$ cm. We know that,

Area of circle $= \pi r^2$

Area of circle $= \pi \cdot \left(\frac{1}{2}\right)^2 = \frac{\pi}{4}\ cm^2$.

Hence, the area of the shaded region is $1 - \frac{\pi}{4}\ cm^2$.

Answer: C

74. Let x be the number of books. If you place the books on the shelf by 3, by 4 or by 5 and one extra book will remain, then $x = 3n + 1, x = 4m + 1$ and $x = 5k + 1$. Therefore, $x - 1$ is divisible by 3, by 4 and by 5 without remainder. Hence, $x - 1 = 3 \times 4 \times 5l = 60l$ and $x = 60l + 1$.

When $l = 1,\ x = 61$, when $l = 2$, $x = 121$, when $l = 3,\ x = 181$, when $l = 4,\ x = 241$, when $l = 5,\ x = 301$.

Minimal number divisible by 7 is 301.

Answer: H

Questions 75 - 80			
75.	Ratio of width to length = $6 : 11$ Therefore, Width = $6x$ m Length = $11x$ m Since shorter side is 18 m, therefore, $6x = 18 \Rightarrow x = 3\ m,$ Length = $11x = 11(3) = 33\ m$ The fence bounds two longer sides and one shorter side of the garden, hence, Length of fence $= 33 + 33 + 18$ $= 84\ m$ **Answer:** A	78.	Probability of choosing black ball $= \frac{1}{6}$ Probability of choosing red ball $= \frac{2}{5}$ We know that, Sum of probabilities is <u>always</u> equal to 1, therefore, Probability of choosing green ball $= 1 - \left(\frac{1}{6} + \frac{2}{5}\right)$ $= 1 - \frac{17}{30} = \frac{13}{30}$ **Answer:** E
76.	$-3 < \frac{x}{3} \leq 6$ Multiply the inequality by 3: $-9 < x \leq 18.$ The solution of the inequality is $(-9,18]$ which is represented by the segment staring from -9 and ending at 18 but with left endpoint -9 excluded, right endpoint 18 included in the solution set. **Answer:** F	79.	The ratio of sisters' ages is $12 : 10 : 6 = 6 : 5 : 3$ Therefore, the money should be divided in the same ratio. Total amount = $\$112$, therefore, $6x + 5x + 3x = 112$ $14x = 112$ $x = 8.$ Hence, the share of sisters will be, First sister = $6x = \$48$ First sister= $5x = \$40$ First sister= $3x = \$24$ **Answer:** D
77.	Let number of coins Willy has = x Number of coins Anna has = y Willy has at least four times as many coins as Anna has, then, $x \geq 4y \quad (i)$ If Willy gives 23 coins to Anna, then number of coins Willy has = $x - 23$ Number of coins Anna has = $y + 23$ These number of coins are the same, so $x - 23 = y + 23 \Rightarrow x = y + 46.$ Substitute it into the inequality (i): $y + 46 \geq 4y$ $46 \geq 3y$ $3y \leq 46$ $y \leq \frac{46}{3} \Rightarrow y \leq 15\frac{1}{3}.$ Therefore, the maximum number of coins Anna could have is 15 coins. **Answer:** C	80.	Since, $LH = HA$, then the right triangle LHA is an isosceles triangle. We know that, Area of triangle = $\frac{1}{2}(Base)(Height)$ $8 = \frac{1}{2} \cdot LH \cdot HA$ Since, $LH = HA$, therefore, $8 = \frac{1}{2}(HA)(HA)$ $16 = (HA)^2$ $HA = 4\ units$ Area of the trapezoid= $\frac{1}{2}(OL + AC)(LH)$ $26 = \frac{1}{2}(4 + AC)(4)$ $13 = 4 + AC$ $AC = 9\ units$ **Answer:** F

Questions 81 - 86

81. Let's enter the given information in two way table in bold and find the number of people who visited none of the cities as:

	Visited London	Not visited London	Total
Visited Paris	**118**	222-118 = 104	**222**
Not visited Paris		690-104 = 586	
Total	**310**	1,000-310 = 690	**1,000**

Answer: D

84. Since, 1 cow = 3 pigs, therefore,
4 cows = 4(3) pigs = 12 pigs,

Since 2 pigs = 5 sheep
12 pigs = 6(2) pigs
12 pigs = 6(5) sheep = 30 sheep

Since 1 sheep = 12 rabbits
30 sheep = 30(12) rabbits
30 sheep = 360 rabbits

Answer: H

82. Let Mrs. Hudson bought x kg of apples and y kg of pears. Therefore,
$x + y = 9 \quad (i)$
If apples were sold by \$1.35 per kg and pears were sold by \$2.52 per kg, then
$1.35x + 2.52y = 18 \quad (ii)$
From eq. (i), plugin $x = 9 - y$ in eq. (ii),
$1.35(9 - y) + 2.52y = 18$
$12.15 - 1.35y + 2.52y = 18$
$1.17y = 5.85 \Rightarrow y = 5$ kg
and $x = 9 - 5 = 4$ kg.
Therefore, she bought 4 kg of apples.

Answer: E

85. We know that,
Average = $\frac{Sum\ of\ quantities}{Number\ of\ quantities}$
The average speed of all transport modes can be calculated as:
Average = $\frac{90+60+30+x}{4}$
$46 = \frac{180 + x}{4}$
$184 = 180 + x$
$x = 184 - 180$
$x = 4\ km/h$

Answer: B

83. The probability of choosing ace from the standard deck is $\frac{4}{52} = \frac{1}{13}$. Then the probability of choosing two aces with replacement is
$\frac{1}{13} \cdot \frac{1}{13} = \frac{1}{169}$

Answer: A

86. Other students = $100\% - (32\% + 24\% + 18\% + 12\% + 6\%)$
Other students = $100\% - 92\% = 8\%$
Total number of students = 1,200
Number of other students who like Math = 1,200 × 8% = 1,200 × 0.08 = 96

Answer: E

Questions 87 - 92

87.
$$3\frac{1}{2}+5\frac{3}{4}+7\frac{1}{8}$$
$$=\frac{7}{2}+\frac{23}{4}+\frac{57}{8}$$
$$=\frac{28}{8}+\frac{46}{8}+\frac{57}{8}$$
$$=\frac{28+46+57}{8}=\frac{131}{8}=16\frac{3}{8}$$

Answer: D

88. Since large rectangle is dilated to small triangle by a scale factor $\frac{3}{4}$, therefore, $L\times\frac{3}{4}=S$, where L represents dimensions of large rectangle and S represents dimensions of small rectangle.
We will use $L=S\times\frac{4}{3}$ to find dimensions of large rectangle as:
Length $6\times\frac{4}{3}=8\ units$
Width= $3\times\frac{4}{3}=4\ units$
Area of large rectangle $=l\times w$
$=8\times 4=32\ units^2$
Area of small rectangle $=3\times 6$
$=18\ units^2$
Area of shaded region $=32-18$
$=14\ units^2$

Answer: F

89. We will find the GCF of 48, 56 and 84.
$48=2^4\cdot 3$
$56=2^3\cdot 7$
$84=2^2\cdot 3\cdot 7$
Then, $GCF(48,56,84)=2^2=4$.
Lily can form 4 identical bouquets with 12 roses, 14 lilies and 21 herbs in each.

Answer: A

90. Blue eyed $=20\%$
Green eyed $=15\%$
Grey eyed $=25\%$
Black eyed $=(100-20-15-25)\%$
$=40\%$
The probability that John's baby will be green-eyed or black-eyed $=\frac{15}{100}+\frac{40}{100}$
$$=\frac{15+40}{100}=\frac{55}{100}=\frac{11}{20}$$

Answer: F

91. Since,
1 kilometer = 3,280 feet, then
120 kilometers = 120 × 3,280 feet.

Similarly,
1 hour = 60 minutes,
1 minute = 60 sec
1 hour = 60 × 60 sec = 3,600 sec

Therefore,
120 km/h = $\frac{120\times 3{,}280}{3{,}600}\ ft/sec$

Answer: A

92. Let Steve's age $=x$ years
Ali's age $=y$ years
Sum of ages of Steve and Ali ages
$=x+y$ years
Difference of Steve and Ali ages,
$=y-x$ years
The sum of the ages is three times the difference of their ages
$x+y=3y-3x$
$4x=2y\Rightarrow y=2x$
$\frac{y}{x}=\frac{2}{1}$

Answer: H

Questions 93 - 98			
93.	First divisible by 6 number after 13 is 18, last divisible by 6 number before 85 is 84. It will make an arithmetic series with $a_1 = 18, a_n = 84$ and $d = 6$. To find the number of terms in series, $a_n = a_1 + (n-1)d$ $84 = 18 + (n-1)6$ $66 = 6(n-1)$ $n - 1 = 11 \Rightarrow n = 12$ To find the sum, use formula: $S_n = \frac{n}{2}(a_1 + a_n)$ $S_{12} = \frac{1}{2}(18 + 84)(12)$ $= 102 \times 6$ $= 612$ **Answer:** B	96.	The ratio in which farmers should divide the money is $(100 \times 6):(120 \times 4):(150 \times 2)$ $= (10 \times 6):(12 \times 4):(15 \times 2)$ $= (10 \times 3):(12 \times 2):(15 \times 1)$ $= (10 \times 1):(4 \times 2):(5 \times 1)$ $= 10 : 8 : 5$ Then the total cost can be represented as: $10x + 8x + 5x = 552$ $23x = 552$ $x = \$24.$ 3rd farmer's share of rent $= 5x$ $= \$24 \times 5 = \$120$ **Answer:** E
94.	If the numbers a, b, c and d are four consecutive odd numbers, then $b = a + 2,\ c = a + 4,\ d = a + 6.$ Let's calculate the differences $b - a$ and $d - c$. $(b - a) = a + 2 - a = 2$ $(d - c) = a + 6 - a - 4 = 2$ Thus, the differences $b - a$ and $d - c$ are the same. **Answer:** G	97.	A round trip can be made in 4 different ways from city S to city T and in 3 different ways from city T to city S because it is desired to take a different route on the way back. Therefore, in total there are $4 \times 3 = 12$ different ways. **Answer:** A
95.	Each week pay = \$325 Per day tip = \$22 Each week tip = $22(7) = \$154$ Earning per week = $325 + 154 = \$479$ Earnings in two weeks $2(\$479) = \$958$ **Answer:** A	98.	$x = 0.\overline{04} = 0.040404 \quad (i)$ Multiplying the equation by 100: $100x = 4.040404 \quad (ii)$ Subtracting eq. (i) by eq. (ii): $100x - x = 4.040404 \ldots - 0.040404 \ldots$ $99x = 4$ $x = \frac{4}{99}$ **Answer:** G

Questions 99 - 104			
99.	To find the dimensions of the maximum size of square wrapping, we will find the GCF of 120 and 96 as: $120 = 2^3 \times 3 \times 5$ $96 = 2^5 \times 3$ $GCF(120, 96) = 2^3 \times 3 = 24$ cm – the maximum length of the square side. Number of square wrapping that can be cut can be calculated by dividing the area of rectangular sheet by the area of square wrapping as: $\frac{120 \times 96}{24 \times 24} = 20$ **Answer:** C	102.	Total coins $= 3 + 6 + 14 + 17 = 40$ If John chooses 2 of these coins at random without replacement, the probability that neither of the 2 coins that John chooses are dimes can be calculated as: $\left(\frac{40-6}{40}\right) \times \left(\frac{39-6}{39}\right)$ $= \frac{34}{40} \times \frac{33}{39}$ $= \frac{17}{20} \times \frac{11}{13}$ $= \frac{187}{260}$ **Answer:** E
100.	The carpenter makes 42 wooden chairs in 28 minutes. We can calculate his rate as: $Rate = \frac{42}{28} = 1.5\ chairs/min$ It means: 1.5 chairs – 1 minute 300 chairs – x minutes We can write the proportion as: $\frac{x}{1} = \frac{300}{1.5}$ $x = 200\ min = 3\ hrs\ 20\ minutes$ **Answer:** H	103.	$\frac{a}{b} = \frac{2c}{d}$ $ad = 2bc \quad (i)$ From eq. (i), we can derive, $\frac{d}{b} = \frac{2c}{a}$ $\frac{d}{c} = \frac{2b}{a}$ and $\frac{ad}{c} = 2b$ But we cannot rewrite eq. (i) as: $\frac{bc}{d} = 2a$ **Answer:** B
101.	$\frac{x+y}{2y} = 5$ $\frac{x+y}{y} = 10$ $\frac{x}{y} + 1 = 10$ $\frac{x}{y} = 9$ $\frac{y}{x} = \frac{1}{9}$ **Answer:** C	104.	Point D lies between points A and B such that $AD = 4$ units, then $BD = AB - AD = 10 - 4 = 6$ units. Point C lies to the right from point B and $BC = 2$ units, then $DC = DB + BC = 6 + 2 = 8$ units. **Answer:** G

Questions 105 - 110			
105.	If n is an even natural number, then $3n$ is an even number too and $3n + 1$ is an odd number. Only this statement is true. **Answer:** B	108.	The favorable outcomes are $(1,6), (2,5), (2,6), (3,4), (3,5), (3,6), (4,3), (4,4), (4,5), (4,6), (5,2), (5,3), (5,4), (5,5), (5,6), (6,1), (6,2), (6,3), (6,4), (6,5), (6,6)$ Total favorable outcomes $= 21$ The total outcomes $= 6 \times 6 = 36$ Probability of obtaining a sum of at least $7 = \frac{21}{36} = \frac{7}{12}$ **Answer:** G
106.	The man is standing at 37th position in the queue. People in front of the man = 36 The girl is standing at 24th position from the end in the queue. People standing behind her = 23 People between the man and the girl = 4 Thus, People behind the man $= 23 - 4 - 1$ $= 18$ people People in the queue $= 18 + 36 + 1 = 55$ **Answer:** F	109.	$5b - 7a = 70$ $7a = 5b - 70$ $a = \frac{5}{7}b - \frac{70}{7}$ $a = \frac{5}{7}b - 10$ **Answer:** A
107.	Use the following formula: $a^2 - b^2 = (a + b)(a - b)$ $(2{,}019)^2 - (2{,}018)^2$ $= (2{,}019 - 2{,}018)(2{,}019 + 2{,}018)$ $= (1)(4{,}037) = 4{,}037$ **Answer:** B	110.	Total surveyed students $= 220$ Students who like first 4 activities $= 75 + 54 + 42 + 33 = 204$ Students who prefer walk with dog $= 220 - 204 = 16$ Therefore, the more students who prefer chat online than walk with dog $= 75 - 16 = 59$ **Answer:** F

Questions 111 - 114			
111.	One bottle contains = $2.5\ l = 2{,}500\ ml$ Each friends gets juice = $300\ ml$ 25 friends will get = 300×25 $= 7{,}500\ ml$ Number of 2.5 ml bottles required $= \frac{7{,}500}{2{,}500} = 3$ bottles **Answer:** B	113.	In the right triangle EBD, $\angle BED = 90° - 23° = 67°$. $\angle BED$ and $\angle BEA$ are supplementary angles, therefore, $\angle BEA = 180° - \angle BED$ $\angle BEA = 180° - 67° = 113°$. Since BE is the bisector of right angle B, therefore, $\angle ABE = 45°$ We know that, sum of interior angles of a triangle is 180°. Hence, in ΔABE, $\angle BAE + \angle BEA + \angle ABE = 180°$ $\angle BAE + 113° + 45° = 180°$ $\angle BAE = 180° - 113° - 45°$ $\angle BAE = 22°$ $\angle BAC = \angle BAE = 22°$ **Answer:** A
112.	Let x years be Denys's age and y years be his sister's age now. After 5 years Denys's age = $x + 5$ years After 5 years Denys' will be as sold as his sister is now, therefore, $x + 5 = y\quad (i)$ Also, after 5 years Denys' sister will be twice as old as Denys is now, hence, $y + 5 = 2x\quad (ii)$ Plugin in $y = x + 5$ from eq. (i) into eq. (ii), $x + 5 + 5 = 2x$ $2x - x = 10$ $x = 10$ Substitute $x = 10$ in eq. (i) to find y: $y = x + 5 = 10 + 5 = 15$ Therefore, Denys' sister is 15 years old. **Answer:** H	114.	First five alphabets = A, B, C, D, E Vowels = A, E, I, O, U. Letters A and E are in both sets, therefore, lets rewrite the favorable outcomes as: Favorable outcomes = A, B, C, D, E, I, O, U Number of favorable outcomes = 8 Total cards = 26 Probability of selecting a card that is one of the first five alphabets or a vowel $= \frac{8}{26} = \frac{4}{13}$ **Answer:** G

TEST 4: ANSWER KEYS

Q #	Answer
58	59
59	20
60	51
61	12
62	0.64
63	C
64	E
65	B
66	H
67	C
68	H
69	B
70	G
71	A
72	G
73	A
74	H
75	B
76	F
77	C

Q #	Answer
78	E
79	D
80	E
81	C
82	F
83	D
84	F
85	C
86	F
87	C
88	G
89	A
90	H
91	C
92	G
93	A
94	F
95	D
96	G
97	A

Q #	Answer
98	H
99	C
100	E
101	C
102	H
103	C
104	G
105	A
106	G
107	B
108	E
109	C
110	F
111	C
112	G
113	D
114	E

Practice Test 4: Answers & Explanations

<table>
<tr><th colspan="4">GRID-IN QUESTIONS</th></tr>
<tr><th colspan="4">Questions 58 - 62</th></tr>
<tr><td>58.</td><td>$\angle AOE$ and $\angle BOF$ are vertical angles and vertical angles are always congruent, therefore,
$\angle AOE = \angle BOF$
$\angle AOC + \angle COE = \angle BOF$
$32° + \angle COE = 91°$
$\angle COE = 91° - 32°$
$\angle COE = 59°$

Answer: 59°</td><td>61.</td><td>Jim has 4 different possibilities of going to school and 3 different possibilities of getting back from school.
Thus, he has $4 \times 3 = 12$ different ways of going to school and getting back home.

Answer: 12</td></tr>
<tr><td>59.</td><td>$Sheep : Geese = 7:4$
Number of sheep = $7x$
Number of geese = $4x$
Each sheep has four legs, then
Number of legs $7x$ sheep have = $28x$
Each goose has 2 legs, then
Number of legs $4x$ geese have = $8x$
Total legs of animals on farm = 180
Therefore,
$28x + 8x = 180$
$36x = 180$
$x = 5.$
Number of geese on the farm = $4x$
$= 4(5) = 20$

Answer: 20</td><td>62.</td><td>Work Wendy has completed = $\frac{9}{25}$
Work left = $1 - \frac{9}{25} = \frac{16}{25}$

Let's convert it to decimal representation:

$\frac{16}{25} = \frac{16 \times 4}{25 \times 4} = \frac{64}{100} = 0.64$

Answer: 0.64</td></tr>
<tr><td>60.</td><td>$5a - 78 = 3a + 24$
$5a - 3a = 24 + 78$
$2a = 102$
$a = 51$

Answer: 51</td><td></td><td></td></tr>
</table>

MULTIPLE CHOICE QUESTIONS			
Questions 63 - 68			
63.	The broken line $RAPS$ consists of three segments RA, AP and PS, then $RA + AP + PS = 13\ cm\ \ (i)$ Perimeter of rectangle ROSE $= 22\ cm$ half of the perimeter $= 11\ cm$ Therefore, $RP + PE + ES = 11\ cm\ \ (ii)$ Add eq. (i) and (ii), $RA + AP + PS + RP + PE + ES$ $= 13 + 11 = 24\ cm$ This sum is the sum of perimeters of two congruent triangles RAP and PSE, thus, Perimeter of triangle $RAP = \frac{24}{2} = 12$ cm. **Answer:** C	66.	Kallis got money $= \$12$ Since Denys got one-third of the money Kallis got, therefore, Denys got money $= \frac{1}{3}(\$12) = \$4$ Since, Simon got twice as much as the other two friends got together, therefore, Simon got money $= 2(\$12 + \$4)$ $= 2(\$16) = \$32$ Thus, total amount Billy had = $\$32 + \$4 + \$12 = \$48$ **Answer:** H
64.	$3a - \frac{b}{c} = \frac{c}{a} + 1$ $\frac{b}{c} = 3a - \frac{c}{a} - 1$ $\frac{b}{c} = \frac{3a^2 - c - a}{a}$ $b = \frac{3a^2c - c^2 - ac}{a}$. **Answer:** E	67.	$12x = 64 - 3y$ $3y = 64 - 12x$ $y = \frac{64}{3} - 4x$ **Answer:** C
65.	Let f years be the age of Jacob's father and s year be Jacob's age. If the father's age is the sum of Jacob's and his mother's age, then, $f = 26 + s\ \ (i)$ After 8 years, Jacob's age $= s + 8$ years Father's age $= f + 8$ years. Since after 8 years, Jacob's age will be $\frac{1}{3}$ times his father's age, then $s + 8 = \frac{1}{3}(f + 8)\ \ (ii)$ Plugin $f = 26 + s$ in eq. (ii), we get, $s + 8 = \frac{1}{3}(26 + s + 8)$ $3s + 24 = s + 34$ $2s = 10 \Rightarrow s = 5$ **Answer:** B	68.	To find the least common multiple of 15, 18 and 210, write the numbers as a product of their prime factors as: $15 = 3 \times 5$ $18 = 2 \times 3^2$ $210 = 2 \times 3 \times 5 \times 7$. Therefore, $LCM = 3 \times 5 \times 2 \times 3 \times 7 = 630$. **Answer:** H

Questions 69 - 74			
69.	John completes the work in 12 hours, it means he does $\frac{1}{12}$ of work per hour. Romi completes the work in 9 hours, hence, she does $\frac{1}{9}$ of work per hour. Together they complete the work in 3 hours, hence, they do $\frac{1}{3}$ of work per hour. Let Sue completes work in x hours, it means she does $\frac{1}{x}$ of work per hour. We can write as: $\frac{1}{12}+\frac{1}{9}+\frac{1}{x}=\frac{1}{3}$ $\frac{1}{x}=\frac{1}{3}-\frac{1}{12}-\frac{1}{9}=\frac{5}{36}$ $x=\frac{36}{5}=7.2$ $= 7\ hours\ (0.2 \times 60)\ minutes$ $= 7$ hours 12 minutes **Answer:** B	72.	If square has side length of 4 cm, then Radius of the circle $= 2\ cm$ Area of circle $= \pi r^2$ Area of circle $= \pi \times 2^2 = 4\pi\ cm^2$ The shaded region is $\frac{3}{4}$ of a circle, therefore, area of shaded region is $\frac{3}{4} \cdot 4\pi = 3\pi\ cm^2$ **Answer:** G
70.	Let $2n$ be the smallest even number, then $2n+2$ and $2n+4$ are the two next even numbers. We know that, $Average = \frac{Sum\ of\ quantities}{Number\ of\ quantities}$ The average of these numbers is: $\frac{2n+2n+2+2n+4}{3} = 38$ $\frac{6n+6}{3} = 38$ $2n+2 = 38$ $2n = 36 \Rightarrow n = 18$ Smallest number in the set $= 2n$ $= 2(18) = 36$ **Answer:** G	73.	m lies to the left of n, therefore $m - n = -2$. Since $n = -2.5$, then $m - (-2.5) = -2$ $m + 2.5 = -2$ $m = -2 - 2.5 = -4.5$ k lies to the right of n, therefore $n - k = -4$. Since $n = -2.5$, then $k = n + 4 = -2.5 + 4 = 1.5$ Therefore, $m \times k = -4.5 \times 1.5$ $= -6.75$. **Answer:** A
71.	The probability that the die A will land on a black face is $\frac{4}{6}=\frac{2}{3}$. The probability that the die B will land on a white face is $\frac{4}{6}=\frac{2}{3}$. Then the probability that dice A will land on a black face and dice B will land on a white face $=\frac{2}{3}\cdot\frac{2}{3}=\frac{4}{9}$ **Answer:** A	74.	If you buy 5 units for $\$k$ each, then Cost of 5 units $= \$5k$ If you buy n units $(n > 5)$, then there are $n-5$ additional units. Every additional unit will cost you $\$m$ less, so Cost for all additional $n-5$ units $= \$(n-5)(k-m)$. Total cost $= \$(5k + (n-5)(k-m))$. **Answer:** H

Questions 75 - 80			
75.	$\frac{a+2b}{3}=\frac{2}{c}$ $c(a+2b)=6$ $a+2b=\frac{6}{c}$ $2b=\frac{6}{c}-a$ $2b=\frac{6-ac}{c}$ $b=\frac{6-ac}{2c}$ $\frac{1}{b}=\frac{2c}{6-ac} \Rightarrow \frac{4}{b}=\frac{8c}{6-ac}$ **Answer:** B	78.	In the sketch, the scale is: 2 in – 7 ft 6.5 in – x ft We can write the proportion as: $\frac{2}{6.5}=\frac{7}{x}$ $2x=6.5\times 7$ $2x=45.5$ $x=\frac{45.5}{2}$ $x=22.75$ ft. **Answer:** E
76	$Hazelnuts: Almonds: Walnuts =$ $= 3:5:7$ Hazelnuts $= 3x$ Almonds $= 5x$ Walnuts $= 7x$ Amount of almonds in bag = 6 pounds $5x = 6$ $x=\frac{6}{5}=1.2$ pounds Amount of walnuts $= 7x$ $= 7(1.2) = 8.4$ pounds **Answer:** F	79.	Since area of ΔBUV is three times the area of the ΔBVW, then $A_{BUV}=3\times 4.5=13.5\ units^2$. Two smaller triangles made by the median of a bigger triangle has the same area. Hence, $A_{VUS}=A_{BUV}=13.5units^2$ Area of the ΔBUS can be calculated as: $A_{BUS}=A_{BUV}+A_{VUS}$ $=13.5+13.5=27\ units^2$ Hence, area of the quadrilateral $SVWU$ is $A_{SVWU}=A_{BUS}-A_{BVW}$ $=27-4.5=22.5\ units^2$ **Answer:** D
77.	Discounted price = \$234 Summer discount = 22% Percent price Brian paid = 100% – 22% = 78% Hence, we can write: $Original\ price \times 78\% = 234$ $Original\ price \times 0.78 = 234$ $Original\ price = \frac{234}{0.78} = \$300$ **Answer:** C	80.	Total readers = 200 People like reading historical novels and mystery novels = $12\%\ of\ 200$ $=\frac{12}{100}\times 200=24$ People like reading historical novels = 85 People like to read only mystery novels are: $200-85-24=91$ people **Answer:** E

Questions 81 - 86			
81.	Multiples of 3 between 1 and 30 are: $3, 6, 9, 12, 15, 18, 21, 24, 27, 30$ Multiples of 5 between 1 and 30 are: $5, 10, 15, 20, 25, 30$ Numbers 15 and 30 are repeating in both the multiples of 3 and 5. Therefore, in total, there are 14 different multiples of 3 and 5. Probability that the card picked is a multiple of 3 or 5 $= \frac{14}{30} = \frac{7}{15}$ **Answer:** C	84.	Area of $\Delta ABC = 10 + 16 = 26\ units^2$ This triangle is isosceles, therefore, area of the ΔLUB is half of the area of ΔLAP. $SU = \frac{1}{2}(BC)$ $UB = CS = \frac{1}{2}(SU)$ Therefore, $A_{\Delta APL} = A_{\Delta LUB} + A_{\Delta PSC}$ (i) Also, $A_{\Delta APL} + A_{\Delta LUB} + A_{\Delta PSC} = 16$ (ii) Plugin $A_{\Delta APL} = A_{\Delta LUB} + A_{\Delta PSC}$ from eq. (i) into eq. (ii), we get, $A_{\Delta APL} + A_{\Delta APL} = 16$ $2(A_{\Delta APL}) = 16 \Rightarrow A_{\Delta APL} = 8$ Therefore, the area of the pentagon $APSUL = 10 + 8 = 18\ units^2$ **Answer:** F
82.	For $x = -4$, $y = -\frac{(-4)^2}{2} + 1 = -7$ For $x = -2$, $y = -\frac{(-2)^2}{2} + 1 = -1$. For $x = 0$, $y = -\frac{0^2}{2} + 1 = 1$. For $x = 2$, $y = -\frac{2^2}{2} + 1 = -1$. For $x = 4$, $y = -\frac{4^2}{2} + 1 = -7$. Y values are $\{-7, -1, 1\}$. **Answer:** F	85.	$\frac{2}{33} = 0.\overline{06}$, $\frac{11}{99} = 0.\overline{1}$, $\frac{8}{125} = 0.064$, $\frac{4}{99} = 0.\overline{04}$. **Answer:** C
83.	Let's calculate the difference of time for each activity. Chatting online: $112 - 44 = 68$ min Watching TV: $118 - 33 = 85$ min Cooking: $68 - 26 = 42$ min Babysitting: $155 - 44 = 111$ min The greatest difference in time appears at babysitting. **Answer:** D	86.	$\frac{4}{216}$ of 3^7 means $\frac{4}{216} \times 3^7$ $= \frac{2^2}{2^3 \cdot 3^3} \times 3^7$ $= \frac{1}{2 \cdot 3^3} \times 3^7$ $= \frac{3^4}{2} = \frac{81}{2} = 40.5$ **Answer:** F

Questions 87 - 92

87. Rabbit:
Let "x" meters be the unknown distance.
Rate $= 2\ m/s$.
Using formula $S = vt$,
Time taken to cover "x" meters $= \frac{x}{2}\ sec$
Wolf:
Distance covered $= (x + 800)$ meters
Rate $= 4\ m/s$.
Time $= \frac{(x+800)}{4}\ sec$
They both spends the same time, hence,
$$\frac{x}{2} = \frac{x + 800}{4}$$
$4x = 2x + 1{,}600$
$2x = 1{,}600 \Rightarrow x = 800$ m.

Answer: C

88. If $a = -2,\ b = 3$, then
$a + b^2 = -2 + 3^2 = -2 + 9 = 7;$
$a^2 + b = (-2)^2 + 3 = 4 + 3 = 7;$
$a + b^3 = -2 + 3^3 = -2 + 27 = 25;$
$a^3 + b = (-2)^3 + 3 = -8 + 3 = -5.$
The greatest answer in the set is 25 that is $a + b^3$.

Answer: G

89. $-5,\ -1,\ 3,\ \ldots$ is an arithmetic series with $a_1 = -5,\ a_2 = -1,\ a_3 = 3$.
The common difference can be calculated as:
$d = a_2 - a_1 = -1 - (-5) = 4$
To find 10th term, use formula,
$a_n = a_1 + (n - 1)d$
$a_{10} = -5 + (10 - 1)4$
$a_{10} = -5 + 9(4) = -5 + 36 = 31$
The sum of first 10 terms in the pattern can be calculated using formula:
$S_n = \frac{n}{2}(a_1 + a_{10})$
$$S_{10} = \frac{10}{2}(-5 + 31) = 5(26) = 130$$

Answer: A

90. Total students $= 1{,}200 + 800 = 2{,}000$
Number of boys who passed the exam $=$
$45\%\ of\ 1{,}200 = 0.45 \times 1{,}200 = 540$

Number of girls who passed the exam $=$
$50\%\ of\ 800 = 0.5 \times 800 = 400$

Total students who passed exams $=$
$540 + 400 = 940$
Students who could not pass the exam $=$
$2{,}000 - 940 = 1{,}060$
Percentage of students who could not pass exam $= \frac{1{,}060 \times 100}{2{,}000} = 53\%$

Answer: H

91. The expression $\frac{x^2-16}{x^3+8}$ has denominator $x^3 + 8$. When the denominator is zero, the expression is undefined. Therefore,
$x^3 + 8 = 0$
$x^3 = -8$
Taking cube root,
$x^3 = (-2)^3$
$x = -2$
Therefore, the expression is undefined at $x = -2$.
Answer: C

92. Total balls $= 50 + 50 + 100 = 200$

Blue balls taken away $= 24\%\ of\ 50$
$= 0.24 \times 50 = 12$ balls
Green balls taken away $= 16\%\ of\ 50$
$= 0.16 \times 50 = 8$ balls

Total balls taken away $= 12 + 8 = 20$
Balls left $= 200 - 20 = 180$ balls

White balls percentage $= \frac{100}{180} \times 100\%$
$= 55.56\% \approx 56\%$

Answer: G

Questions 93 - 98			
93.	Exterior angle $\angle C = 80°$, Interior angle $\angle C = 180° - 80° = 100°$ We know that, the sum of the measures of all interior angles of a quadrilateral is always 360°. Therefore, $110° + 130° + 100° + \angle D = 360°$ $340° + \angle D = 360°$ $\angle D = 360° - 340° = 20°$ **Answer:** A	96.	Selecting at least 3 men for a committee of 4 persons means that either 3 or 4 men should be selected. First case: 3 men and 1 woman: $C_3^6 \cdot C_1^5 = 20 \times 5 = 100$ Second case: 4 men: $C_4^6 = 15$ Total different ways $= 100 + 15 = 115$ **Answer:** G
94.	Since, $a : b = 3 : 7$, then $a = 3x,\ b = 7x$ Also, $b : c = 4 : 5$, then $b = 4y,\ c = 5y$. Since, $b = 7x$ and $b = 4y$, therefore, $7x = 4y \Rightarrow y = \frac{7}{4}x \quad (i)$ Plugin $y = \frac{7}{4}x$ from eq. (i) to $c = 5y$, $c = 5\left(\frac{7}{4}\right)x = \frac{35}{4}x$ Now, $a : c = 3x : \frac{35}{4}x$ $a : c = \frac{12}{4} : \frac{35}{4} = 12 : 35$ **Answer:** F	97.	In 25 liters of solution there is $25 \times 0.15 = 3.75\ L$ of juice concentrate. Let "x" liters be the amount of water added to the solution, then Amount of new solution $= (25 + x)\ L$ In this new solution, $3.75\ L$ of juice concentrate form 10%, therefore, $(25 + x)\ L \rightarrow\ 100\%$ $3.75\ L \rightarrow\ 10\%$ We can write the proportion as: $\frac{(25 + x)}{3.75} = \frac{100}{10}$ $25 + x = 37.5$ $x = 37.5 - 25 = 12.5$ L **Answer:** A
95.	The point where the medians of a triangle intersect each other is known as centroid and its coordinates can be calculated as: $\left(\frac{x_1 + x_2 + x_3}{3}, \frac{y_1 + y_2 + y_3}{3}\right)$ Therefore, the centroid of ΔABC is: $x_O = \frac{-3 + 6 + 9}{3} = \frac{12}{3} = 4$ $y_O = \frac{1 + 2 - 3}{3} = 0$ Therefore, the coordinates of point where medians of triangle meet are $(4, 0)$. **Answer:** D	98.	Let, number of coins Pamela has $= x$ be Number of coins Samantha has $= 3x$ After 6 days: $3x + (2 \times 6) = 2(x + (3 \times 6))$ $3x + 12 = 2(x + 18)$ $3x + 12 = 2x + 36$ $x = 24$ (Pamela's coins) Samantha's coins $= 3x = 3(24) = 72$ Let n be the number of days after which they have equal number of coins, then, $72 + 2n = 24 + 3n$ $n = 72 - 24 = 48$ days. **Answer:** H

Questions 99 - 104			
99.	The segment KL is the midline of the triangle ACD, therefore, $KL = \frac{1}{2}AC = \frac{1}{2} \times 12 = 6$ units. The height of the triangle BLK is $\frac{3}{4}$ of BD, hence, $h = \frac{3}{4} \times 8 = 6$ units. $Area\ of\ triangle = \frac{1}{2}(base)(height)$ Area of triangle BKL $= \frac{1}{2}(KL)(h)$ $= \frac{1}{2}(6)(6) = 18\ units^2$ **Answer:** C	102.	First die: Probability of getting a 3 $= \frac{1}{6}$ Second die: Probability of not getting 5 $= \frac{5}{6}$ Using the product rule, the probability of getting a 3 on the first die and not getting 5 on the second die can be calculated as: $\frac{1}{6} \cdot \frac{5}{6} = \frac{5}{36}$ **Answer:** H
100.	18 pineapples = 6 × 3 pineapples 18 pineapples = 6 × 228 olives 18 pineapples = 1,368 olives 18 pineapples = 12 × 114 olives 18 pineapples = 12 × 32 mandarins 18 pineapples = 384 mandarins **Answer:** E	103.	If $\frac{S}{M} = 12$, then $M = \frac{S}{12}$. Since $M < -4$, we get: $\frac{S}{12} < -4$ $S < -48$. The greatest possible value for S is -49. **Answer:** C
101.	Are of circle C $= A = \pi r^2$ Circumference of circle C $= C = 2\pi r$ Since, twice the area of a circle C is equal to 3 times the circumference, so, $2A = 3C$ $2\pi r^2 = 3(2\pi r)$ $2\pi r^2 = 6\pi r$ $r = \frac{6}{2} = 3\ units$ Since, radius of circle O is half as that of the radius of circle C, therefore, Radius of circle O $= r_1 = \frac{3}{2} = 1.5\ units$ Area of circle O $= \pi(r_1)^2$ $= \pi(1.5)^2 = 2.25\pi\ units^2$ **Answer:** C	104.	In the right triangle ACD, $\sin 30° = \frac{CD}{AD}$ $0.5 = \frac{4}{AD} \Rightarrow AD = \frac{4}{0.5} = 8\ units$ $\angle CDA = 90° - 30° = 60°$ The trapezoid ABCD is isosceles, therefore, base angles are congruent. $\angle A = \angle CDA = 60°$ and $\angle B = \angle C = 180° - 60° = 120°$. In the ΔABC, $\angle BCA = 120° - 90° = 30°$ $\angle BAC = 60° - 30° = 30°$ Since two of the angles of ΔABC are congruent, hence, ΔABC is isosceles and $AB = BC = CD = 4\ units.$ Perimeter of trapezoid $ABCD$ is $AB + BC + CD + AD$ $= 4 + 4 + 4 + 8 = 20$ units **Answer:** G

Questions 105 - 110

105. The first ten prime numbers are:
2, 3, 5, 7, 11, 13, 17, 19, 23, 29.

$$Average = \frac{Sum\ of\ quantities}{Number\ of\ quantities}$$

Sum of prime numbers $= 2 + 3 + 5 + 7 + 11 + 13 + 17 + 19 + 23 + 29 = 129$

Average $= \frac{129}{10} = 12.9$

Answer: A

106. Let the numerator of the fraction $= x$
Denominator $= x + 5$
Fraction $= \frac{x}{x+5}$.
When 8 is added to both numerator and denominator, the new fraction becomes $\frac{3}{4}$.
Therefore, we can write:

$$\frac{x+8}{x+5+8} = \frac{3}{4}$$

$$\frac{x+8}{x+13} = \frac{3}{4}$$

$4(x + 8) = 3(x + 13)$
$4x + 32 = 3x + 39 \Rightarrow x = 7$
Initial fraction $= \frac{x}{x+5} = \frac{7}{7+5} = \frac{7}{12}$
Answer: G

107. If n is an even number, $2n$ is an even number too. If m is an odd number, $3m$ is an odd number too.
$3m$ is an odd number, so $3m + 1$ is an even number. The sum of two even numbers $2n$ and $3m + 1$ is always an even number.
Answer: B

108. A regular hexagon consists of 6 equal equilateral triangles as shown below.

Each side of triangle is 2 cm.
Height of triangle $\sqrt{2^2 - 1^2} = \sqrt{3}\ cm$
Area of one triangle $= \frac{1}{2}(2)\sqrt{3}$
$= \sqrt{3}\ cm^2$
Area of hexagon = 6(Area of triangle)
$= 6\sqrt{3}\ cm^2$
The height of triangle is the same as the radius of the circle. $r = \sqrt{3}\ cm$
Area of the circle $= \pi r^2 = \pi(\sqrt{3})^2$
$= 3\pi\ cm^2$.
The area of the shaded region is:
$6\sqrt{3} - 3\pi\ cm^2$.
Answer: E

109. Diameter $= 21\ cm$
Circumference of circle $= \pi d$
$= 21\pi\ cm$
Using the approximation $\pi = \frac{22}{7}$, the circumference will be:
Circumference $= 21\pi = 21 \times \frac{22}{7}$
$= 3 \times 22 = 66\ cm$

Answer: C

110. The given infinite sequence consists of the pattern 1,2,3,4,5,6 that has a length of 6 numbers. Now,
$2019 = 336 \times 6 + 3$,
Then, the number at 2019th position in the sequence is the same as the 3rd number 3.
Answer: F

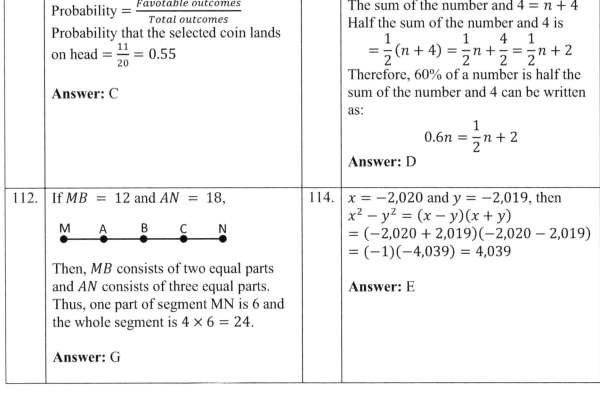

Questions 111 - 114			
111.	Total coins = 10 Total heads on 10 coins = 11 Total tails on 10 coins = 9 Total number of outcomes = 20 Probability = $\frac{Favotable\ outcomes}{Total\ outcomes}$ Probability that the selected coin lands on head = $\frac{11}{20} = 0.55$ **Answer:** C	113.	Let n be unknown number. 60% of n = 60% $\times n$ $= \frac{60}{100} \times n = 0.6n$ The sum of the number and 4 = $n + 4$ Half the sum of the number and 4 is $= \frac{1}{2}(n+4) = \frac{1}{2}n + \frac{4}{2} = \frac{1}{2}n + 2$ Therefore, 60% of a number is half the sum of the number and 4 can be written as: $0.6n = \frac{1}{2}n + 2$ **Answer:** D
112.	If $MB = 12$ and $AN = 18$, M A B C N Then, MB consists of two equal parts and AN consists of three equal parts. Thus, one part of segment MN is 6 and the whole segment is 4 × 6 = 24. **Answer:** G	114.	$x = -2{,}020$ and $y = -2{,}019$, then $x^2 - y^2 = (x-y)(x+y)$ $= (-2{,}020 + 2{,}019)(-2{,}020 - 2{,}019)$ $= (-1)(-4{,}039) = 4{,}039$ **Answer:** E

TEST 5: ANSWER KEYS

Q #	Answer
58	45
59	80
60	2
61	120
62	4.15
63	C
64	F
65	A
66	F
67	A
68	G
69	A
70	F
71	A
72	E
73	A
74	E
75	B
76	E
77	A

Q #	Answer
78	H
79	B
80	G
81	B
82	G
83	A
84	F
85	B
86	G
87	D
88	G
89	A
90	G
91	C
92	E
93	D
94	F
95	D
96	E
97	B

Q #	Answer
98	E
99	B
100	F
101	A
102	F
103	D
104	G
105	D
106	H
107	B
108	F
109	B
110	F
111	C
112	H
113	D
114	E

Practice Test 5: Answers & Explanations

GRID-IN QUESTIONS			
Questions 58 - 62			
58.	If EB is perpendicular to AC, then $\angle CBE$ is equal to 90°. Therefore, $\angle ABD$ and $\angle DBE$ are complementary, this means that: $\angle ABD + \angle DBE = 90°$. Since $\angle DBE = 45°$, therefore, $\angle ABD + 45° = 90°$ $\angle ABD = 90° - 45° = 45°$ **Answer**: 45°	61.	Tariq wants to visit New Jersey, Maryland, South Carolina, Washington and Fayetteville, in total 5 states. He can choose: 1st state in 5 different ways, 2nd state in 4 different ways, 3rd state in 3 different ways, 4th state in 2 different ways, last 5th state in 1 ways only. Thus, he has $5 \times 4 \times 3 \times 2 \times 1 = 120$ different ways of selecting the order of states to be visited. **Answer:** 120
59.	$Students : Teachers = 4 : 1$ Number of students $= 4x$ Number of teachers $= x$ Total people in the center = 400 then $4x + x = 400$ $5x = 400$ $x = \frac{400}{5} \Rightarrow x = 80$ Hence, there are 80 teachers in the center. **Answer:** 80	62.	Distance travelled = $4\frac{3}{20}$ km To convert to decimal form, we will find the decimal form of $\frac{3}{20}$ only as: $\frac{3}{20} = \frac{3\times5}{20\times5} = \frac{15}{100} = 0.15,$ Therefore, $4\frac{3}{20}$ km = 4.15 km **Answer:** 4.15 km
60.	$10x + 20 = 40$ $10x = 40 - 20$ $10x = 20.$ Divide the equality by 10: $x = \frac{20}{10} = 2$ **Answer:** 2		

MULTIPLE CHOICE QUESTIONS			
Questions 63 - 68			
63.	The triangle HMA is isosceles right triangle (because the quadrilateral $MATH$ is a square). Since the triangle HMA is isosceles, then, $MH = MA$. By the Pythagorean theorem, $(MH)^2 + (MA)^2 = (AH)^2$ $(MH)^2 + (MH)^2 = 4^2$ $2(MH)^2 = 16$ $(MH)^2 = 8 \Rightarrow MH = \sqrt{8}\ cm$ Area of the square= $side\ \times side$ Area of the square= $\sqrt{8}\ \times \sqrt{8} = 8\ cm^2$ **Answer:** C	66.	Let, Amount of money Benjamin lent = $\$x$ Brother got = $\frac{2}{3}x$ Remaining amount = $x - \frac{2}{3}x = \frac{1}{3}x$ If each friend receives $\frac{1}{2}$ of the remaining amount, then, Each friend got = $\frac{1}{2} \times \frac{1}{3}x = \frac{1}{6}x$ Since each friend got \$5,000, hence, $\frac{1}{6}x = 5{,}000 \Rightarrow x = \$30{,}000$ **Answer:** F
64.	First, simplify the expression $a^2 - (b + c) + b$ $= a^2 - b - c + b$ $= a^2 - c$ Plugin $a = -3$ and $c = 2$, we get, $a^2 - c = (-3)^2 - 2 = 9 - 2 = 7$ **Answer:** F	67.	$10a + 5b = 20$, then $10a = 20 - 5b$ $a = \frac{20 - 5b}{10}$ $a = \frac{20}{10} - \frac{5b}{10}$ $a = 2 - \frac{b}{2}$ **Answer:** A
65.	Let Noah's age = x years Liam's age = y years If Liam is 3 times as old as Noah, then $y = 3x\ \ (i)$ After 3 years, Liam will be 8 years more than two third of Noah's age, then $y + 3 = \frac{2}{3}(x + 3) + 8\ \ (ii)$ Substitute $y = 3x$ from eq. (i) into eq. (ii), $3x + 3 = \frac{2}{3}(x + 3) + 8$ $9x + 9 = 2x + 6 + 24$ $7x = 21 \Rightarrow x = 3$ **Answer:** A	68.	The teacher needs to make groups of 3 students from 9 students in a class. Then the teacher has $C_3^9 \cdot C_3^6 = \frac{9!}{3! \cdot (9-3)!} \times \frac{6!}{3! \cdot (6-3)!}$ $= \frac{9!}{3! \cdot 6!} \times \frac{6!}{3! \cdot 3!}$ $= 84 \times 20$ $= 1{,}680$ Therefore, 1,680 different combinations of groups can be made. **Answer:** G

Questions 69 - 74

69. Note that
$600 = 2 \times 300 = 2 \times 2 \times 150$
$= 2^2 \times 2 \times 75 = 2^3 \times 3 \times 25$
$= 2^3 \times 3 \times 5^2$
Therefore, the prime factorization of 600 is $2^3 \times 3 \times 5^2$.

Answer: A

70. If John can finish a certain job in 3 hours, then he completes $\frac{1}{3}$ of a job per hour.

Bobby can finish this job in 2 hours, then he completes $\frac{1}{2}$ of a job per hour.

Together they complete $\frac{1}{3} + \frac{1}{2} = \frac{5}{6}$ of a job in an hour.

Therefore, together they need $\frac{6}{5}$ hours to complete the job.

$\frac{6}{5}$ hours $= 1\frac{1}{5}$ hours.

Answer: F

71. Let $2k$ be the smallest even integer, then $2k,\ 2k+2,\ 2k+4$ are three even consecutive integers. Their sum is
$2k + 2k + 2 + 2k + 4 = 1{,}206$
$6k + 6 = 1{,}206$
$6k = 1{,}206 - 6$
$6k = 1{,}200$
$k = 200$
Least even integer $= 2k$
$= 2(200) = 400$
Greatest even integer $= 2k + 4$
$= 2(200) + 4 = 404$
Average of least and greatest even integers is
$= \dfrac{400 + 404}{2} = \dfrac{804}{2} = 402$
Answer: A

72. Total coins $= 3 + 5 + 10 + 7 = 25$
If Ethan selects 2 coins at random, without replacement, the probability that the first coin is a quarter and the second coin is a dime can be calculated as:
$\dfrac{10}{25} \times \dfrac{5}{24} = \dfrac{2}{5} \times \dfrac{5}{24} = \dfrac{1}{12}$

Answer: E

73. Side length of square = 6 units
Area of the square $= length \times length$
$= 6 \times 6 = 36\ units^2$
The diagonal of the square is the diameter of the circle, therefore, to find the diagonal, we will use Pythagorean theorem,
$d^2 = 6^2 + 6^2$
$d^2 = 36 + 36 = 72$
$d = 6\sqrt{2}$ units
Radius $= r = \frac{d}{2} = 3\sqrt{2}$ units
Area of the circle $= \pi r^2$
$= \pi \cdot \left(3\sqrt{2}\right)^2 = 18\pi\ units^2$
The area of the shaded region will be:
$(18\pi - 36) units^2$

Answer: A

74. $y = -1.5$
Also
$|y - z| = 10.5$
Since $y < z$, therefore, $y - z < 0$, hence
$y - z = -10.5$
$-1.5 - z = -10.5$
$z = 10.5 - 1.5 = 9$
Now,
$|x - z| = 30.5$
Since $x < z$, therefore, $x - z < 0$, hence
$x - z = -30.5$
Plugin $z = 9$, we get,
$x - 9 = -30.5$
$x = 9 - 30.5 = -21.5$

Answer: E

Questions 75 - 80			
75.	Cost for first 10 minutes = k cents Cost for each additional minute= g cents Since, $m > 10$ minutes, then First 10 minutes cost = k cents Remaining $(m-10)$ minutes will cost $= (m-10)g$ cents Total cost $= k + (m-10)g$ cents. **Answer:** B	78.	Let, original price of the gift = $\$x$, then Discount received = 15% Price percentage paid $= (100-15)\%$ $= 85\%$ Since, Jackson paid \$68 after getting 15% discount, therefore, $x \times 85\% = 68$ $x \times 0.85 = 68$ $x = \frac{68}{0.85} = \$80$ **Answer:** H
76.	$\frac{k+g}{a} = \frac{4}{m}$ $(k+g)m = 4a$ $a = \frac{m(k+g)}{4}$ Then $\frac{a}{6} = \frac{m(k+g)}{24}$ **Answer:** E	79.	Scale used on the map is $\frac{3}{4} in = 1{,}000\ km$ Distance between two villages on the map $= 1\frac{7}{8}\ in = \frac{15}{8} in$. Now, $\frac{3}{4}\ in = 1{,}000\ km$ $\frac{15}{8}\ in = x\ km$ We can write the proportion as: $\frac{x}{1{,}000} = \frac{15}{8} \div \frac{3}{4}$ $x = \frac{15}{8} \times \frac{4}{3} \times 1{,}000 = 2{,}500\ km.$ **Answer:** B
77.	Let Jacob's age = j years Sofia's age = s years Lucas's age = l years Since, Jacob is six times as old as Sofia, then, $j = 6s \quad (i)$ Jacob is $2\frac{3}{4}$ times as old as Lucas is, then $j = 2\frac{3}{4}l \quad (ii)$ From eq. (i) and (ii), we can write: $6s = 2\frac{3}{4}l$ $6s = \frac{11}{4}l$ $24s = 11l$ $\frac{l}{s} = \frac{24}{11} = 2\frac{2}{11}$ **Answer:** A	80.	Since, $AH = HT$, then ΔAHT is an isosceles triangle. Since $\angle AHT = 120°$, then $\angle HAT + \angle HTA = 180° - 120° = 60°$ In the isosceles ΔAHT, angles HAT and HTA are congruent, hence, $\angle HAT = \angle HTA = 30°$ Segments AH and TH bisect $\angle MAT$ and $\angle MTA$ respectively, then $\angle MAT = \angle MTA = 60°$. In ΔAMT, $\angle MAT + \angle M + \angle MTA = 180°$ $\angle M = 180° - \angle MAT - \angle MTA$ $\angle M = 180° - 60° - 60° = 60°$. **Answer:** G

Questions 81 - 86			
81.	Total donors $= 400$ Percent donor of AB type blood $= 11\%$ Number of donors having AB blood type $= 400 \times 11\%$ $= 400 \times \frac{11}{100}$ $= 44$ donors **Answer:** B	84.	Average $= \frac{Sum\ of\ quantities}{Number\ of\ quantities}$ Average of David's score: $\frac{70+85+90+88+97+89}{6} = \frac{519}{6} = 86.5$ Average of Camilia's score: $\frac{76+80+85+95+100+92}{6} = \frac{528}{6} = 88$ The difference between the average scores of David and Camilia's is: $88 - 86.5 = 1.5$ **Answer:** F
82.	Jar A: Total marbles $= 7$ Red marbles $= 4$, Blue marbles $= 3$ $P(x = Red\ marble) = \frac{4}{7}$ Jar B: Total marbles after placing one marble from Jar A to jar B $= 7 + 1 = 8$ Black marbles $= 5$, Yellow marbles $= 2$ If the marble placed into Jar B is red, then, the probability of choosing red marble is $\frac{1}{8}$. Therefore, the probability of choosing a red marble from Jar B is $\frac{4}{7} \cdot \frac{1}{8} = \frac{1}{14}$ **Answer:** G	85.	2 0.5 1 3 3 5 We know that, Area of rectangle $= length \times width$ Area of big rectangle $= (3 + 5 + 1) \times (2 + 3)$ $= 9 \times 5 = 45\ units^2$ Sum of area of two small dotted rectangles $= (3 \times 3) + (4.5 \times 1)$ $9 + 4.5 = 13.5\ units^2$ Area of given polygon $= 45 - 13.5$ $= 31.5\ units^2$ **Answer:** B
83.	$-2x + 4 > 12$: $-2x > 12 - 4$ $-2x > 8$ $2x < -8$ $x < -4$ If x is an even integer, then the greatest possible value of x is -6 **Answer:** A	86.	Let $x = 1.\bar{4} = 1.4444 \ldots$ $10x = 14.4444 \ldots$ Subtracting both equations, we get: $10x - x = 13$ $9x = 13$ $x = \frac{13}{9} = 1\frac{4}{9}$ **Answer:** G

Questions 87 - 92

87. $\frac{1}{4}$ of 2^{20} is

$\frac{1}{4} \times 2^{20}$

$= \frac{1}{2^2} \times 2^{20}$

$= 2^{20-2}$

$= 2^{18} = (2^2)^9 = 4^9$

Answer: D

88. Make a two way table with given data.

	Toyota	No Toyota	Total
BMW	20		275
No BMW		50	
Total	250		

Fill in the table as:

	Toyota	No Toyota	Total
BMW	20		275
No BMW	**230**	50	**280**
Total	250		**555**

Therefore, there are 555 people in the community.

Answer: G

89. When $x = -1$, then:

$-4x^2 = -4(-1)^2 = -4(1) = -4$,

$3x^3 = 3(-1)^3 = 3 \cdot (-1) = -3$,

$x = -1$,

$\frac{x^3}{2} = \frac{(-1)^3}{2} = -\frac{1}{2}$,

1

The smallest number in the set is -4 i.e. $-4x^2$.

Answer: A

90. Between 1,040 and 3,060, first number that is divisible by 3 is 1,041 and last number divisible by 3 is 3,060. Then we can make an arithmetic series of multiples of 3 between 1,040 and 3,060 as:

1,041, 1,044, 1,047, 1,050, …, 3,060

$a_n = a_1 + (n-1)d$

$3{,}060 = 1{,}041 + (n-1)3$

$2{,}019 = 3(n-1)$

$n - 1 = 673 \Rightarrow n = 674$

Answer: G

91. People supporting Team A = 30

People supporting Team B = 40

Total people = 70

Let x be the number of additional team A supporters to make 60%. Then

$70 + x$ - 100%

$30 + x$ - 60%

$\frac{70 + x}{30 + x} = \frac{100}{60}$

$\frac{70 + x}{30 + x} = \frac{5}{3}$

$3(70 + x) = 5(30 + x)$

$210 + 3x = 150 + 5x$

$2x = 60 \Rightarrow x = 30$

Answer: C

92. The expression $\frac{x-4}{x^3-27}$ is undefined when the denominator $x^3 - 27$ becomes 0.

$x^3 - 27 = 0$

$x^3 = 27$

$x = 3$

Therefore, the expression $\frac{x-4}{x^3-27}$ is undefined at $x = 3$.

Answer: E

Questions 93 - 98			
93.	Initial number of students = 2,000 Final number of students = 2,600 We know that percent increase can be calculated using formula: $\frac{New\ Value - Old\ Value}{Old\ Value} \times 100\%$ $= \frac{2{,}600 - 2{,}000}{2{,}000} \times 100\%$ $= \frac{600}{2{,}000} \times 100\% = 30\%$ **Answer:** D	96.	$A(-4,3), B(5,-1)$ Since, point C is the midpoint of the points A and B, therefore, coordinates of point C are: $\left(\frac{-4+5}{2}, \frac{3+(-1)}{2}\right)$ $= \left(\frac{1}{2}, \frac{3-1}{2}\right)$ $= \left(\frac{1}{2}, \frac{2}{2}\right) = \left(\frac{1}{2}, 1\right)$ **Answer:** E
94.	A regular pentadecagon is a 15-sided polygon with all congruent interior angles and congruent sides. We know that, sum of interior angles of any n sided polygon is $(n-2) \times 180°$. Therefore, the sum of all interior angles of pentadecagon can be calculated as: $(15-2) \times 180° = 2{,}340°$ Since, all angles of a regular pentadecagon are congruent, therefore, measure of each interior angle is: $\frac{2{,}340°}{15} = 156°$ **Answer:** F	97.	Since triangles ABC and DEF are similar triangles, then corresponding angles are congruent. Hence, $\angle A = \angle D = 70°$ $\angle C = \angle F = 60°$ $\angle B = \angle E$ Since, sum of interior angles of a triangle is always 180°, therefore, $\angle A + \angle B + \angle C = 180°$ $70° + \angle B + 60° = 180°$ $\angle B + 130° = 180°$ $\angle B = 180° - 130° = 50°$ **Answer:** B
95.	Diameter of a hydrogen atom = 10^{-10} m Diameter of red blood cell = 8×10^{-6} m To find the number of times, the diameter of a red blood cell is bigger than the diameter of a hydrogen atom, we proceed as follows: $\frac{8\times10^{-6}}{10^{-10}}$ $= 8 \times 10^{-6-(-10)}$ $= 8 \times 10^{-6+10}$ $= 8 \times 10^{4}$ **Answer:** D	98.	14 people can sit on a bench. Total people in community center = 379 To find the number of people on the farthest right bench, when each bench can accommodate 14 people only, we can write 379 as: $379 = 14 \times 27 + 1$ Therefore, there will be only 1 person on the bench that is farthest to the right. **Answer:** E

Questions 99 - 104			
99.	Let n be the number of months needed by Oliver and Aria to have the same number of marbles. Number of marbles Oliver has = 500 Marbles Oliver gets each month = 50 After n months, Marbles Oliver has $= 500 + 50n$ (i) Number of marbles Aria has = 800 Marbles Oliver gets each month = 20 After n months, Marbles Aria has $= 800 + 20n$ (ii) marbles. Aria has 800 marbles and receives 20 marbles per month from her aunt, then she will have $800 + 20n$ Equating eq. (i) and (ii) $500 + 50n = 800 + 20n,$ $30n = 300 \Rightarrow n = 10$ months **Answer:** B	102.	Radius $= r = 14$ inches Circumference of circle $= 2\pi r$ Circumference$= 2\pi \times 14 = 28\pi$ inches Revolutions the wheel make = 24 Distance the bicycle travelled $= 24 \times 28\pi$ $= 24 \times 28 \times \frac{22}{7}$ $= 24 \times 4 \times 22$ $= 2{,}112$ inches We know that, $12\ inches = 1\ ft$ $1\ inch = \frac{1}{12}\ ft$ $2{,}112\ inches = \frac{2{,}112}{12}\ ft = 176\ ft$ **Answer:** F
100.	Consider the right triangle FAE. Using Pythagorean theorem, $(AF)^2 = (AE)^2 + (FE)^2$ $5^2 = 3^2 + (AE)^2$ $(AE)^2 = 25 - 9 = 16$ $AE = 4$ ABDE is a square, therefore, $AB = 4$ $FC = 3 + 4 + 3 = 10$ Area of trapezoid AFCB is: $\left(\frac{AB + FC}{2}\right) AE = \left(\frac{4 + 10}{2}\right) 4$ $= \left(\frac{14}{2}\right) 4 = 28\ units^2$ **Answer:** F	103.	Red flowers = 10 White flowers = 5 Mixed flowers = 3 Total flowers = 10 + 5 + 3 = 18 The probability that one flower picked at random will be a white flower $= \frac{5}{18}$ **Answer:** D
101.	3 apples = 4 bananas (i) 3 bananas = 9 cherries (ii) We need to find how many cherries can John buy at the cost of 1 apple. From eq. (i): 1 apple $= \frac{4}{3}$ bananas 1 apple $= \frac{4}{9} \times 3$ bananas 1 apple $= \frac{4}{9} \times 9$ cherries from eq. (ii) 1 apple = 4 cherries **Answer:** A	104.	The diagonals of the rhombus are perpendicular, therefore, ΔHMO is right triangle. By the Pythagorean theorem, $(HM)^2 = (HO)^2 + (MO)^2$ $10^2 = 6^2 + (MO)^2$ $(MO)^2 = 100 - 36 = 64$ $MO = 8$ units Hence, lengths of the diagonals of rhombus are $12cm$ and $16cm$. Area of rhombus $= \frac{12 \times 16}{2} = 96\ cm^2$ **Answer:** G

<table>
<tr><th colspan="4">Questions 105 - 110</th></tr>
<tr><td>105.</td><td>$\frac{20}{K} = y \quad (i) \qquad y > 20 \quad (ii)$
From eq. (i) and (ii), we can write:
$\frac{20}{K} > 20 \Rightarrow \frac{1}{K} > 1$
Since k is in the denominator, it cannot be equal to zero, also it cannot take negative values, because for negative values inequality will not hold. Hence,
$\frac{1}{K} > 1 \Rightarrow 1 > K \Rightarrow K < 1$
All value between 0 and 1 will satisfy the inequality. $K \in (0,1)$ or $0 < K < 1$

Answer: D</td><td>108.</td><td>If $K + C = 10 \quad (i)$
$K - C = 20 \quad (ii)$
Adding eq. (i) and (ii),
$K + C + K - C = 10 + 20$
$2K = 30 \Rightarrow K = 15$
Plugin $K = 15$ in eq. (i), we get,
$K + C = 10$
$15 + C = 10 \Rightarrow C = -5$
Hence,
$K^2 + 2C = (15)^2 + 2(-5)$
$= 225 - 10 = 215$

Answer: F</td></tr>
<tr><td>106.</td><td>Speed during first 10 hours = 50 miles/hr
Distance covered in 10 hours $= 50 \times 10$
$= 500$ miles
Total distance covered $= 500 + 300$
$= 800$ miles
Fuel needed in 20 miles = 1 gallon
Fuel needed in 800 miles $= \frac{800}{20}$
$= 40$ gallons
Cost of each gallon = \$3.20
Cost of 40 gallons $= 3.20 \times 40 =$ \$128

Answer: H</td><td>109.</td><td>Each angle of equilateral ΔABC measures 60°. Hence,
Angle subtended by arc AC = 60°
Which is $\frac{1}{6}$ of the full rotation 360°.
Hence, length of arc AC will also be $\frac{1}{6}$ of the circumference of the circle.
Length of arc AC $= \frac{1}{6}(2\pi r) = \frac{1}{3}\pi r$
$= \frac{1}{3}\pi(6) = 2\pi \; units$
Perimeter of shaded region
$= 2\pi + 6 \; units$
Answer: B</td></tr>
<tr><td>107.</td><td>In a garden, Rose : Dahlia = 3: 2
Number of roses $= 3x$
Number of dahlias $= 2x$
$3x + 2x = 100 \Rightarrow x = 20$
In the shop Rose : Dahlia = 1: 4
Number of roses $= y$
Number of dahlias $= 4y$
Combined Roses $= 3x + 2y$
Combined dahlias $= 2x + 4y$
$\frac{3x + y}{2x + 4y} = \frac{1}{2}$
$6x + 2y = 2x + 4y$
$4x = 2y \Rightarrow 2x = y$
$y = 2(20) = 40$
Total number of flowers in flower shop =
$y + 4y = 5y = 5(40) = 200$.

Answer: B</td><td>110.</td><td>Eggs sold in April = 100 dozens
Eggs sold in May = 250 dozens

Percent increase can be calculated using formula:
$\frac{New\ Value - Old\ Value}{Old\ Value} \times 100\%$
$= \frac{250 - 100}{100} \times 100\%$
$= \frac{150}{100} \times 100\%$
$= 150\%$

Answer: F</td></tr>
</table>

Questions 111 - 114			
111.	$0, 2, 4, A, B$ The first symbol in the password can be chosen in 4 different ways because 0 cannot be at 1st position. the last symbol – in 3 ways, because 0 cannot be at last position. the 2nd symbol – in 3 ways the 3rd symbol – in 2 ways the 4th symbol – in 1 way Total ways = $4 \times 3 \times 3 \times 2 \times 1$ = 72 ways **Answer:** C	113.	Let the number of adults $= x$ Number of children $= y$ Then, $x + y = 40 \ldots (i)$ The entry ticket to the park cost \$20 per adult and \$10 per child, hence, $20x + 10y = 500 \ldots (ii)$ From the eq(i), $x = 40 - y$, substitute it in eq(ii), $20(40 - y) + 10y = 500$ $800 - 20y + 10y = 500$ $300 = 10y$ $y = 30$ Therefore, 30 children were on the trip. **Answer:** D
112.	$3^a \times 7^b = 3087 \ldots (i)$ Let's write 3087 as a product of its prime factors: $3087 = 3 \times 3 \times 7 \times 7 \times 7$ $3087 = 3^2 \times 7^3 \ldots (ii)$ Comparing eq(i) and (ii), we get: $a = 2$ and $b = 3$. Thus, $(a - b)^2 = (2 - 3)^2$ $= (-1)^2 = 1$ **Answer:** H	114.	Since, $a * b = a^2 - b$, therefore, $2 * 7 = 2^2 - 7 = 4 - 7 = -3$ $(2 * 7) * 4 = -3 * 4 = (-3)^2 - 4$ $= 9 - 4 = 5$ **Answer:** E

TEST 6: ANSWER KEYS

Q #	Answer
58	8.45
59	9
60	10
61	45
62	9000
63	B
64	G
65	D
66	F
67	A
68	F
69	C
70	E
71	C
72	F
73	A
74	H
75	B
76	E
77	C

Q #	Answer
78	G
79	B
80	E
81	B
82	H
83	A
84	E
85	B
86	G
87	B
88	F
89	D
90	G
91	A
92	G
93	D
94	E
95	D
96	F
97	C

Q #	Answer
98	E
99	A
100	H
101	B
102	F
103	A
104	G
105	A
106	H
107	C
108	E
109	B
110	H
111	B
112	E
113	B
114	H

Practice Test 6: Answers & Explanations

GRID-IN QUESTIONS			
Questions 58 - 62			
58.	Tariq drives $8\frac{9}{20}$ kilometers. To convert it to decimal, we will find the decimal form of the fractional part as: $\frac{9}{20} = \frac{9 \times 5}{20 \times 5} = \frac{45}{100} = 0.45$ Then, $8\frac{9}{20} = 8.45.$ **Answer:** 8.45	61.	We know that, Distance = Speed×Time Distance covered in $\frac{1}{2}$ hr $= 60 \times \frac{1}{2}$ $= 30\ miles$ Distance covered in $1\frac{1}{2}$ hr $= 40 \times 1\frac{1}{2}$ $= 40 \times \frac{3}{2} = 60\ miles$ Total distance $= 30 + 60 = 90\ miles$ Total time taken $= \frac{1}{2} + 1\frac{1}{2} = 2\ hrs$ Speed $= \frac{Distance}{Time} = \frac{90}{2} = 45\ mph$ **Answer:** 45 mph
59.	$\frac{a+3}{a-9}$ is undefined, when the denominator $a - 9$ becomes zero. $a - 9 = 0 \Rightarrow a = 9$ Therefore, then given expression is undefined at $a = 9$. **Answer:** 9	62.	Since, the passcode cannot start with 0, therefore, to set a 4-digit passcode: 1st digit in can be chosen in 9 ways, 2nd digit – in 10 ways 3rd digit – in 10 ways 4th digit – in 10 ways. Therefore, $9 \times 10 \times 10 \times 10 = 9{,}000$ different passcodes can be made. **Answer:** 9,000
60.	4 pencils cost as much as 2 pens, then 2 pencils cost as much as 1 pen. 5 pens cost as much as one book, 1 book = 5 pens, 1 book $= 5 \times 2 = 10$ pencils. **Answer:** 10		

MULTIPLE CHOICE QUESTIONS			
Questions 63 - 68			
63.	$6k + 7m = 14$ $7m = 14 - 6k$ $m = \frac{14}{7} - \frac{6}{7}k$ $m = 2 - \frac{6}{7}k$ **Answer:** B	66.	Total crayons in Box $X = 5 + 6 = 11$ Black crayons = 5, Blue crayons = 6 Probability of selecting a blue crayon from box $X = \frac{6}{11}$ Total crayons in box Y after placing one crayon selected from box $X = 8 + 3 + 1$ $= 12$ Probability of selecting a blue crayon from box $= \frac{6}{11} \times \frac{1}{12} = \frac{1}{22}$ **Answer:** F
64.	Total marbles $= 5 + 6 + 7 = 18$ Probability of choosing a blue marble first $= \frac{6}{18} = \frac{1}{3}$ Since the blue marble is no replaced, there are 17 marbles left now. The probability of choosing the 2nd marble white $= \frac{7}{17}$ Then the probability that the 1st marble is blue and the 2nd marble is white is: $\frac{1}{3} \times \frac{7}{17} = \frac{7}{51}$ **Answer:** G	67.	$\frac{1}{8}$ of 2^{10} is $= \frac{1}{8} \times 2^{10}$ $= \frac{1}{2^3} \times 2^{10}$ $= 2^{10-3}$ $= 2^7$ **Answer:** A
65.	Let, Jackson's age $= x$ years, then Alexander's age $= 3x$ years Let, Grace's age $= y$ years, then Alexander's age $= 5y$ years Thus we can write: $3x = 5y$ $y = \frac{3}{5}x = 0.60x$ This means that Grace's age is 60% of Jackson's age. **Answer:** D	68.	Since, ΔCAT and ΔXYZ are similar, hence, their corresponding sides are proportional. Therefore, $\frac{CA}{XY} = \frac{AT}{YZ}$ $\frac{4}{6} = \frac{AT}{10}$ $AT = \frac{4}{6} \times 10$ $AT = \frac{2}{3} \times 10 = \frac{20}{3} = 6\frac{2}{3}$ **Answer:** F

Questions 69 - 74			
69.	Male Employees : Female Employees $= 1:3$ Number of male employees $= x$ Number of female employees $= 3x$ $x + 3x = 200 \Rightarrow 4x = 200 \Rightarrow x = 50$ Male Customers : Female Customers $= 1:5$ Number of male customers $= y$ Number of female customers $= 5y$ When employees and customers are combined, the ratio of male to female is $1:4$, therefore, $\frac{x+y}{3x+5y} = \frac{1}{4} \Rightarrow \frac{50+y}{3(50)+5y} = \frac{1}{4}$ $200 + 4y = 150 + 5y$ $y = 50$, Customers visit coffee shop on Sunday $= y + 5y = 6y = 6(50) = 300$ **Answer:** C	72.	Let $2n + 1$ be the smallest odd integer, then $2n + 3$ and $2n + 5$ are the two next odd integers. The sum of these consecutive odd integers in 1,437, therefore, $2n + 1 + 2n + 3 + 2n + 5 = 1{,}437$ $6n + 9 = 1{,}437$ $6n = 1{,}437 - 9$ $n = \frac{1{,}428}{6} = 238$ Least odd integer $= 2n + 1$ $= 2(238) + 1 = 477$ Greatest odd integer $= 2n + 5$ $= 2(238) + 5 = 481$ The sum of the least and the greatest odd integer is $477 + 481 = 958$. **Answer:** F
70.	Write 1,728 as a product of its prime factors as: $1{,}728 = 2^6 \times 3^3$ Compare it with $2^c \cdot 3^k = 1{,}728$, we get, $c = 6,\ k = 3$ $c + k = 6 + 3 = 9$ **Answer:** E	73.	Let, original price of book $= x$ Price after 10% discount $= x - 0.1x$ $= 0.9x$ Tax paid $= 0.08 \times 0.9x = 0.072x$ Saqib paid $= 0.9x + 0.072x = 0.972x$ Therefore, $0.972x = 97.20$ $x = \frac{97.20}{0.972} = 100$ Therefore, original price of the book is \$100. **Answer:** A
71.	$(m + A)^2 - (T - H)^2 =?$ Plugin the values of m, A, T and H: $= \left(-3 + (-2)\right)^2 - \left(3 - (-1)\right)^2$ $= (-3 - 2)^2 - (3 + 1)^2$ $= (-5)^2 - 4^2 = 25 - 16 = 9$ **Answer:** C	74.	Area of rectangle $= Length \times Width$ $A = (x + 3)(x + 2)$ $A = x^2 + 2x + 3x + 6$ $A = x^2 + 5x + 6$ **Answer:** H

Questions 75 - 80			
75.	Let n be the number of years after which Jack and David will have the same amount of money. After n years, amount of money Jack will have = $50{,}000 + 1{,}500n$ After n years, amount of money, David will have =$60{,}000 + 500n$ They will have same amount, hence, $50{,}000 + 1{,}500n = 60{,}000 + 500n$ $1{,}000n = 10{,}000$ $n = 10$ years **Answer:** B	78.	Total shirts purchased = 20 Cost of 2 shirts = $\$x$ Cost of remaining 18 shirts = $\$18y$ Thus, Total cost of 20 shirts = $\$(x + 18y)$ **Answer:** G
76.	Let, the numbers of adults = x Number of children = y Then, $x + y = 50 \quad (i)$ Since, tickets cost \$20 each adult and \$10 each child, then, $20x + 10y = 700 \quad (ii)$ Substitute $x = 50 - y$, from eq. (i) into eq. (ii), then $20(50 - y) + 10y = 700$ $1{,}000 - 20y + 10y = 700$ $10y = 300$ $y = 30$ The number of adult tickets sold were: $x = 50 - 30 = 20$ **Answer:** E	79.	Number of students who weigh more than 150 pounds = $7 + 5 = 12$ Total students in class = 40 Percentage = $\frac{12}{40} \times 100\% = 30\%$. **Answer:** B
77.	Total people in meeting = 80 Unemployed = $\frac{1}{5} \times 80 = 16$ Employed = $80 - 16 = 64$ Engineers = $\frac{3}{8} \times 64 = 24$ Employed people who were not engineers = $64 - 24 = 40$ **Answer:** C	80.	Number of employees in 2014 = 400 Number of employees in 2016 = 300 Percent decrease = $\frac{Old\ Value - New\ Value}{Old\ Value}$ Percent decrease = $\frac{400-300}{400} \times 100\%$ $= \frac{100}{400} \times 100\% = 25\%$ **Answer:** E

Questions 81 - 86			
81.	Diameter of car's wheel = $28\ inches$ We know that, Circumference of circle = πd Circumference of wheel = $28\pi\ inches$ $= 28 \times \frac{22}{7} = 88\ inches$ Distance covered by car = $176\ ft$ $= 176 \times 12\ in = 2{,}112\ in$ Number of revolutions = $\frac{2{,}112}{88} = 24$ **Answer:** B	84.	Write 1,176 as a product of its prime factors as: $1{,}176 = 2 \times 588$ $= 2 \times 2 \times 294$ $= 2^2 \times 2 \times 147$ $= 2^3 \times 3 \times 49$ $= 2^3 \times 3 \times 7^2$ **Answer:** E
82.	Total books = 4 He can choose: The 1st book in 4 different ways, the 2nd book – in 3 ways, the 3rd book – in 2 ways and the last book – in 1 way. Total different combinations: $= 4 \times 3 \times 2 \times 1 = 24$ **Answer:** H	85.	The triangle HAT is a right isosceles triangle with hypotenuse $4\sqrt{2}\ units$. By Pythagorean theorem, $(HT)^2 + (TA)^2 = \left(4\sqrt{2}\right)^2$ $(TA)^2 + (TA)^2 = 32$ $2(TA)^2 = 32 \Rightarrow (TA)^2 = 16$ $TA = HT = 4\ units$ Area of square MATH = 4×4 $= 16\ units^2$ Area of circle = $\pi r^2 = \pi \times 2^2$ $= 4\pi\ units^2$ Area of shaded region = $16 - 4\pi$ $= 4(4 - \pi)\ units^2$ **Answer:** B
83.	Let, Jackson's age = x years Jacob's age= y years Jacob is three times as old as Jackson, so, $y = 3x \ldots (i)$ In 4 years, Jacob will be 14 years more than $\frac{1}{4}$ of Jackson: $y + 4 = \frac{1}{4}(x + 4) + 14$ Substitute $y = 3x$ from eq(i): $3x + 4 = \frac{1}{4}(x + 4) + 14$ $12x + 16 = x + 4 + 56$ $11x = 44 \Rightarrow x = 4$ Jackson is 4 years old now. **Answer:** A	86.	Let, David's age = x years Bobby's age= $1\frac{1}{5}\ x$ years Let, Rose's age = y years Bobby's age = $1\frac{1}{2}\ y$ year Then, $1\frac{1}{5}\ x = 1\frac{1}{2}y$ $\frac{6}{5}x = \frac{3}{2}y$ $12x = 15y$ $y = \frac{12}{15}x = \frac{4}{5}x$ Therefore Rose's age is $\frac{4}{5}$ of David's age. **Answer:** G

Questions 87 - 92			
87.	Total students $= 2{,}000$ Algebra students percentage $= 14\%$ Number of students who take Algebra class $= \frac{14}{100} \times 2{,}000 = 280$ students **Answer:** B	90.	The measure of each interior angle of a regular n-sided polygon is $\frac{(n-2)\times 180°}{n}$. Therefore, $\frac{(n-2)\times 180°}{n} = 144°$ $180° \times (n-2) = 144° \times n,$ $180n - 360 = 144n$ $180n - 144n = 360$ $36n = 360 \Rightarrow n = 10.$ **Answer:** G
88.	We know that, Perimeter of square $= 4 \times Side\ length$ Perimeter of square $= 4 \times 3 = 12\ units$ If x is the side length of the equilateral triangle, then, Perimeter of equilateral triangle $= 3x$ Since perimeter of equilateral triangle and perimeter of square are the same, therefore, $3x = 12 \Rightarrow x = 4\ units$ Area of equilateral triangle $= \frac{\sqrt{3}}{4}x^2$ is $= \frac{\sqrt{3}}{4} \times 4^2 = 4\sqrt{3}\ units^2$ **Answer:** F	91.	The goal of writing a number in scientific notation is to have a decimal number, with one digit to the left of the decimal point, followed by a power of 10 as 10^a. Thus, 563.18×10^3 $= 5.6318 \times 100 \times 10^3$ $= 5.6318 \times 10^5$ **Answer:** A
89.	$3a(5b - 5a) = 30$ Plugin $a = -2,$ $3(-2)\big(5b - 5(-2)\big) = 30$ $-6(5b + 10) = 30$ $(5b + 10) = -\frac{30}{6}$ $5b + 10 = -5$ $5b = -15$ $b = -\frac{15}{5} = -3$ **Answer:** D	92.	$J = 2^2 \times 3 \times 7^2$ $K = 2 \times 3^4 \times 7.$ Then $LCM(J, K) = 2 \times 3 \times 7 \times 2 \times 3^3 \times 7$ $= 2^2 \times 3^4 \times 7^2$ **Answer:** G

Questions 93 - 98			
93.	Total letters from A to P $= 16$ Since, $417 = 16 \times 26 + 1$, Therefore, 417th sharpie will be marked with 1st letter A. **Answer:** D	96.	For any integer k, $3k$ is multiple of 3. Then $3k+3,\ 3k+6$ and $3k+9$ are next three multiples of 3. **Answer:** F
94.	Let's find the percent increase during each period. Percent increase formula is: $\frac{New\ Value - Old\ Value}{Old\ Value} \times 100\%$ The percent increase during: $2003 - 2006: \frac{8-4}{4} \times 100\% = 100\%$ $2006 - 2009: \frac{15-8}{8} \times 100\% = 87.5\%,$ $2012 - 2015: \frac{40-22}{22} \times 100\% \approx 82\%,$ $2015 - 2018: \frac{70-40}{40} \times 100\% = 75\%.$ **Answer:** E	97.	Let, total chocolates in the box $= x$ On Monday, Jason ate $= \frac{1}{7}$ of chocolates $= \frac{1}{7} \times x = \frac{x}{7}$ On Tuesday, Jason ate $= 16$ chocolates Total chocolates Jason ate $= \frac{x}{7} + 16 \quad (i)$ Chocolates left in box $= \frac{2}{3}x$ Chocolates Jason ate $= x - \frac{2}{3}x = \frac{x}{3} \quad (ii)$ Eq. (i) and (ii), both represent the number of chocolates, Jason ate, therefore, $\frac{x}{3} = \frac{x}{7} + 16$ $7x = 3x + 336$ $4x = 336 \Rightarrow x = 84$ **Answer:** C
95.	Each of the angle of all four equilateral triangles is 60°. Also, we know that the sum of all the angles about a common vertex, forming a circle, is always 360°, therefore, $a° + 60° + b° + 60° + c° + 60° + d° + 60° = 360°$ $a° + b° + c° + d° = 360° - 240°$ $a° + b° + c° + d° = 120°$ Hence, the average of all four angles is $\frac{a° + b° + c° + d°}{4} = \frac{120°}{4} = 30°$ **Answer:** D	98.	Cost of k pencils $= \$x$, Cost of one pencil $= \$\frac{x}{k}$ At the same rate, y pencils will cost $\$\frac{x}{k} \times y = \$\frac{xy}{k}$ **Answer:** E

Questions 99 - 104			
99.	Since, $B * A = 2A - B$, then $3 * 2 = 2 \times 2 - 3 = 4 - 3 = 1$ Also, $A \Delta B = 3B$, so $2\Delta 3 = 3 \times 3 = 9$ Hence, $(3 * 2) * (2\Delta 3) = 1 * 9$ $= 2 \times 9 - 1 = 18 - 1 = 17$ **Answer:** A	102.	$\sqrt{(-8+1)^2 + (-5+4)^2}$ $= \sqrt{(-7)^2 + (-1)^2}$ $= \sqrt{49 + 1}$ $= \sqrt{50}$ $= \sqrt{25 \times 2}$ $= 5\sqrt{2}$ **Answer:** F
100.	The worst situation is if 9 quarters were pulled, then 8 dimes and then 3 nickels. So, minimum coins to be pulled $= 9 + 8 + 3 = 20$ **Answer:** H	103.	1 USD = 2.12 Fijian dollars then 1 Fijian dollar $= \frac{1}{2.12}$ USD $= \frac{100}{212} = \frac{25}{53}$ USD 318 Fijian dollars = $318 \times \frac{25}{53}$ USD $= 150$ USD **Answer:** A
101.	We know that, Area of triangle $= \frac{1}{2} \times Base \times Height$ Base is the distance between the points (3,3) and (6,3), which can be calculated by subtracting the x-coordinates as: Base $= 6 - 3 = 3\ units$ Height is the distance between the point (5,7) to the base, which can be calculated by subtracting the y-coordinates of (5, 7) and any of the point on the base as: Height $= 7 - 3 = 4$ $Area = \frac{1}{2} \times 3 \times 4 = 6\ units^2$ **Answer:** B	104.	The pattern $-4,\ -6,\ -10,\ -18,\ \_,\ -66,\ \_$ The difference between every two terms of the sequence is: $-2, -4, -8, -16, -32, -64$ ... It means -6 is obtained by adding -2 to the first term -4, -10 is obtained by adding -4 to the second term -6 and so on. Therefore, 5th term is $-18 - 16 = -34$ 7th term is $-66 - 64 = -130$. The average of the 5th and the 7th terms is $\frac{-34 + (-130)}{2} = \frac{-34 - 130}{2}$ $= -\frac{164}{2} = -82$ **Answer:** G

Questions 105 - 110			
105.	<u>Jordan</u> Clean the whole room = 45 minutes Cleaning per minute $= \frac{1}{45}$ of room <u>Clara</u> Clean the whole room = 30 minutes Cleaning per minute $= \frac{1}{30}$ of room <u>Together</u> Cleaning per minute $= \frac{1}{45} + \frac{1}{30}$ $= \frac{5}{90} = \frac{1}{18}$ of room Therefore, together they will take 18 minutes to clean the room. **Answer:** A	108.	David's per day earning $= \frac{2{,}170}{31} = \$70$ The store owner pays \$80 per day to every other employee, therefore, Ruby Earned for David's shift = \$80 More money paid to Ruby $= 80 - 70$ $= \$10$ **Answer:** E
106.	Let $x = 5.\overline{3} = 5.3333\ldots$ $10x = 53.3333\ldots$ $10x - x = 53.3333\ldots - 5.3333\ldots$ $9x = 48$ $x = \frac{48}{9} = \frac{16}{3}$ Let $y = 6.\overline{6} = 6.6666\ldots$ $10y = 66.6666\ldots$ $10y - y = 66.6666\ldots - 6.6666\ldots$ $9y = 60$ $y = \frac{60}{9} = \frac{20}{3}$ Then $5.\overline{3} + 6.\overline{6} = x + y$ $= \frac{16}{3} + \frac{20}{3} = \frac{16+20}{3} = \frac{36}{3} = 12$ **Answer:** H	109.	Angles a, b, c, d, e, f are exterior angles of hexagon. We know that, the sum of all exterior angles of any polygon is always 360°, therefore, $a + b + c + d + e + f = 360°$ **Answer:** B
107.	Only one number 4 is divisible by 4, so the probability that she will spin the number divisible by 4 is $\frac{1}{6}$. There are 3 odd numbers: $1, 3, 5$, therefore, the probability of spinning the odd number is $\frac{3}{6} = \frac{1}{2}$. Hence, the probability that she will get a number divisible by 4 in the first spin and an odd number in the second spin is $\frac{1}{6} \times \frac{1}{2} = \frac{1}{12}$ **Answer:** C	110.	Let the number be x, then, $200\% \times x = 4n$ $\frac{200}{100} \times x = 4n$ $2x = 4n$ $x = 2n$ 50% of the number will be: $50\% \times x = 50\% \times 2n$ $= \frac{50}{100} \times 2n = \frac{1}{2} \times 2n = n$ Therefore, 50% of that number is n. **Answer:** H

Questions 111 - 114

111.	$\left(\frac{a+b}{b-a}\right)\cdot\left(\frac{a-b}{a+b}\right)\cdot(-7)$ $=\frac{(a+b)(a-b)}{(b-a)(a+b)}.(-7)$ $=\frac{(a+b)(a-b)}{(-1)(a-b)(a+b)}.(-7)$ $=\frac{(-7)}{(-1)}=7$ **Answer:** B	113.	Height of tank = $h = 10\,ft$ Volume of tank = $V = 1{,}540\,ft^3$ We know that, Volume of cylinder = $V = \pi r^2 h$ Substituting known values, we get: $1{,}540 = \pi r^2 \times 10$ $\pi r^2 = 154$ $r^2 = \frac{154}{\pi}$ $r^2 = \frac{154 \times 7}{22}$ $r^2 = 49$ $r = 7\,ft$ Therefore, radius of the tank is 7 feet. **Answer:** B
112.	Distance covered on 1st day = 50 miles Distance covered on 2nd day = 70 miles Distance covered on 3rd day = 75 miles Distance covered on 4th day = 85 miles Let, Distance covered on 5th day = x miles Average distance covered = 72 miles We know that, Average = $\frac{Sum\ of\ quantities}{Number\ of\ quantities}$, Substituting the known values, we get, $\frac{50+70+75+85+x}{5} = 72$ $280 + x = 360$ $x = 80$ miles Therefore, Cooper drives 80 miles on the 5th day. **Answer:** E	114.	All integers from 50 to 110 are, $50, 51, 52, \ldots, 110$ It makes an arithmetic sequence with a common difference 1. $a_1 = 50,\ a_n = 110,\ d = 1$ We know that, $a_n = a_1 + (n-1)d$ $110 = 50 + (n-1)1$ $60 = n - 1$ $n = 61$ The sum of a finite arithmetic sequence can be calculated as: Sum = $\frac{n}{2}(a_1 + a_n)$ Sum = $\frac{61}{2}(50 + 110)$ $= \frac{61}{2}(160) = 61(80) = 4{,}880$ Therefore, the average of all the integers from 50 to 110 will be: $\frac{4{,}880}{61} = 80$ **Answer:** H

Made in United States
North Haven, CT
11 June 2022

20122804R00141